WHAT WOMEN REALLY WANT

HOW AMERICAN WOMEN ARE QUIETLY ERASING
POLITICAL, RACIAL, CLASS, AND RELIGIOUS
LINES TO CHANGE THE WAY WE LIVE

Celinda Lake and Kellyanne Conway

WITH CATHERINE WHITNEY

FREE PRESS
New York London Toronto Sydney

ƒP

FREE PRESS
A Division of Simon & Schuster, Inc.
1230 Avenue of the Americas
New York, NY 10020

FREE PRESS and colophon are trademarks
of Simon & Schuster, Inc.

Designed by Kris Tobiassen

For information regarding special discounts for bulk purchases,
please contact Simon & Schuster Special Sales at 1-800-456-6798
or business@simonandschuster.com

Manufactured in the United States of America

10   9   8   7   6   5   4   3   2   1

Library of Congress Cataloging-in-Publication Data Control Number 2005053136

ISBN-13: 978-0-7432-7382-4
ISBN-10:   0-7432-7382-6

To our mothers
who opened doors and inspired our dreams

and to the women
whose voices are never heard

ACKNOWLEDGMENTS

We often say that women succeed through collaboration, and nothing demonstrates that more than the process of writing this book. We relied on countless associations—from the professionals who guided us, to the friends and family who supported us, to the men and women across the nation who shared their thoughts, stories, and ideas.

First and foremost, our gratitude goes to our agent, Fredericka Friedman. Fredi had the vision and the determination that brought this book into being. We have benefited greatly from her insights about publishing, and her ability to ask the right questions, always probing beneath the surface to force us to more fully articulate the trends.

Catherine Whitney, who is an experienced nonfiction book collaborator, helped us to focus on what we do best—research and analysis—by organizing the structure of the book and translating our data and conclusions into prose that is both a fascinating read and a significant statement about the future of women in America. We also appreciate the valuable input of Catherine's agent, Jane Dystel.

We couldn't have asked for a better publishing home than Free Press at Simon & Schuster. Our editor, Leslie Meredith, has always been enthusiastic about the work, even as she pushed us to make our material stronger. We are very lucky to have her shepherding our book through every stage of publishing and marketing. Leslie's assistant, Kit Frick, has been on top of every detail, and we appreciate her hard work.

Our staffs—at Kellyanne's company, THE POLLING COMPANY, INC.;

and Celinda's company, Lake Snell Perry Mermin/Decision Research—have been invaluable. In particular, Angela Reale, Claire Meehan, and Monica Kemp at THE POLLING COMPANY, and Caitlin Murphy, Erica Stanley, and Alyssia Snell, at Lake Snell Perry Mermin, have repeatedly gone above and beyond the call of duty to organize the polls and disseminate the data. Celinda Lake would also like to thank Sharon Kolling Perin.

Kellyanne would also like to thank those family members and friends whose unconditional love, quiet sacrifice and loud encouragement help to make this book—and so much else—possible and enjoyable, namely: husband George, babies George Anthony and Claudia Marie, mother Diane, father John, Pop Pop Jimmy, Aunts Marie, Rita and Angela, Uncle Eddie, Reneé, Ron, Jay, Angel, Alexa, Astin, Giovanna and Jimmy, and in loving memory of and eternal admiration for grandmothers Antoinette and Claire.

Finally, we are grateful to the women who make what we do possible—the quiet revolutionaries who are transforming the way we live in America.

CONTENTS

PREFACE: A Radical Collaboration
by Catherine Whitney · xi

INTRODUCTION: America in HER Image · 1

TREND 1: Singular Sensations · 9

TREND 2: "Altared" States · 27

TREND 3: Baby Flux · 45

TREND 4: Open-Collar Workplaces · 63

TREND 5: The Electric Hive · 103

TREND 6: The Mouse Race · 119

TREND 7: Generational Compression · 141

TREND 8: Beauty in Action · 167

TREND 9: Purse-String Power · 181

TREND 10: Just-in-Time Politics · 197

CONCLUSION: What Do Women Really Want? · 215

APPENDIX A: Polling Methodology and Results · 221

APPENDIX B: Two Sides Speak: The 2004 Election · 289

APPENDIX C: Selected Notes · 301

Index · 309

A RADICAL COLLABORATION

The day after the 2004 election, Republican pollster Kellyanne Conway and Democratic pollster Celinda Lake spoke on the phone. Even though the contest between President Bush and Senator Kerry had been the most contentious in recent history, their conversation was collegial, and they were eager to shake off their red and blue cloaks as they returned to a project that had engaged them for two years—an unprecedented collaboration to track the real trends in the lives of American women.

The two women couldn't have been more different. Lake, 52, was a member of the baby boom generation, single, and liberal. Conway, 37, was on the front end of Generation X, married in her thirties, a new mom of twins born sixteen days before the election, and conservative. Over the years, they had found themselves on opposite sides of some of the country's most polarizing debates. Lake and her firm, Lake Snell Perry Mermin & Associates, represented organizations like Planned Parenthood, the AFL-CIO, and the Democratic National Committee. Conway and her firm, THE POLLING COMPANY, represented organizations like the Family Research Council, the Heritage Foundation, and the Republican National Committee. Many people would find it mind-boggling, if not impossible, that these two could be colleagues rather than combatants—especially in November 2004. This is how it came about.

As the most prominent female pollsters and analysts in the country, Lake and Conway spend much of their time traveling the nation listening to the views of ordinary people from all walks of life. Political polling is only a piece of it. They are in the business of measuring attitudes and behaviors in many arenas—to discover what people buy, what they believe, how they work, how they live, what they care about, what they fear, and what they want. They aren't natural collaborators on a political stage, although they've occasionally been part of bipartisan projects.

As often happens with women, however, they stumbled unexpectedly on a point of commonality. As they surveyed the nation's women in the years after 9/11, they independently reached a surprising conclusion: Even though the political rhetoric was more heated and polarizing than ever, the divisions didn't seem to be there in many other areas. In the very places they expected disagreement they found agreement. Even when they viewed the results through the prisms of their different political leanings, each saw the same big trend: **The emergence of a new vital center—a united power base among women that was reshaping America more than politics. Women were acting in ways that blurred and, in some cases, erased all the usual lines of division—politics, race, religion, age, and class.**

What was going on? So intrigued were Lake and Conway about this discovery that they decided to explore further, and what they found was a radical new way of looking at women's influence.

One of the first things they realized was that in order to authentically examine the question of what women really want, they had to make a distinction between politics and other arenas of life. By its very nature, politics is divisive. Its goal is to have winners and losers, and its process is to choose one party, candidate, and platform over another. Politics tracks the population according to its differences, constantly separating the red from the blue. As pollsters for vying political interests, Conway and Lake each hold very strong views—and client stakeholders to match—on the hot-button issues. But life is about much more than politics. While the media likes to focus on dissent because it is dramatic, the daily operation of society is all about commonality, with everyone striving to minimize the differences. A million silent agreements form the etiquette of society that keeps commerce humming, that allows neighborhoods to function, that maintains an orderly flow on highways. This etiquette isn't political, but its cultural weight is heavier and more lasting than the shifting winds of political opinion.

Once Lake and Conway had examined women's trends in a broader terrain than the political, they found that women were increasingly operating as trend-shapers and not just trend-responders. The feminist movement had matured, and a wider array of choices and opportunities had become available to women. They were no longer pursuing models of success that didn't enrich their lives. Women from all walks of life and political persuasions were saying, by their words and actions, that they were no longer content to let the old (primarily male) norms shape their choices. *They* had become the norm, and they wanted an America that reflected their needs and values.

But what *were* those needs? Obviously, there is no prototypical American woman. She has many faces. She is a senior, a baby boomer, or maybe even a "grandboomer." She is a Gen Xer and a millennial baby, often a mother or a not-yet-mom. She is white, black, Latina, and Asian. She is just as likely to be single as married, and she might be comfortable living with a partner to whom she is not wed. She could be second wife by 37 or a new mom at 50. She works full-time or part-time at a job or a career, or she stays at home with her kids. She often has a home-based business or entrepreneurial aspirations. She controls the family purse strings, worries about health care and security, and never has enough time to sleep.

Lake and Conway understand that women are not homogenous. They are complex. And they share a gut-level consensus that exists under the radar of conventional polls. Tracking polls, which blanket the national consciousness on a weekly basis, often fail to measure the intensity of beliefs and commitments, and they aren't always sensitive to the distinctions women want to make about their lives. Even voting behaviors don't necessarily reflect the most important values. Two women can vote for different candidates but want the same result—for example, an improvement in health care or secure retirement benefits.

As they continued to collect data showing that the most important national trends are driven by women and transcend political differences, Lake and Conway decided to launch a major independent study that would answer the seemingly trite but somewhat elusive question of what women really want. During the early months of 2005, they conducted two national polls, using sampling controls to ensure that a proportional and representative number of female adults were interviewed from such demographic groups as age, race and ethnicity, and geographic region. The margin of error was calculated at plus or minus 3.5%, meaning that in 19 out of 20 cases, the results obtained would differ by no more than 3.5 percentage points in either direction if the entire female population nationwide were to be surveyed. (Margins for subgroups are higher.)

The construction of a poll requires a sensitive blending of knowledge and curiosity. Lake and Conway make their livings listening to people, especially women, and they know how to ask questions that elicit more than superficial answers and without leading a respondent to a preferred position. They developed the polling questions for this book, looking for opportunities to dig deeper and to distinguish these polls by their long-term implications. The American public is assaulted with constant polls that track the opinion and fashion *du jour*. Thousands of trivial factoids vie for our attention every hour. Tracking polls are like one-night stands—intense and appealing in the moment, but gone the next day. These flash-in-the-pan polls are even more prevalent during election years, complete with labels that simplify the differences between the sexes and marginalize women's true influence and diversity. The 2004 election was a perfect example of the slippery nature of polls. The Lake-Conway polling was unique in its depth and sensitivity to women. By delving beneath the radioactive hot-button debates, they found something different—an uplifting account of women's power to invent the good life for the new century.

The analysis that Lake and Conway bring to the polling data is a crucial part of this book, but they're quick to qualify that pollsters don't gaze into crystal balls to predict the future. Rather, they study the seeds of emerging trends and gauge their direction, in the same way an arborist studies a tree's early leanings, branch and leaf patterns, to determine how it will grow. This book is the product of that work, and it is an exhilarating ride into the future. Women will cheer to find their views, their ideals, and their very *selves* reflected in the analysis of trends and the voices of women like them.

One of the first opinion polls ever conducted was used by Warren Harding in 1920 to find out how American women would cast their first vote ever. Smart move; he won the election. In the 85 years since, people have never stopped wanting to know what women think, how they feel, where they're going, and what they want. Read on to hear an invigorating and inspiring take on the new ways American women are changing and improving our world.

—*Catherine Whitney*

AMERICA IN HER IMAGE

At a recent focus group composed of working women and men, a male executive stated, "A successful day for me is when I don't have to talk to anyone." As several men in the room nodded in agreement, the women stared at him incredulously. They just didn't get it.

If men feel more in control when they are left alone, women thrive on collaboration within a collection of interconnecting networks. "For me a successful day is when all my relationships are clicking," countered a woman in the focus group.

It's not exactly news that men tend to isolate while women communicate; the news is the way this one simple reality has sparked a movement. **Cubicle by cubicle, neighborhood by neighborhood, on playgrounds, in coffee bars, on commuter trains, at community and school functions, in shops and health clubs, at conferences and retreats, informal female networks are relaying information, offering support, solving problems, and making a difference.**

A REVOLUTION WITHOUT FANFARE

Eileen, an internist in her forties who specializes in women's health, likes to tell the story of her first anatomy class in medical school. "Our anatomy texts referred to the male as the human prototype, the biological ideal. Female anatomy was only discussed when it digressed from the male standard. Smaller bones, a uterus, breasts that interfered with easy dissection, a weaker musculature. It was ludicrous—like saying children are merely miniature adults. But that was the attitude in the medical community. Some of those anatomy texts are still around, even though we know better today. Women aren't just smaller, weaker versions of men. They're unique."

The medical model that Eileen describes is a fitting metaphor for what it has meant to be a woman in America. Although women have made tremendous advances toward equality and self-determination in the past century, the strides were usually measured by how successfully they adapted to the male standard. The canvas was already painted. The mold was already cast. Women were left to add the final touches, the accessories—a dab of color here, a high-heeled shoe there. Success in business meant showing she could be tough like a man. Success in marriage and motherhood meant satisfying the needs of her family. Few women in their right minds remained single by choice; status accrued with marriage and children.

Even in recent, more enlightened times, women have typically been defined not by what they are but by what they are not. A woman on her own is *un*married. She is child*less*. If she is at home raising children, she is *non*working. Many women have thus been diminished by the language of the day.

Politically, women's influence for most of the 85 years since they earned the vote has been relegated to "soft" issues—education, health, and family values. Candidates didn't talk to female audiences about the stock market, business, crime, or the military. They talked about schools or the environment. While these issues are still dear to them, women have broadened their scope of concern as their influence has grown.

The women's movements of the last century have accomplished a great deal in improving access and opportunity for women in business, education, and the military. Today, we are in a decidedly post-feminist age. More and more, women are not fighting for a place in the establishment. They *are* the establishment.

Without fanfare, almost stealthily, America has become women-

centric, reaching its full expression in the first decade of the twenty-first century. As a not-so-silent majority of women—from seniors to boomers to Generations X and Y—confront the singular challenge of recasting the nation in their image, they are shaking the culture to its core. Some grew weary of pounding at the seemingly immovable fortress of the male norm. Some gave the male norm the heave-ho altogether.

As pollsters and analysts, we've noticed the shifting patterns in family and work practices, lifestyle choices, and voting trends for many years. But when we probed more deeply, we discovered a fundamental new reality that statistics alone couldn't measure. Women from all walks of life and political persuasions are saying, in effect, that they no longer define issues in accordance with male standards. Women have become the norm, and they want an America that better reflects their image.

EIGHT ARCHETYPES

What exactly does this female norm look like?

When we polled a representative sample of American women, we identified eight distinct archetypes, proving that women come from diverse experiences and points of view, even as they share many common goals. **We didn't always find agreement on the means, but we often found agreement on the ends.** These eight archetypes are not abstract; they are based on the real women we surveyed. Along a broad continuum of change, some women are forceful advocates, while others are waging quieter revolutions, and still others are on the sidelines waiting to be lifted up.

These are the faces of American women, portrayed in our polling.

Feminist Champion: A politically engaged liberal, this highly educated, upwardly mobile woman is an activist for women's and children's issues. She tends to be more secular than others and holds strongly pro-choice views. She represents a mix of ages (the largest percentage being between 40 and 49) and she may be married or single. Devoted to her career and community, she is strongly motivated by values of equality and opportunity. You might find her at a pro-choice rally, a benefit for third world women, or working on a political action committee.

Suburban Caretaker: She is the lynchpin of home and community, typically a white, suburban wife and mother in her thirties and forties. A comfortable family income allows her to stay home with the kids, if she chooses, or to work part-time. Spirituality, and often religion, are important to her, and she views herself as the caretaker of the emerging generation, making her deeply invested in the moral standards of her community and nation. She focuses on education and health care and now tends to be a conservative "values" voter. You might find her at a PTA meeting, organizing a church event, or cheering her son or daughter at the fieldhouse or dance recital.

Alpha-Striver: She didn't get the memo that women can't "have it all," and she is determined to excel both professionally and personally. Her high income, investments, and advanced education give her a wide array of options. She is likely to be a "junior senior," between the ages of fifty and sixty-four, either married or single, and often a mom. Relatively liberal and engaged politically, she views herself as an agent of change. You might find her at a corporate conference, a county board planning meeting, or taking her high schooler on college interviews.

Multicultural Maverick: Young, single, urban, and multiethnic (White, Latina, African American, Asian), she is an individualist rather than a joiner, attracted to entrepreneurial endeavors. Her childless status gives her greater freedom, although she is strongly connected to her parents and siblings and may live at home. Although she tends to be liberal in her political views, she is somewhat indifferent about voting, and she distrusts most politicians. You might find her at the health club, coffee bar, or bistro, hanging out with friends, at a family barbecue, or attending an Earth Day concert.

Religious Crusader: Deeply committed to faith and family, she is more likely to view issues through the prism of "right vs. wrong" than "right vs. left." A politically active Christian conservative or church-going Catholic, this woman in her forties is financially upscale, married, and a mother. If she works outside the home it is in her own business or in a career that provides a great deal of flexibility. You are most likely to see her at a religious service, a pro-life rally, or home schooling her children.

Waitress Mom: Usually a blue collar or service worker, this middle class mom is most concerned about achieving balance in her life and greater educational and financial opportunities for her children. While the majority of this group is married, the remaining third is split between single, divorced, and widowed. She tends to be a conservative-leaning moderate, a reliable voter who may "swing" to support candidates who address her core concerns of health, security and the economy. She considers herself a person of faith, but she does not regularly attend religious services. You are most likely to see her working a forty-hour week, grocery shopping at night, and taking her kids to the mall on weekends.

Senior Survivor: This over-65 grandmother is security- and health-conscious and may be either financially struggling or financially set, depending on her retirement means and monthly prescription bills. Politically centrist, she votes in nearly every election, and tends to support incumbents and the status quo. She may be married, widowed, or single. If her health is good, you might find her taking care of her grandchildren, getting involved in community organizations, working or volunteering part-time, and traveling. If she is frail or in poor health, you are most likely to find her at home, living with her children or in an assisted-living apartment—relying on her daughter to take her shopping and to medical appointments.

Alienated Single: Economically marginal and politically disengaged, this woman tends to be young—under 45. Divorced or never married, she may or may not have children. She is the least religious and the least educated of any group. Lacking a meaningful affiliation with a religious organization or supportive community, she tends to fly under the radar.

She feels that she has little control over her future and worries about how she will take care of herself as she ages and is faced with health issues. Although she identifies herself as politically independent, she is usually not registered to vote. You are likely to see her in a low-wage job, rental apartment, and riding the bus or subway instead of driving. She is the least likely to be an agent of change, but she may be the beneficiary of changes others produce.

While our eight archetypes are incredibly diverse, we found it remarkable how often they voiced common dreams for themselves and their families, and how optimistic they were about the future. Even those on the lower end of the economic scale said their personal and work lives were much better than those of previous generations. In each category we found women who had by design or circumstances strayed from a self-limiting path to open up new options.

Even the most traditional of the women we surveyed recognized that they are living in a time when the cultural plates are shifting, opening up options that never existed before. As we interviewed them, we detected 10 major trends that are being driven by women in the categories of family life, work life, home life, aging, and public engagement. In these profound ways women are defining the terms of their lives—and the nation's life—according to what they want, what they believe, and what feels right. They are dispelling myths, not with loud words but through quiet action:

- The rapidly growing population of single women demonstrates that they're not ladies-in-waiting, but living fully. They're buying homes, building retirement portfolios, enjoying sex, and even having children. They are debunking the glum notion that being single is an anxious state that leads to panic as they approach 40. For the first time in memory, a woman's status in the world does not accrue solely with marriage and children.

- Women are looking at the culture of work in America and saying, "We can do better." Instead of rushing to join the rat race and elbowing their way to the top of the frenzied pack,

women are engineering a new work mode in entrepreneurial ventures and nontraditional environments.

• Women are orchestrating their home and work lives in ways
that improve their satisfaction and lower their stress. They
are refusing to buy into the effort to have it all—at least, not
all at once. The Mommy Entrepreneur or Mommy Telecommuter tracks are increasingly common examples of
women redefining their place in the world and at home.

• Women are unmasking the lies in the culture that are repeated so often that most people have come to believe them
without question. For example, the reality of the belea-
guered midlife woman "sandwiched" between the burdens
of child care and parent care is not as common as we've been
led to believe. The majority of seniors—especially senior
women—are care*givers*, not care*takers*. Mixed-generational
families most often live in homes owned and operated by the
senior generation.

• Women are compressing the generation gap, negotiating
the best of both youth and aging. They are first-time moms
at 50, entrepreneurs at 65. They are replacing linear notions
of age with stage of life, a fluid, borderless definition that reflects the way they really live.

• Generational compression has unified the fractured trends
that once separated women by age. For the first time in history, women of different generations find they are more
alike than not.

Women are erasing traditional lines of separation, sometimes meeting in the middle, eager for consensus, but often at least extending a
hand to try to get there. As Arthur Schlesinger said many decades ago,
"The middle of the road is definitely not the vital center. It's the *dead*
center." The movement we're describing is definitely not middle-of-
the-road. It's off-road and into the future.

The vision of the future detected in these trends is optimistic and often exhilarating. That in itself is a big change from the past, when women were defined by their struggles. A new age of opportunity will find women taking creative alternative routes to the centers of influence—doing it their way and in the process forging a better way. "The events in our lives happen in a sequence in time," Eudora Welty wrote, "but in their significance to ourselves they find their own order . . . the continuous thread of revelation."

SINGULAR SENSATIONS

Single women are becoming the most desirable demographic—fervently courted by industry and politicians, independent, happy, and not putting their lives on hold until Mr. Right comes along.

Remember the children's card game called Old Maid? Players collect pairs of cards as they try to avoid being left holding the Old Maid card— a scary representation of a witchlike crone. The player holding the Old Maid at the end loses the game and also *becomes* the Old Maid. For little girls, losing at Old Maid could provoke a slight twinge of dread—the fear that someday she might be grown-up and single.

Today, you'd never hear an unmarried woman described as an old maid. In fact, by the 1990s, the card game Old Maid was so outdated that one savvy game designer created Old Bachelor. There, players collect pairs of cards depicting accomplished women while they try not to get stuck with the Old Bachelor.

In the past, control over the marriage proposal and thus the prospect of marriage rested solely with the man. Men did the proposing. Women did the waiting, hoping, and praying. An unmarried woman was a woman who hadn't been asked. Even nuns became brides of Christ, and they took their vows wearing actual wedding gowns which they then replaced with habits. A woman who *chose* to remain unmarried was considered eccentric and maybe even deranged.

BY THE NUMBERS

22 MILLION
The number of unmarried women

60
Percentage of women ages 40 to 69 who are single

26
Percentage of households run by unmarried adults

Today, one-third of American women are unmarried—a huge number that reflects a significant trend. One thing is certain: 22 million women are not just sitting around waiting for a proposal!

Our survey revealed just how dramatic this shift is. When asked an open-ended question about the reasons they thought women were single, not one respondent said, "Because they haven't been asked" or "Nobody has proposed." Rather, a plurality volunteered the primary reason as "Haven't found the right person" followed by "Personal choice/never wanted to be married."

We chose "Singular Sensations" as the number one trend, because **for the first time in history, unmarried women as a group have a significant influence on the culture.** By virtue of their numbers and the ways they choose to live, they have set in motion a cascade of other trends in virtually every area of society, including family and parenting, housing and work styles, politics, and the way we age.

SINGLE WOMEN: A MIXED DEMOGRAPHIC

Who are the unmarried women of America? The stereotype of the free-wheeling single party girl who spends $500 on Manolo Blahniks doesn't sum up this category any more than the widowed blue-haired granny who ventures out on a solo weekly drive. Single women are represented

BEING SINGLE

	THEN	NOW
Reason	Men were single by choice. Women were single because they hadn't been asked.	Women are choosing to be single—either permanently or for the foreseeable future.
Economics	Men married down. Women married up. Women needed marriage to improve their economic status.	Women don't need a man or marriage to be self-sufficient and climb the economic ladder.
Sex	Celibate or slut	"She is in control"
Babies	"First comes love, then comes marriage, then comes Daddy with the baby carriage."	Maybe: "First comes baby."
Fear	Being an Old Maid	Getting stuck with an Old Bachelor
Models	The spinster aunt	Oprah

in every demographic category, and their primary concerns differ depending on their status. However, across the board they are more secular and progressive, and they tend to be more economically vulnerable than other groups.

Not surprisingly, **unmarried Feminist Champions reinforce the ideals of equality and independence that have been the hallmarks of feminism.** They tend to be over 40, and some have been married in the past. The never-marrieds in this group are not opposed to the idea, but they are living fully, are financially stable, and have strong community and family ties.

Multicultural Mavericks—young, ethnically diverse, and primarily urban—are the cultural trendsetters of Generations X and Y. They tend to be individualists who say that marriage is in their future, but on their terms and according to their time lines. It is important to them to be established in careers and financially stable before they start families.

Many of the Alpha Strivers in our survey are married, but the singles in this category are young (in their thirties) and have achieved notable career success. They have delayed marriage and children for professional development, but expect to marry and have children, confident of their ability to balance career and family.

Single Waitress Moms, as the label implies, are busy juggling jobs and kids, leaving them little time to develop social relationships or independent interests. They are split between divorced and never-marrieds, and the younger women in this group aspire to be in healthy, permanent marriages at some time in the future. They worry about the economic future of being unmarried.

Unmarried Senior Survivors come from a generation when more than 80% were married. As a result, they're primarily widows, although a growing percentage in this age group is divorced. Most Senior Survivors are also mothers and grandmothers and have full family lives. Between 10% and 15% of them are the primary caretakers of grandchildren. However, according to a CBS Evening News report (July 11, 2005), they haven't stopped looking for love. One million Americans 65 years and older are using the Internet to meet a companion/find a date, and senior membership on match.com has tripled in the past five years.

Alienated Singles form the often invisible working poor, mothers with children who live from paycheck to paycheck and without a safety net. They need the support of others to buoy them, either through official social programs or informal community assistance.

MS. "RIGHT NOW"

You don't have to be a sociologist to figure out why women traditionally equated fulfillment with marriage. Before the 1960s, women had few opportunities to thrive, or even survive, on their own. Marriage was a blessed union that bestowed on a woman not only her right to sexual expression and motherhood, but also a respected status in the community and a better shot at financial solvency. A young married woman appeared to have grabbed the gold ring. With marriage came permission to leave her usually low-paying, unsatisfying job and/or restrictive parents for a life in which she could be independent and have a small power base in her own home.

Unmarried women fared poorly by comparison. Even if they managed to earn enough for a comfortable existence, they were isolated from the vibrant mainstream of family life that went on all around them. They were the odd women out, the proverbial third wheel in a culture that traveled in twos.

Today, this picture has changed dramatically, and **the search for Mr. Right has been edged aside by the quest to become Ms. Right Now.** Women are on their own by choice more than circumstance. They are Ladies-tired-of-waiting, with varied interests, packed schedules, and meaningful pursuits. They're not waiting for Mr. Right to own a home, enjoy sex, invest and build retirement nest eggs, or even to have children.

The numbers do not lie. **More than 22 million American women live alone—an 87% increase in the past two decades.** About 12 million have never been married, 8 million are widowed, and nearly 2 million are divorced.

Only 25% of these unmarried women are under age 35, dispelling the myth that most singles are young. In fact, since the majority of married women outlive their husbands by five years or more, most women spend part of their later years being single, and statistics show that fewer widowed and divorced women are remarrying. The population of women on their own spans all age groups and economic circumstances— although those without children tend to be more economically upscale.

Unmarried women are demanding attention from marketers, politicians, and businesses, and they are forcing change in public policy and the workplace. They often find themselves at the top of the "fastest-growing segment" charts. They are the fastest-growing segment of new home and second-home buyers, car purchasers, travelers, graduate school students, new investors—the list goes on. Single women are a thriving demographic. While the prevalence of married-couple households has declined from 80% in the 1950s to just 50.7% today, the ranks of singles have expanded. They comprise 42% of the workforce, 40% of home buyers, and 35% of voters.

When we talk to never-married women in their forties or older, we find this theme repeated over and over: They always planned to get married, assumed they would be married, but for one reason or another, it never happened. Some of their stories sounded like the popular comic greeting card of the 1990s, with a shocked woman proclaiming, "Oh, my God, I forgot to get married!" Others came close to being married, and some were even married briefly when they were younger and are disappointed that they never found the right life partner. Often, even the older unmarried women say that they might still marry. The subject isn't closed, the view not totally jaded. Here's the distinction, though. **They aren't on hold, and they certainly aren't hopeless. They feel a strong sense of personal identity and entitlement. They peek at the future with optimism but are fully living their lives in the present.**

Lynn,* 46, an Atlanta bank officer, lived with a man for five years when she was in her twenties. After that relationship ended, she rented an apartment for a few years before buying a condominium when she was in her midthirties. "I expected to marry the man I lived with in my twenties," she said, "and after we broke up, I figured I'd meet someone else within a couple of years, but I never did. Now I'm in my forties, and I would say that my identity is that of a single person. I still may get married someday, but it would have to be a very special man to disrupt the good life I have."

* The names of interviewees have been changed to protect their privacy.

When they talk about their passions, unmarried women are more apt to talk about having children than having husbands. Nearly half of them are single mothers—usually by circumstance, but increasingly these days by choice. That, too, is an arena that is opening itself up to unmarried women—a factor we'll discuss in Trend 3.

"I'm the One I Want"

For me to marry I'd have to find the male equivalent of me.
That hasn't happened yet.

—FRAN, 42

Studies show that men thrive when they're married, but women tend to be happier and more successful and live longer when they're single. While never-married women are reaching the peaks of their careers and personal lives, never-married men are the least attractive demographic. Sara, 42, an unmarried Chicago marketing executive, offered an example that illustrates this point. "When I was growing up, my Uncle Bert was what they called a 'confirmed bachelor.' He dated various women, lived in a nice apartment, and had plenty of money—unlike my parents, who had three kids to raise and were always struggling to make ends meet. My mother and her sisters were constantly plotting to set Uncle Bert up with a nice woman so he would settle down, but he'd laugh and ask why he'd want to trade his life for one like theirs, and he seemed to have a good point. We all thought Uncle Bert was sexy and fabulous. But today, when I meet a man my age who has never been married, I am immediately suspicious. It's probably unfair, considering I haven't been married either, but I wonder if something may be wrong with him. The point is, I'm the great catch, not him."

This fact may be one reason why our survey respondents stated that the main reason for women being unmarried was they "haven't found the right person." Does that mean they're too picky or just less willing to settle? Mindful of the 50% divorce rate, and eager to achieve their personal goals, they may not be looking as hard or as early for a husband. As women get older, better educated, and more successful, the "right person" is actually harder to find. In our survey, college-educated and pro-fessional women were more likely than college-educated men to say that their main reason for being single was because they hadn't found the right person.

These data makes sense when you consider that, traditionally, men married down and women married up. As women grow more success-ful, the pool of available men on the "up" side shrinks. The culturally ingrained notion that men should be more financially and profes-sionally successful than their wives or girlfriends has not yet been pierced, although there is anecdotal evidence that the customs are changing.

The popular television series *Sex and the City* grappled with this question. Miranda, the hard-charging lawyer, agonized over being with the sensitive, financially middling bartender, but finally overcame her fears for the sake of a baby she had not planned to have. Carrie, on the other hand, ultimately could not endure life with her Birkenstocks-clad furniture builder, or even the Russian artist. She ended up with Mr. Big (the aptly-named successful man whose appetites match his bank account), after all. The desperately seeking and twice-divorced Charlotte fell for a man who, though financially successful, is short and bald and doesn't fit her picture of Prince Charming. As for saucy Saman-tha, after a lifetime working her way through corporate boardrooms and countless bedrooms, she finally found love with a much younger, less es-tablished man. Four women, four choices that converge into a cultural reality.

We found a disparity in the way men and women viewed the rea-sons for being single. Overall, single women were more likely than single men to state that the reason they themselves were still single was not having found the right person (38% to 32%), and Black women were more likely than Black men to give this reason.

While our survey respondents chose "haven't found the right per-son" as the main reason women were unmarried, women also cited "personal choice" as the secondary rationale for being single. Not sur-prisingly, women with postgraduate degrees were most likely to say being single was a personal choice.

Thinking for a moment about single Americans, why do you think people are or remain unmarried?

Total	Men	Women	
31%	**28%**	**34%**	**HAVEN'T FOUND THE RIGHT PERSON**
14%	13%	15%	PERSONAL CHOICE/NEVER WANT TO BE MARRIED
8%	7%	9%	WANT INDEPENDENCE FOR A WHILE
8%	8%	8%	WANT TO SPEND TIME ON CAREER
8%	8%	8%	BAD PREVIOUS RELATIONSHIPS
8%	7%	8%	JUST NOT READY FOR SPOUSE AND/OR CHILDREN
6%	5%	7%	WANT TO GAIN MORE FINANCIAL SECURITY FIRST
5%	5%	6%	DEMANDS OF CAREER AND JOB GET IN THE WAY
5%	5%	4%	DEMANDS OF LIFESTYLE AND OTHER GOALS GET IN THE WAY
2%	2%	2%	SAW OTHERS IN BAD RELATIONSHIPS
2%	2%	1%	GAY OR LESBIAN
1%	1%	2%	OTHER FAMILY RESPONSIBILITIES
4%	6%	3%	OTHER (VOLUNTEERED)
5%	5%	4%	ALL OF THE ABOVE (VOLUNTEERED)
1%	1%	1%	NONE OF THE ABOVE (VOLUNTEERED)
5%	5%	5%	DO NOT KNOW (VOLUNTEERED)
*	*	*	REFUSED (VOLUNTEERED)

Unmarried Women:
Top 2 Reasons for Singlehood (By Income)

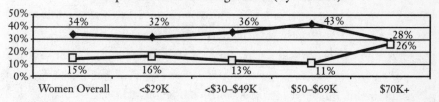

◆ Haven't Found the Right Person   □ Personal choice/Never Want to be Married

Overall, single women were slightly more likely than single men to say that the reason why they haven't married was personal choice (17%

to 11%). We also saw an indication that as single women get older, better educated, and more professionally successful, they are more inclined to view their status as a choice. Women with post-graduate degrees were more likely than men with post-graduate degrees to say that being single is a choice. Women aged 35 to 54 were somewhat more likely than younger women, 18 to 34, to say being single was a personal choice (17% to 11%). And unmarried women earning $70,000 or more were among the most likely to call being single a matter of personal choice. Or, as one 44-year-old respondent put it, "In my twenties, I was single because I wanted the independence and to focus on my schooling and

THE JAPAN FACTOR

If the "liberation" of American women from the marriage market strikes some as not a particularly radical trend, one need only look across the ocean to Japan to conclude that it is significant. Tradition and freedom make strange bedfellows, but in this culturally old-fashioned society, where gender roles are strictly prescribed, the percentage of women staying single is even greater than in the United States. Over the past decade, the portion of Japanese women aged 25 to 29 who never married has surged from 40% to 54%. Among women aged 30 to 34 the never-married group has increased from 14% to 27%. In a recent poll, 73% of single Japanese women said they were happy to remain single.

What is most interesting about this trend is that it seems to be driven by the heavy traditional burden placed on married women. In the 1980s, a woman unmarried by 25 was dismissed as "Christmas cake"—thrown out on December 26. She was considered unattractive and outside the mainstream. But many Japanese women complain that men are still stuck with old-fashioned ideas about marriage, and they have begun to resist an institutional structure that often puts an end to their independence, careers, and personal growth.

According to Frances Rosenbluth, professor of political science at Yale University, who has studied social trends among Japanese women,

"Women are not satisfied with the old way, but they don't have a new way. They're stuck. The way they cope with that is by at least having some career before getting married. They figure once they get married, it's going to be all over."

Adding to the appeal of the single life is the complete absence of ex-pectations for unmarried women. They often live at home, supported by their parents, while they spend their own earnings on leisure activities and travel.

Not too long ago, many Japanese hotels would not even allow women traveling alone to spend the night, fearing they were looking for a place to commit suicide. Now single women have become some of their best customers.

career. In my thirties, I was single because I had not found the right person. In my forties, I'm single because I've made a choice. I bought a house; I have my own life. By the time I get to my fifties, who knows? The point is, I can do anything I want to do."

TABLE FOR ONE

Are single women lonely? In our survey, one in four respondents named "loneliness or isolation" as the main downside of being single, but probing deeper we found substantial futurizing in that response. That is, unmarrieds are not necessarily feeling lonely or isolated *now*, but they worry about solitary confinement as they age.

"I sometimes worry about growing old alone," admitted Margaret, who is 46. "It's a vague anxiety. I'm certainly not feeling isolated now. I've heard people say you should have kids so they can take care of you in your old age, but I don't agree with that. What I really think is that most of us worry about being alone when we're older, whether we're married or single."

"I think singles have a knee-jerk fear of having no one in their lives who puts them first," said Jamie, 39. "But, you know, it's often an idealized view. If I'm feeling sorry for myself for one reason or another, I'll think, 'Oh, boo hoo, I'm all alone. Nobody cares.' But people *do* care. I get tremendous support from my friends, my three sisters, my parents, my church. My best friend, who is married and has two children is more isolated than I am because she doesn't have time for friends. It's a trade-off"

One thing is clear: Women are providing their husbands or male partners more emotional support than they're receiving from them. A Harris Interactive study conducted for *Psychology Today* found that while 76% of men turned to their partners for emotional support, only 36% of women turned to their partners—a two-to-one differential that reflects our own findings. Women tend to seek out other women when they need to vent, want sympathy, or seek a sense of belonging. Men are far more likely than women to say that their most important relationship is with their wife or significant other.

So who holds the perception that the downside of being single is loneliness and isolation? The breakdown among our survey respondents was revealing. Across the board, single men were somewhat more likely than single women to say that isolation was the most difficult aspect of being single (27% to 21%). The difference may reflect several realities. One is the relative ease women have establishing emotionally supportive relationships with both male and female friends. Another factor is that far more single women are raising children. Additionally, single women generally tend to maintain stronger ties (and sometimes closer proximity) to their parents than their male counterparts.

Regardless of your marital status, which of the following best describes the downside, if any, to remaining single and unmarried?

Total	Men	Women	
25%	24%	26%	**LONELINESS OR ISOLATION**
12%	13%	11%	NOTHING/THERE IS NO DOWNSIDE
11%	13%	10%	LACK OF MEANINGFUL RELATIONSHIPS
10%	7%	13%	HANDLING ALL THE RESPONSIBILITIES ALONE

10%	11%	10%	BEING ON YOUR OWN IN DIFFICULT TIMES/WHEN OLDER
7%	7%	7%	NOT HAVING CHILDREN
6%	4%	8%	LESS FINANCIAL SECURITY
5%	5%	5%	DIFFICULTY MEETING PEOPLE LATER IN LIFE
5%	6%	4%	FEELING LIKE YOU'RE "MISSING OUT" BY NOT BEING MARRIED
3%	3%	3%	SOCIETAL PRESSURE
3%	3%	3%	PRESSURE FROM OTHER FAMILY MEMBERS
1%	1%	*	OTHER (VOLUNTEERED)
4%	4%	3%	ALL OF THE ABOVE (VOLUNTEERED)
2%	1%	3%	NONE OF THE ABOVE (VOLUNTEERED)
5%	4%	5%	DO NOT KNOW (VOLUNTEERED)
1%	1%	2%	REFUSED (VOLUNTEERED)

For unmarried Americans, the importance of familial relationships seems to depend upon the presence of children. When an unmarried man or woman has a child, that relationship becomes the most important. In our survey, single women with children were 13 points more likely than married women with children to say that their most important relationship was with their child (33% to 20%). When men are childless, this relationship seems weighted toward a partner, whereas for women, this relationship is heavily shifted toward a parent.

There are economic realities that trigger a sense of isolation. Men and women with annual incomes between $30,000 and $49,000 were among those most likely to say that isolation was the greatest downside for singles (29% and 30%, compared to 24% and 26%, respectively).

The practical side of living alone was viewed differently by the sexes. Women were 6 points more likely than men to say that handling day-to-day responsibilities on one's own was the main disadvantage to being unmarried (13% to 7%). Our polling numbers show that this transcends mere loneliness. They worry about flying solo into an uncertain future, with financial, physical, and emotional support all up to them.

Twelve percent of our respondents said there was *no* downside to re-

DID YOU KNOW?

Mary Richards, the single heroine of the Mary Tyler Moore Show, *which aired from 1970 to 1977, was in her thirties. Her best friend, Rhoda Morgenstern, was also in her thirties, and she was 34 when she married Joe on her own show,* Rhoda. *By statistical averages of the 1970s, these two TV favorites had already passed the average age of marriage by well over a decade.*

maining unmarried, with negligible differences between the sexes. These non-conformists may be among those who are moving this "trendlet" into a lifestyle to which marketers and politicians are beginning to respond.

HAPPILY NEVER MARRIED

"This is a true story," recounts Eileen, 38. "I was seeing a therapist because I thought I should try to figure out why I wasn't married. Maybe I had an intimacy problem or a fear of commitment. I wanted to get to the bottom of it. My therapist was a very bright lady, about my age, married with two kids. She helped me realize that I did have some issues, but they weren't what I thought. The turning point came after I'd been seeing her for about seven months. I was telling her about refusing a date with this guy from my church because I just wanted to order in a pizza and watch TV in my ratty old pajamas. I remember giving an embarrassed little laugh and saying something like, 'Isn't that pathetic?' Then I noticed the look on my therapist's face. There was so much longing there it almost knocked me over. I realized with amazement that this woman who had the perfect life was jealous of me! She probably never had a peaceful moment. I began to look at my life with new perspective and I saw that it didn't need to be fixed."

Many single women, especially those who were childless, recounted similar "aha" moments, occasionally even expressing a wicked glee at the relative ease of their lives compared to their overstretched married friends. Some of them insist that the choice to be unmarried can be as dignified and satisfying as the choice to be married, and this has given rise to a new industry aimed at symbolizing the state. A successful example is the Ah ring.

The brainchild of Ruva Fox, a New York single entrepreneur with a lot of happy, single friends, the Ah ring doesn't require a Prince Charming or a bended knee, and for that reason it's selling like hotcakes among single women. "Engaged women have their engagement rings and married women have their wedding bands," said Fox, "but there was nothing on the market specifically designed for single women." She decided to market the Ah ring, the first diamond ring made for single women. The Ah stands for "available" and "happy." Worn on the pinkie and priced to sell at $295, the ring is a 14-karat, white-gold band of 11 round, full-cut diamonds (about 1/4-karat altogether), with "Ah" engraved inside.

Thanks in part to an early endorsement by Oprah, Fox has turned her idea into a multimillion-dollar company. She has also expanded her concept. In 2002, when she found herself too busy for a planned vacation to Greece, she created the Tranquility Cross. "It reminded me of the Greek blue sky and sea. It's very peaceful." She's also produced the Snowflake Necklace ("no two are alike") and plans soon to offer diamond earrings shaped like daisy petals. It will be themed, "He loves me; he loves me not."

QUIRKYALONE AND LOVING IT

The morning after yet another kissless New Year's Eve, Sasha Cagen, 30, found herself reflecting upon exactly what term would define her status. She lit upon "quirkyalone," and from that came a movement, a book—*Quirkyalone: A Manifesto for Uncompromising Romantics*—and an International Quirkyalone Day (February 14), an alternative to the couple-centered Valentine's Day that includes and celebrates everyone, single or coupled.

Who are the quirkyalones? In her original manifesto, Cagen wrote, "We are the puzzle pieces who seldom fit with other puzzle pieces. Romantics, idealists, eccentrics, we inhabit singledom as our natural resting state. In a world where proms and marriage define the social order, we are, by force of our personalities and inner strength, rebels. . . . For the quirkyalone, there is no patience for dating just for the sake of not being alone. . . . Better to be untethered and open to possibility: living for the exhilaration of meeting someone new, of not knowing what the night will bring. We quirkyalones seek momentous meetings."

Cagen points out that there have always been quirky *loners*—take Emily Dickinson as an example—but quirkyalones are not loners. It would be pretty hard to make a movement composed of loners. Quirkyalones are social animals who appreciate periods of solitude and independence. They assert that family, friendship, and even passion do not require being joined at the hip.

With quirkyalones, Cagen hit on two themes that are gaining traction with young and old alike, especially women. The first is the importance of individuality. In a mass-oriented culture, women are increasingly looking for ways to highlight their uniqueness. The second theme is the revival of the friend as a significant other. Younger singles are pioneering new ways of being close, often substituting a circle of committed platonic and same-sex relationships for an early trip to the altar. In urban areas, a tribal culture has emerged, with singles of both sexes forming supportive coalitions that replace traditional family units. They share holiday meals, take vacations together, and nurse each other when they're ill. The Internet has expanded the connectivity of singles. According to Match.com, online dating revenue rose to $313 million in 2003. But it's not just romance that's driving this trend. Singles are using the Internet to make friends, engage in political activism, and chat about shared interests. This solitary connectedness also manifests itself in settings where individuals can do things alone, "together" with other individuals doing them alone—e.g., coffee bars, chat rooms, and health clubs.

NEW RULES

In 1996, Ellen Fein and Sherrie Schneider's book, *The Rules: Time-Tested Secrets for Capturing the Heart of Mr. Right*, was published to great fanfare. Its premise was that single women were failing to find marriage partners because they were not playing by the time-honored rules of the seduction game. With its retro flavor (A few gems: never call a man, never accept a date for the weekend after Thursday, never offer to pay for dinner) *The Rules* served up a chiding collection of behavioral makeover tips for contemporary independent single women.

The Rules was popular for a while, and its spin-off books and workshops still attract many followers. After all, the emergence of an empowered, fulfilled, single-by-choice woman doesn't mean that little girls don't dream of wedding days or craft frilly white wedding gowns out of old lace curtains. Nor does it mean that women don't seek romance, lasting love, and commitment. **But the very fact that so many women remain unmarried by choice—either for a while or forever—is a clear demonstration that their dreams have undergone a change since the days when "I do" meant "I must." Even among those who eventually walk down the aisle, there is an increasing likelihood that "I do" will be preceded by "I may," or "I probably will."**

Considering that *The Rules* author Ellen Fein filed for divorce in September 2004 after 16 years of marriage, women are right to question who makes the rules. It seems they are concluding that they'll write their own.

THE NEXT 10 YEARS

What are our projections for the rising numbers of self-reliant single women forming a permanent, stable population? The implications of a vast cohort of unmarried adults living alone are enormous, especially in the arenas of public policy, housing, consumerism, and fertility technologies.

- We project that in the coming elections (especially 2006 and 2008), unmarried women will be the number one "get" for

candidates, in the way Soccer Moms were in 1992 and
Nascar Dads were in 2004. In particular, Alienated Singles—economically marginal, nonvoting women—will be
drawn into the political arena by candidates who address
their primary issues: jobs, social security, and housing. With
these efforts, the number of nonvoting single women will
decline.

• The question of "Who will care for me?" will become front
and center for single women, affecting law and policy in life-
and-death matters. Living wills and health proxies may become as common as insurance policies.

• In 2006, the largest group of single women, the baby
boomers, will hit 60. As single women age and married
women become widowed, new family constructs will
emerge, including communities of older women.

• Commitment ("to me") ceremonies and non-bridal registries will become big business as single women demand acknowledgment of their status.

• The "adoption option" will become more attractive to singles. Others will continue to boost the growing trend of fertility treatments.

"ALTARED" STATES

Choice is the new consensus when it comes to marriage, and a large number of women are exercising that choice to delay a trip to the altar, vow out altogether, or join an increasingly diverse set of alternative family styles.

During the year that Jodie, 34, was planning her wedding, two stories briefly dominated the tabloids, several months apart. The first was the extravagant wedding spectacle of a celebrity bride-to-be, known as "Bridezilla," whose materialistic chutzpah included selling sponsorships to vendors who vied for a piece of the big day. The second story involved Jennifer Wilkins, dubbed in the media as the "Runaway Bride," who bought a bus ticket to notoriety when she disappeared a week before her nuptials, triggering a nationwide woman hunt and 600 guests being left at the altar. In the period following her reappearance, the more sympathetic commentators suggested that perhaps Wilkins had been overwhelmed by the eight bridal showers, exhausted by the effort to co-ordinate twelve bridesmaids, and spooked by the sheer size of the event, which, of couse, she had created. The would-be bride agreed to counseling, and the obligatory prime-time interview.

As a professor of social sciences, Jodie was fascinated by the way these two stories exposed extremes of the same cultural phenomenon: even as the rate of marriage is declining and women delay, defer, or deny marriage altogether, weddings themselves seem to be taking on more grandiose characteristics.

Jodie speculated that traditionally a woman's wedding day had been romanticized as the stuff of dreams because girls had precious little else to dream about. Perhaps brides-to-be were encouraged to become control freaks because so little in their lives was within their control. If nothing else, they could have this one day.

But those old notions no longer were true. Young girls had plenty to dream about beyond their weddings, with seemingly infinite choices and opportunities. Maybe Bridezilla and the Runaway Bride were extreme examples of a cultural emphasis that tends to the wedding day, and not the mariage. Jodie was quite proud of the tasteful small service she had planned. She and her fiancé, Ben, were more interested in saving for a down payment on a house than in blowing a bundle on a big party—and neither would dream of asking parents to foot any part of the bill. Their ceremony would be simple, followed by a modest reception, and they'd return to work the following day. The honeymoon would have to wait.

Today's woman is penciling in marriage and motherhood on her lifetime To Do list, and a trip to the altar, although still desired, is no longer urgent. It may be second or third on the wishlist, or not there at all. This "altared" state of the family has not occurred by chance but by design. Choice is the new consensus when it comes to family. Women today have both the freedom and the opportunity to choose from a wide menu of lifestyles, and the time lines grant them a lot more latitude.

Those who long for the good old days of traditional families might be surprised to learn that the institutional family has always been in a state of flux, expanding and contracting to meet the needs of the times. Furthermore, the so-called good old days were not exactly that for married women, who were for legal purposes considered chattel— the property of their husbands and subject to whatever treatment they received. Until the late 1970s, it wasn't considered a crime for a man to beat or rape his wife in most jurisdictions. The evolution of the institution of marriage has primarily been pushed forward by women. That's not to say that women take an "anything goes" approach to this most sacred of unions. Far from it. They're just looking for ways to make it stronger,

NUCLEAR FAMILY

	THEN	NOW
Definition	*Dad, Mom, and 2.2 kids*	*The family nucleus has expanded to include a wide range of lifestyles and combinations, including single parents, stepfamilies, committed unmarried partners, and gay and lesbian couples and parents.*
Women's power	*The two M's—marriage and motherhood*	*Personal fulfillment and individual timelines*
Marriage time line	*18 to 20*	*25 to 30*
Style	*Dependence*	*Interdependence*
Rewards	*Status and security*	*Intimacy and mutual support*

more meaningful, and more intimate. For the first time in history, women are saying that a strong marriage requires a happy wife.

Our second trend, Altared States, piggybacks the first, since lower numbers of married women means higher numbers of singles. But the two trends also converge on another point—a fundamental alteration in the way marriage and family are defined and lived in America today.

Marriage Can Wait

I'm 23, the age my mother was when she got married. I think she was ready to settle down then, but I don't feel the least bit ready. When people ask me if my boyfriend and I are planning to get married anytime soon, I always say I don't think I'll get married and have kids until *I'm* not a kid myself.

—MICHELLE, 23

For the first time in history, women do not gain power and influence solely through the two M's—Mrs. and Mom. While they still value marriage and children, they are developing their own time lines. For many, education precedes marriage, rather than marriage precluding education. The median age of women getting married is rising. While 25.1 years (compared to 20.8 years in 1970) may not seem so advanced, the real-world translation is that larger numbers of women are getting married in their thirties. The figure keeps edging upward. Once married couples with children comprised the biggest demographic—the engine that drove everything from home-buying to support for public education, to retail sales. Now only 24% of the population fits this demographic, below married couples with no children (27%) and singles (26%).

Beneath the surface of these trends are significant shifting sentiments about the meaning of marriage and children in a woman's life. **In a 1965 survey, three out of four college women said they would marry a man they didn't love if he fit their criteria in every other way. Not anymore. Today 80% of women say they'd rather have a partner who can communicate his feelings than one who makes a good living.**

Women are living in an age when demands on personal and professional lifestyles are seriously affecting the dynamics of their relationships. They are examining and reexamining their career choices, personal commitments, and motherhood, wondering if they've decided to do the right things at the right times. Younger women who watched their baby boomer moms struggle to "have it all" are reevaluating the sequence of their choices—and that often means delaying marriage and family until their careers are established or they're in a position to take time off for family. These women are more aware of what economists call the "opportunity cost" to women who trade in corporate stilettos for casual sneakers, which is whatever they give up to have a family, including loss of freedom, salary, career advancements, and other opportunities. And they're more intent on sorting out their lifetime goals before they take the big plunge.

Nuclear Explosion

My partner and I have lived together for twelve years, and we consider ourselves life mates. We have powers of attorney, health care proxies, and we own a home (joint tenants with rights of survivorship). Marriage isn't for us. Both of us have been there, done that, and in our fifties we don't see the point. But I find myself introducing him to strangers as my "husband" because it's easier than having to explain. No other word adequately describes our status.

—MARYANN, 51

It has been clear for some time that the definition of nuclear family has undergone a big change, with baby boomers on the leading edge. However, it's been a difficult change to track. For one thing, it wasn't until the 1990 Census that "unmarried partner" was even included among a list of possible categories that respondents could choose to identify household relationships. Census 2000 data shows that there are significantly more nontraditional families compared to 10 years earlier. **Only one-fourth of Americans currently live in a "traditional" family composed of a married couple and their children.** Until the advent of Medicare and Medicaid in the last 40 years, a "traditional" family often included an elderly parent living at home with the married couple and children.

Even with the arrival of a statistical box for unmarried partners, the trends are slippery, especially when people refuse to acknowledge or define their status. For example the 2000 Census reported about 600,000 gay and lesbian households—an estimate that is probably low.

The 2000 Census counted 4.9 million homes in which the head of the household lived with an unmarried partner of the opposite sex—up from 3 million in 1990. Polling shows that 37% of Americans report living together before marriage—a trend that applies across all age groups. In the past, cohabitation was viewed as a preparatory step toward marriage, but that seems to be changing. Studies show that between 25% and 30% of women cohabitating do not plan to marry their partner.

The family nucleus has expanded to include a wide range of lifestyles and combinations, including single parents, stepfamilies, committed unmarried partners, and gay and lesbian couples and parents.

Institutionally, America has not yet adapted to the trend. According to the U.S. General Accounting Office, there are more than 1,000 federal laws in which marriage is a factor. Unmarried couples lose out on married couples' rights to inherit a spouse's estate tax-free or Social Security benefits. On the other hand, elimination of the marriage penalty tax offered couples more even treatment when filing federal returns.

Insurers tend to offer lower rates to married people for everything from auto to renters coverage. An assortment of health clubs, country clubs, and automobile clubs typically have family memberships that are less expensive for married couples. The list goes on. According to Thomas Coleman, executive director of the American Association for Single People, "the lion's share of benefits go to people who are married,

BY THE NUMBERS

37
Percentage of adults living together before marriage

4.9 MILLION
Number of households with unmarried partners living together

1,049
The number of federal laws in which marriage is a factor

whether they are employment benefits, taxation breaks, or consumer discounts."

Even couples who are getting married are not necessarily fitting traditional molds. Another significant neotraditional trend is seen in the rapid rise in mixed marriages—those marriages that reach across normally restricted racial, ethnic, and religious boundaries. Only 42% of single women feel that it is important to marry a man of the same religious faith, and the old taboos nearly evaporate when teens are questioned. Interestingly, while more than 90% of teens approve of marriages between people of different races, ethnicities, and religions, only 56% of people ages 15 to 29 approve of marriage between homosexuals, with girls being twice as likely as boys to support gay marriage.

Openness to intermarriage is showing up where you'd least expect it. According to the American Jewish Committee's Survey of American Jewish Opinion, more than half of American Jews disagree with the statement, "It would pain me if my child married a gentile," and 50% agree that "It is racist to oppose Jewish-gentile marriages."

There are currently more than 2 million interracial marriages, accounting for about 5% of all marriages in the United States. Black-white marriages number approximately half a million. It's still difficult, though. According to a University of Houston study, interracial couples have a 30% greater increase in stress.

According to a *New York Times* series on class in America, the majority of cross-class marriages now involve women marrying men with less education—the reverse of an old trend. It is also, writes author Tamar Lewin, the combination most likely to end in divorce.

On the surface, such a variety of family forms and expressions might seem a sure road to divisiveness, but at the vital center women are remarkably cohesive in their core values regarding family. **Single or married, parents or childless, semicommitted or significant others—women are committed to the necessity and importance of family, even as they redefine its makeup.** In fact, according to both male and female respondents to our survey, family life has never been better. A huge 81% said that the quality of their family life was better

---

DID YOU KNOW?

- *Latinas are more likely than other demographic groups to be part of traditional nuclear families.*
- *The Northeast has the lowest percentage of married people (52.7%) and the highest percentage of those never married (29.3%).*
- *Naperville, Illinois, has the most married people—67.7% of its population—while Gary, Indiana, has the most "formerly married" people, with 27.2% of its population divorced, separated, or widowed.*

---

than that of their parents at the same age, with 50% of those saying it was much better.

UNWEDDED BLISS

According to researchers at the National Marriage Project, a bipartisan group affiliated with Rutgers University, the number of unmarried partners has shot up dramatically in the last generation. This group is defined as couples who are sexual partners, not married to each other, and sharing a household. In over half of all first marriages, the couples live together first, compared to virtually none 50 years ago. There are currently about 11 million people living with unmarried partners, including both same-sex and opposite-sex couples. While cohabitation is most common among the young and is often viewed as a prelude to marriage, an emerging trend involves couples cohabiting as an alternative to marriage.

Exactly who is cohabiting? Cohabitation is more common among those of lower educational and income levels. Recent data show that among women in the 19-to-44 age range, 60% of high school dropouts have cohabited, compared to 37% of college graduates. Not surprising, cohabitation is also more common among those who are less religious than their peers, those who have been divorced, and those who have experienced parental divorce, fatherlessness, or high levels of marital discord during childhood. Almost 40% of these households contain children.

The jury is still out on whether cohabitation before marriage leads to more stable unions. While cohabitors tend to be somewhat more likely to separate or divorce once they do marry, researchers remain uncertain about whether this is due to cohabitation or other factors. A national study of women published in the *Journal of Marriage and the Family* found that premarital cohabitation, including premarital sex, when limited to a woman's future husband, was not associated with an elevated risk of marital disruption. However, studies repeatedly show that living together before marriage as a way of trying out the relationship before the fact, does not seem to make marriage better or protect it from divorce.

A new category of cohabitants is found in a group where one might least expect it—the elderly. The past decade has shown a 73% increase in the numbers of couples 65-plus who were—as they used to say— "shacking up." The Census count shows 266,600 unmarried couples over age 65 cohabiting without benefit of marriage, but most experts believe the number is much higher, as elders are often reluctant to acknowledge their arrangements. In any case, the trend will certainly grow as baby boomers hit 65 and live 20 to 30 years past that.

The biggest reason for this trend is economics—especially health benefits. For example, widows who retain their late husbands' pension, medical benefits, and Social Security risk losing them if they remarry. Others face complex family finances, with adult children circling the wagons to be sure a surviving parent's assets aren't depleted by a new spouse.

Meanwhile, seniors are living longer and more vibrantly than ever, and many want a significant other to share their interests and passions.

"We used to call it 'living in sin,' " said Joan, a 68-year-old widow who has lived with 72-year-old Jules for two years. "I would have been furious if either of my daughters had done it, and I wouldn't have believed I would do it either. But I weighed up the pros and cons, and in the end it just felt silly not to enjoy these years with a man I love." Joan acknowledged, however, that in the beginning, she and Jules tried to keep their arrangement a secret, for fear their children would disapprove. She laughed heartily at the memory. "We were sneaking around," she said, and we finally looked at each other and said, 'What are we doing?' "

WHO LOVES YA, BABY?

The relationship a person holds with his or her spouse or significant other has typically been "the one." We don't call them significant others or our "better half" for nothing! But our survey found a wide gap between men and women on this point. **While 45% of men named their spouse or significant other as their most important relationship, only 34% of women did.** Three in ten women said that their deepest connection was with their children—nearly twice the number of men. Separated, divorced, or widowed women were 20 points more likely than their male counterparts to say that their most important relationship was with their child (54% to 34%).

For you personally, what is the MOST important relationship in your life? Your relationship with . . .

Total	Men	Women	
39%	45%	34%	**SPOUSE OR SIGNIFICANT OTHER**
23%	16%	30%	CHILD
7%	6%	8%	MYSELF
6%	6%	6%	PARENT
6%	7%	5%	EXTENDED FAMILY MEMBER
4%	4%	3%	FRIEND
3%	3%	3%	BROTHER OR SISTER
2%	2%	1%	MEMBER OF THE CLERGY
1%	1%	*	PROFESSIONAL MENTOR
7%	6%	8%	OTHER (VOLUNTEERED)
2%	2%	1%	DO NOT KNOW (VOLUNTEERED)
1%	1%	1%	REFUSED (VOLUNTEERED)

Most Important Relationship

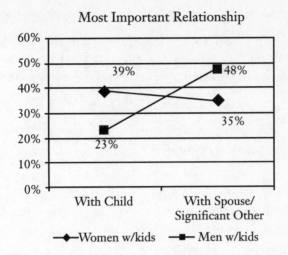

The relationship with their child was more important to low-income women, whereas the relationship with their spouse was most important to high-income women. A similar correlation with income did not exist for men.

Among races, the relationship with their child was most important to Hispanic women (49%), followed by Black women (39%), then white women (28%).

Childless women were 22 points more likely (22% to 6%) than those overall to cite their relationship with their mother or father as most important.

The conclusion? Women bond most strongly with their children

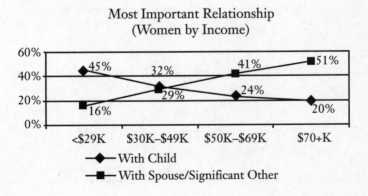

OPPOSITES ATTRACT,
BUT SIMILARS ENDURE

According to David Popenoe and Barbara Dafoe Whitehead, prominent researchers on marriage and the family, the evidence points to 10 key factors that can determine the success or failure of a marriage.

1. *Marrying in one's teens carries two to three times the risk of divorce as marrying in one's twenties or older.*
2. *An introduction through family, friends, or acquaintances is still the best way to find a marriage partner.*
3. *The more similar people are in their values, backgrounds, and life goals, the more likely they are to have a successful marriage.*
4. *Women have a significantly better chance of marrying if they do not become single parents before marrying.*
5. *Both women and men who are college-educated are more likely to marry, and less likely to divorce, than people with lower levels of education.*
6. *Living together before marriage does not prove useful as a "trial marriage."*
7. *Marriage helps people to generate income and wealth.*
8. *People who are married are more likely to have emotionally and physically satisfying sex lives than single people or those who just live together.*
9. *People who grow up in a family broken by divorce are slightly less likely to marry, and much more likely to divorce when they do marry.*
10. *The risk of divorce is far below 50% for educated people going into their first marriage, and lower still for people who wait to marry at least until their midtwenties, haven't lived with many different partners prior to marriage, or are strongly religious and marry someone of the same faith.*

and their parents. This may have something to do with a caretaker mentality. That is, adult women find their most significant relationships to
be with those they care for (children and older parents), while men find
their most significant relationships to be with those who care for them
(wives and partners).

VOWING IN AND OUT

A problem called emotional infidelity is on the rise. Couples are struggling with a feeling of betrayal that comes from one partner sharing
non-sexual intimacies with people outside the marriage. For instance,
when Brad and Colleen pledged to forsake all others on their wedding
day, they thought they knew what that meant. They would be sexually
monogamous, and they would love and adore each other. And that's
what they did. They had a happy marriage, and within five years Colleen
gave birth to two children. Everything was complete—until Brad started
fooling around on the computer.

Since it was so far beyond her power to imagine, it took Colleen a
long time to catch on to Brad's activities. The first thing she noticed was
that he was often leaving their bed in the middle of the night and going
downstairs to his home office. He offered several explanations—indigestion, insomnia, a report that was due the following day.

Brad's absence from the bed started to upset Colleen's sleep
rhythms, and sometimes she would go downstairs to see if she could
coax her husband back. When she appeared in the door of his study, he
would hurriedly press a key to darken the computer screen.

"What are you doing?" she asked him more than once.

"Working," he'd reply. Or he'd tell her he was just reading or
browsing.

Brad's peculiar middle-of-the-night behavior continued for months.
Sometimes he never made it to bed at all, heading for his study after dinner and staying there until two or three in the morning. He was spending less time with Colleen and the children, and their marriage was
suffering. Colleen felt abandoned.

"You love that computer more than you love us," she said one day, hoping to make Brad come to his senses. He didn't respond, so she cried. "It's like you're having an affair with the computer."

That got Brad's attention. He turned a bright shade of red—guilty red, Colleen thought—and stormed out of the room. The next day while Brad was at the office, Colleen went to his computer. She cracked his password, and before she knew it she was perusing the correspondence files of a single guy named Brett, who had a very full social life. There were many flirtatious e-mails from women, and the transcripts of some private conversations from online chat rooms that were extremely sexually graphic.

Colleen was horrified, but when she confronted Brad, he shrugged it off as nothing more than computer game-playing. "It's not real," he assured her. "I'm here every night, aren't I?"

Brad did not consider his online assignations as infidelity, but his wife, Colleen, did. She insisted that he stop his computer activities immediately and that they seek counseling. Eventually they separated and then divorced.

"To this day, Brad insists that he wasn't doing anything to hurt our marriage," Colleen says. "He didn't see that his behavior was emotional infidelity. He was withdrawing from us even as he pursued a fantasy life online. The fact that he didn't physically go out and pick up women doesn't mean he was being faithful."

A New Sort of Affair

Infidelity expert Dr. Shirley Glass found that 82% of unfaithful people she treated had "fallen" into an affair with someone who was, at first, "just a friend." These days, friendships and work relationships and Internet liaisons are interfering with marriages. And more women are having affairs than before. Dr. Glass reported, in her book *Not Just Friends*, that from 1982 to 1990, 38% of wives she treated who were unfaithful had been involved with someone they worked with. But from 1991 to 2002, the number of women having work affairs increased by 50%.

Obviously, men are also having affairs, and most of them are with people they work with. Among the people Dr. Glass treated, about 62% of unfaithful men met their affair partners at work.)

The other surprising news that Dr. Glass discovered is that *most people mistakenly think that infidelity isn't really infidelity if there's no sex.* Not true. "In the new infidelity, affairs do not have to be sexual," according to Dr. Glass. Many, including even Internet affairs, are primarily emotional. "Today's affairs are more frequent and more serious than they used to be because more men are getting emotionally involved and more women are getting sexually involved."

Dr. Glass notes the following, sobering statistic: "At least one or both parties in 50 percent of all couples, married and living together, straight and gay, will break their vows of sexual or emotional exclusivity during the lifetime of the relationship. . . . After reviewing twenty-five studies, however, I concluded that 25 percent of wives and 44 percent of husbands have had extramarital intercourse."

Leaving Mr. Right

Divorce rates continue to hold steady at around 50%. That is, one in two married couples are vowing out after an average of eight years. Overall, 27% of Americans have been divorced, and that doesn't even count the 58 million couples who are separated but not divorced. Divorce rates increase with multiple marriages. Although the divorce numbers haven't moved that much in recent decades, there is a signifi-

DID YOU KNOW?

According to an AARP poll, among divorcees ages 40 to 80, men suffer more than women. Men in this group report an increase in happiness when they are able to find a new partner postdivorce, while women report being happy regardless of whether they find a new partner.

cant change in who is doing the divorcing. Today, 66% of divorces are instigated by women, and the numbers are even higher among women in their fifties and sixties. Well-educated and economically self-sufficient, women no longer need to stay in bad marriages. They have options.

Traditionally, older women have been risk-adverse. But we're now seeing older women taking the leap after decades of marriage, striking out on their own to start businesses, travel, and invent new lives. In addition, the number of women who report cheating on their spouses is increasing. With almost 60% percent of women working outside the home, interactions with coworkers, frequency of business trips, the use of Internet dating sites, and, again, financial emancipation, have provided some women with both motive and opportunity to engage in extramarital affairs.

The federal government is making it more difficult to track these very significant trends; it has stopped collecting marriage and divorce statistics. Now they're only compiled at the state level—and some states are opting out of collecting them at all.

One positive sign in an otherwise grim statistical picture is the in-

BY THE NUMBERS

27
The percentage of Americans who have been divorced

8 YEARS
The average duration of a first marriage

66
The percentage of divorces initiated by women

43
The percentage of marriages that are remarriages

TROUBLE AHEAD?

According to statistics compiled by Jupiter Media Matrix, more than 30% of visitors to online singles sites are already married.

creasing momentum of collaborative divorces—amicable alternatives to messy, protracted court battles. These problem-resolution methods are now available in 35 states and much of Canada. Unlike traditional divorces, success in a cooperative setting is not measured by which party "wins," but by reaching a decision that is reasonable and acceptable to both parties. Prior to representing their clients, lawyers sign a pledge to withdraw from the case if either party decides mediation is not for them.

CAN THIS INSTITUTION BE SAVED?

"I admit that I worry about getting married because I don't want to end up divorced like my parents," said Erin, 27. "I'm not sure how to avoid it. They loved each other once, and then they stopped. They were so hostile in the end. It's scary. My friends who come from divorced families feel exactly the same way. The other day I heard a woman say, 'This is my starter marriage.' I thought that was pretty offensive."

Marriage remains the core institution in societies across the globe. Most people aspire to be married and consider it a crucial setting for raising children. From a socioeconomic standpoint, marriage creates a ring of protection around vulnerable individuals, and many social scientists believe that strengthening the family will reap benefits by strengthening the community at large—reversing the cycle of poverty, reducing the crime rate, improving health, and guaranteeing a better future for children. President Bush's Healthy Marriage Initiative grew out of this thinking.

Others believe that the best way to encourage stable families is to recognize that not every family looks—or needs to look—the same. Proponents of domestic partnerships and gay marriages argue that these unions are as solid as "traditional" marriages, and the proof is in the behavior, not the label.

As these trends continue, so, too, do the underlying debates. The "altared" state of marriage in America has some raising their eyebrows and others shrugging their shoulders, as all struggle to find the right social and personal recipe for a perfect union.

THE NEXT 10 YEARS

What are the implications of the seismic changes in the institution of marriage? While our society continues to encourage traditional marriage as a healthy and protective construct necessary for strong communities and thriving children, the definition of family grows more diverse.

- The median age of marriage will continue to rise. While this trend has usually been seen as having a long-term negative effect on family finances, we project that this negative impact will be countered by a positive reduction in the rate of divorce for the first time in 30 years.

- The greatest public policy change will occur in the arena of domestic benefits. While we don't expect the debate over gay marriage to be fully resolved in the next decade, we expect that committed partners, both gay and heterosexual, will achieve more domestic benefits—not by law but as a corporate recruiting tool.

- Expect to see changes in pension and Social Security policies that will enable widows to remarry without sacrificing their benefits.

- Generation Y'ers will slow the rise of the median age for first-time marriages, and trot down the aisle sooner than their commitment-adverse Gen X predecessors.

- More couples will be discussing their online habits before they get married, agreeing on parameters and accountability.

TREND 3

BABY FLUX

There are fewer babies being born than ever, but kid-centricity is on the rise. We are a child-obsessed nation, but where are the children?

Margaret, a Philadelphia caterer, was used to making frequent trips cross-country to Denver to visit her parents and three siblings. Since her husband's job was less flexible than hers, she usually made the trips alone. Then, when Nate was born, she thought nothing of packing him up and making him an infant frequent flier. She recalls her first trip with Nate in tow. "My seat was near the back of the plane, and as I walked down the aisle, I noticed that people were physically recoiling from me and turning their heads away. I could almost hear them thinking, 'Don't sit here, don't sit here.' When I reached my row, the man sitting on the aisle gave me a dirty look and said, 'Oh, great,' in a sarcastic voice. I felt like making a public apology for bringing a baby on board."

It's a paradox of modern life: **We are a child-centric nation, that lavishes time, attention, and material goods on our offspring, even as we are less than enthusiastic about having them around.** This "not in my neighborhood, not in my restaurant, not in my row" mentality is to some extent the customary attitude of adults who believe children have a time and a place, and should be seen and not heard. Sometimes the child aversion runs deeper, however, influencing the way mothers perceive they are treated. A joint study conducted by the University of Connecticut and the University of Minnesota found that one in five mothers feels "less valued by society since becoming mothers."

Baby booms and baby busts punctuate our nation's history. There have even been baby burps—somewhere between boom and bust. But what we're experiencing now can only be described as a baby boggle. On the one hand, fewer babies are being born to fewer women. According to the report "Fertility of American Women," **44% of all women of childbearing age (defined as age 15 to 44) are childless.** On the other hand, there is increasing evidence that we are obsessed with children. What gives?

We've called our third trend Baby Flux because we are experiencing our choices in entirely new ways. Try to imagine a woman in the 1960s handing over her fertilized eggs for another woman to incubate. Try to imagine a 1960s woman in her forties and even fifties giving birth to a healthy baby, after undergoing in vitro fertilization. And try to imagine a sixties kindergarten class where two-thirds of the parents are over 40. High-tech prescription drugs and fertility treatments have converged with delayed marriage and childbearing to create a brave, and very uncertain, new world.

The Graying of the American Mom

I was 46 when my son was born. Now when I take him to the playground people are constantly telling me how cute my *grandson* is. It makes me cranky, but it's worth it.

—SARAH, 50

With motherhood, women are again illustrating the desire to make decisions if and when they feel the time is right. Due to personal struggles between time for career and time for self, motherhood often gets delayed well into middle age, resulting in a higher likelihood of medically assisted pregnancies and aging parents. This trend is critical for policy redefinition. For example, with a delay in the start of a family, children have to assume financial and medical responsibility at an earlier

HAVING BABIES

	THEN	NOW
Social context	The purpose of marriage was to raise children	The purpose of marriage is to find personal satisfaction and commitment. Children may or may not be part of the deal.
Testing, testing	Pregnancy test	Fertility test
Birth method	Natural childbirth	Prescheduled cesarians (and if the delivery is vaginal, don't hold the epidural)
Single moms	Having babies out of wedlock was a crisis and a stigma	Single mothers are attractive to marketers.
Adoption	Live babies	Frozen embryos

age, and older couples must struggle to fund their retirements and their children's college educations simultaneously. **According to a July 4, 2004, *New York Times* report, seniors (65-plus) have the fastest growing share of personal debt. The primary drain on their finances, apart from health care and precription drugs, is support for adult children, in particular, paying for education and their children's first homes.** With older moms, that pressure will increase even more. It is particularly acute when the economy is struggling and we see a record number (52%) of adult children returning home to live.

Motherhood is still a priority, but women are delaying it to finish their educations and start careers. The result is a graying of the

American mom. More couples are joining the IV (in vitro) line as new fertility technology resets biological clocks and allows women to conceive well into their forties. The number of births to women aged 45 to 54 rose to 4,565 in 2000. According to the Centers for Disease Control, this is the highest number ever recorded for that age group, and the trend shows no sign of waning.

The remarkable increase in the number of single-mother households with women who have never married signals a dramatic shift to childbearing outside marriage. **The number of births to unmarried women grew from less than 90,000 per year in 1940 to more than 1.3 million per year in 1999. Single mother–led households have traditionally been economically marginal—21% currently live in poverty, but the emerging population of single mothers-by-choice tends to be more financially secure.**

Women are again illustrating the desire to make decisions when they feel the time is right. Because of personal struggles between time for career and time for self, motherhood often gets delayed well into

THE MOTHERHOOD CONTINUUM

Neil Gilbert, Chernin professor of social welfare at UC–Berkeley, makes an interesting case about the relationship between family size and women's personal goals. He posits that women make four basic lifestyle choices, which can be pictured along a continuum. At one end of the continuum are women with three or more children. These women tend to identify strongly as mothers, and their sense of worth comes from the traditional childrearing responsibilities and from practicing the domestic arts. "In 1976, about 59 percent of women over 40 years of age had three or more children," Gilbert observed. "But as women gained control over procreation and employment opportunities opened, fewer of them took this traditional route. Today, only 29 percent of the women over 40 years of age have three or more children."

At the opposite end of the continuum are women who are childless—often by choice. These women tend to be work-centered and achievement-oriented. In the last 30 years, this group has almost doubled among women over 40.

At the broad center of Gilbert's continuum, are the 52 percent of women over 40 who have one or two children. These women are interested in finding ways to balance employment and family. Gilbert divides the center into two categories. The first, "neotraditional" group, contains families with two children whose working mothers are physically and emotionally invested more in their home life than their jobs, which are often part-time. Since 1976 the proportion of women over age 40 with two children has increased by 75 percent and currently amounts to about 35 percent of the women in that cohort. The second, "modern" group involves a working mother with one child. These women are more career-oriented and devote greater time and energy to their paid employment than neotraditional women. The proportion of women over 40 with one child has climbed by almost 90 percent since 1976, and currently amounts to 17 percent of the women in that cohort.

middle age, resulting in a higher likelihood of medically assisted pregnancies and aging parents.

Hooked Up to a Different Kind of IV Line

I consider couples who spend small fortunes on fertility treatments so they can conceive in their forties to be self-indulgent. Hasn't anyone heard of adoption?

—JANICE, 33

Older couples who cash in their 401(k)s or max out their credit cards to become parents demonstrate the inherent desire of women to have biological children. Today, *one child in every hundred is conceived via fertility treatments in the United States.*

Here's one example. While there has always been a plethora of publications for pregnant and new mothers, new magazines target couples who are having trouble getting pregnant or are becoming parents later in life. *Conceive* magazine, started by two women who experienced infertility, covers issues such as miscarriages, fertility injections, and alternative therapies for conception, such as diet changes, stress reduction, and acupuncture. *Plum*, sponsored by the American College of Obstetricians and Gynecologists, is a free publication for women over 35.

Fertility treatment requires enormous commitment. The financial and emotional costs can be extraordinary. Depending on the number of attempts, the price tag can rise into the hundreds of thousands of dollars. The entire experience can place strains on the marriage. Even the strongest couples can be shaken by the loss of intimacy, the scheduled lovemaking, the embarrassment, and the guilt and blame. Many women find it a bitter irony that they're unable to have a baby when they've succeeded in every other way, personally and professionally. It may be easy to forget the agonies when you're cradling your bundle of joy, but for countless numbers of people, the joy (and the baby) never arrive.

The fertility industry is still largely unregulated, and there is no way to know exactly how many successes there have been—and how many attempts had to be made before a baby was conceived and carried to term. According to the industry itself, there is a 70% failure rate for each attempt.

According to the Centers for Disease Control, which compiles national statistics for all assisted reproductive technology techniques, success rates for IVF vary depending on a number of factors, including the reason for infertility, where the procedure is being done, and the age of the participants. The most recent CDC report from 2000 found:

- Successful pregnancy was achieved in 30.7% of all cycles.

- About 69% of the cycles carried out did not produce a pregnancy.

- Less than 1% of all cycles resulted in an ectopic pregnancy.

- About 11% of these pregnancies involved multiple fetuses.

- About 83% of pregnancies resulted in a live birth.

- About 17% of pregnancies resulted in miscarriage, induced abortion, or a stillbirth.

The average cost of an IVF cycle in the U.S. is $12,400, according to the American Society of Reproductive Medicine. This price will vary depending on region of the country, the amount of medications involved, the number of IVF cycles, and the amount—if any—of reimbursement by insurance companies. Although some states have enacted laws requiring insurance companies to cover at least some of the costs of infertility treatment, many states haven't.

Fertility technology brings with it a host of ethical challenges regarding the disposal of unused embryos. The debate about stem-cell research is an example of the difficult choices that face the nation as technology unleashes formerly unimagined possibilities. Clinics often prepare more embryos than a couple needs, because multiple implantations are the rule. So the question is: What should be done with the spare embryos? In the United States, no laws govern their storage and disposal. Each of the 400 or so fertility clinics registered with the Society for Assisted Reproductive Technology stands alone, creating and enforcing its own policies.

The increasing reliance on fertility treatments has also affected the adoption market. Couples who would once have chosen adoption because it was their only option, might pass it over if they have a chance to have their own baby—even if it utilizes someone else's sperm or egg. Indeed, the fastest-growing trend on the adoption front is frozen embryo adoption programs.

WOMB FOR HIRE

When Teresa Anderson, 25, delivered quintuplets last year, she was elated. So was the babies' genetic mother, Luisa Gonzalez, 32. "I've been waiting for this for a long time," she said, praising Teresa, the surrogate mother who provided the womb.

Gonzalez, a homemaker, and her husband Enrique Moreno, a landscaper, had been trying to start a family for 10 years, with no success. They met Teresa Anderson through a surrogacy website, and decided to go that route. Eggs were harvested from Luisa's ovaries and fertilized in a laboratory with Enrique's sperm. Teresa was then implanted with five embryos to increase the chance that one would bear fruit. All five were successful.

Teresa, who has two children with her own husband, decided to forego the $15,000 fee, because she knew the new family of seven needed the money.

The decisions we make about fertility have consequences that extend beyond individual families. The consensus has yet to be formed on this delicate matter of hired wombs, although in some legal proceedings the jury is *in*. The 1980s "Baby M" case in New Jersey made national news when state courts ruled the surrogate agreement null and void, and returned the infant to the surrogate mother, stating that she had not relinquished her rights to her birth child. Other courts have followed suit.

In your view, which word best describes a single woman who decides to have a child, either naturally or by adoption?

Total	Men	Women	
27%	**24%**	**30%**	**COURAGEOUS**
26%	26%	26%	LOVING
10%	11%	10%	FINANCIALLY SECURE
9%	9%	9%	NAÏVE
8%	8%	8%	MATURE
8%	9%	7%	SELFISH
4%	6%	2%	IMMATURE
3%	3%	2%	OTHER (VOLUNTEERED)
5%	5%	6%	DO NOT KNOW (VOLUNTEERED)
*	1%	*	REFUSED (VOLUNTEERED)

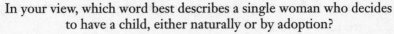

In your view, which word best describes a single woman who decides
to have a child, either naturally or by adoption?

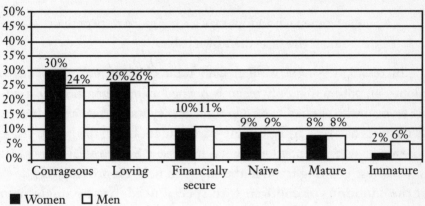

MOTHER COURAGE

Twenty-six percent of the nation's mothers are single women—some by
choice, some through circumstance. Our survey shows that both men
and women are becoming more accepting of a single woman who gives
birth to a baby or adopts. When asked, "Which word best describes a
single woman who decides to have a child, either naturally or by adoption?", 24% of men and 30% of women chose "courageous," followed
by "loving" (26% apiece). To call a woman who chooses to have children
alone courageous and loving is a dramatic departure from the stigmatiz-
ing descriptions of yore, when children who were born "out of wedlock"
were called "bastards," and the women who birthed them called worse.

Our survey detected a number of interesting facts.

- Women want children, even when they don't want a spouse.
  The pull of motherhood may be the strongest desire of all.
  In that respect, it makes sense that some single women
  would have children in cultures where it is not stigmatized.

- Although both men and women in our survey overwhelmingly favored having two parents in the household (a mother

and a father), they also approved of single women choosing
to have a child.

- Single women who adopt may garner more respect than single women who bear their own babies.

Increasingly, single women who want children are choosing to
adopt—an option that only recently opened up to them. In 1970, a single woman who applied to an adoption agency was turned away. In fact,
some states had laws against single-parent adoption. In the last 20 years,
however, single-parent adoption has increased. Some researchers say it
is the fastest-growing trend in the adoption field. **Approximately 25%
of the adoptions of children with special needs are by single men
and women,** and it is estimated that about 5% of all other adoptions are
by single people. The outlook for single-parent adoption is encouraging
as it becomes more widely accepted.

REALITY CHECK, PLEASE

While our survey respondents indicated that single women choosing
motherhood or adopting were probably financially secure, a parallel
track of single mothers is not doing so well. These are the underclass of
single women running households, who constitute 60% of all families
living in poverty. **Approximately 38% of never-married mothers are
below the poverty line.**

Over the past two decades, the number of poor, female-headed
households grew by 45%, faster than all poor families and poor married-
couple families (which grew by 39% and 24%, respectively). In recent
research, the Institute for Women's Policy Research (IWPR) has inves-
tigated the unique obstacles that low-income single mothers face in
moving their families out of poverty. Among low-income families (defined as having family incomes of less than 200% of the official poverty
line), single-mother families are the most impoverished group: 50%
were poor, compared with only 17% of low-income married-couple
families. Their higher poverty rates result from several causes: Single
mothers receive only small amounts of child support; they lack the in-

come-stabilizing effect of an additional earner that many married-couple families enjoy; and their earnings tend to be less than those of male breadwinners. These developments have enormous implications for public policy, as we will examine in later trends.

KINDER, GENTLER BIRTHING

Doulas, birthing tubs, labor massages, early epidurals—labor and delivery have come a long way in the last two decades alone. Women are combining new technology with old-fashioned folk wisdom to make the birth experience more comfortable, more meaningful, and less stressful all around. Deluxe wings are being built in hospitals to offer the height of luxury to new moms and their families, including private rooms, spouses, sofa beds, and Jacuzzis.

The biggest trend may be in the use of cesarian deliveries, which now comprise about 23% of all births in the United States. Once the method of last resort, the improved safety and increased availability of cesarians are making them an attractive option—especially to women accustomed to planning their lives and scheduling their days. More than 22% of cesarians are scheduled ahead of time at the mother's request.

FAVORITE AUNTIES

Our surveys show that most women are child-centered, even when they don't have or want children of their own. When it comes to involvement with children, single women on their own hardly lead a "barren" existence. Nearly every single woman we know is a devoted aunt, big sister, godmother, or friend to the children of her relatives, co-workers, and friends. These relationships are often extremely close, and single women often talk about how enriching it is to be involved in a mentor or confidante relationship, without having the obligations of parenthood.

DID YOU KNOW?

Gift registries aren't just for brides anymore. One in four mothers-to-be is registered at Babies "R" Us.

LACTIVISM RISING

On June 7, 2005, 200 breast feeding women gathered outside ABC studios in New York City for a nurse-in after Barbara Walters made a derogatory remark about public breast-feeding on her talk show, *The View*. The rally was an example of an increasingly vocal population of "lactivists" who are tired of being relegated to office storage rooms, bathrooms, closets, and other points of invisibility when they feed their babies. Many women say they have become frustrated by the mixed messages they receive about breast feeding. Today, nearly 70% of new mothers breastfeed—proof that the message about the demonstrable health benefits of breast milk has reached the mainstream. At the same time, mothers are often made to feel like pariahs when they try to feed their babies in public.

Watch this issue develop both in the business arena and legislatively. Already six states have passed laws giving women the right to breast-feed wherever they are "otherwise authorized to be." Even with the passage of laws, more work will need to be done to cross the murkier terrain of attitudes, beliefs, and biases. The trend is clear, however. Women are bringing their babies out of the back rooms, breasts and all.

CAUTION: ALPHA MOM ZONE

Alpha moms—those hyperperfectionist mothers with impossibly high standards—can suck the self-esteem out of a room faster than you can say, "My baby speaks three languages." Many mothers are feeling increased pressure to keep pace with the competitive craze to nurture baby Einsteins, while lavishing their children with more elaborate toys and scheduling them into more activities. Overhead on the playground: A woman explaining to a child of 5 who was having a meltdown because she didn't want to leave, "Alice, you know we have to do flash cards for 30 minutes before dinner. You do want to get into Harvard, don't you?" Huh?

Alpha moms raise the bar for all mothers, some of whom are just plain fed up. That's what inspired Judith Warner to write, *Perfect Madness: Motherhood in the Age of Anxiety*. Warner's book tapped into the rising tide of fear and doubt. Warner, a mother of two, states that American women are driving themselves (and their children) crazy with an obsessive quest to achieve motherhood perfection, as defined by the alpha moms. (It's sort of like taking nutritional advice from an anorexic. In fact, the "perfect mom" syndrome may be contributing to eating disorders in young women attempting to live up to expectations.) This quest overstresses moms and kids and squeezes the life out of child's play.

NEW TIMES, NEW TERMS

Familymoon: *A honeymoon in which the bride and groom bring their children from previous marriages.*

Helicopter parent: *A parent who hovers over his or her kids.*

Nanny-cam: *A special video camera, small enough to be concealed, used to spy on the babysitter.*

Parallel parenting: *Divorced parents assume different duties with the kids while avoiding contact with each other.*

Stealth parenting: *Performing child care duties while pretending to be at a business meeting or other work-related function.*

Trophy child: *A child used to impress others and enhance the status of a parent or parents.*

A little extra stress for a good cause never hurt anyone, but the problem with today's hyperparents is that they often measure perfect mothering by status symbols—getting their child into the "right" preschool, or catering the most elaborate birthday party. Children as young as 2 or 3 years old have multiple extracurricular activities. One 3-year-old we know takes ballet, swimming, and Spanish classes.

Of course, it takes time and money to be an alpha mom, which raises two questions: Is alpha mom striving for the kids' sake or her own? Accustomed to professional success, personal self-indulgence, and a rigorous schedule, she is not about to lose status or cede control because Junior wants to be a "normal" kid. And, secondly, are we as a society comfortable with parenting goals that promote materialism and further divide the haves from the have-nots? If they were being perfectly honest, some parents would say yes.

THE HYBRIDS

Another trend is remarriage—with children. More people are part of second marriages than first marriages, and *more than 65% of all remarriages involve kids. There are 20 million stepfamilies in the United States.* Today, when you ask a woman how many children she has, she may answer something like this: "Two of mine, one of his, and two of ours." Hybrid offspring are increasingly becoming the norm. Thus the familymoon. Encore brides and grooms are taking the kids and stepkids along on family vacations—familymooning at Disneyworld or other vacation spots. Yet, much as we'd wish that every stepfamily could model the Brady Bunch, the documentary version of this sugary sitcom is often more sobering. Creating harmony takes time and patience, and sometimes it never happens. There is no such thing as an instant family.

PET-TERNAL INSTINCT

Meet Furkid. He's cute and cuddly and he's got his father's eyes. He doesn't cry in the night, and he offers constant adoration—especially when treats are on hand. If you haven't guessed, Furkid is an animal. (Some even claim the word "pet" is politically incorrect, implying that animals can be *owned* by humans.)

There are more pets than people in the U.S., and they are sometimes treated better. From doggy day care, to doggy spas, to pet psychiatrists, to haute couture, people are treating their pets like surrogate offspring. Even Oprah devoted a show to introducing her "daughter," a cocker spaniel named Sophie.

A couple of our acquaintance with two cats named Osborne and Inkwell were looking at houses with a real estate agent. "Do you have any children?" the agent asked.

"Yes," the woman replied without missing a beat. "Our son Osborne is 12, and our daughter Inkwell is 8."

The real estate agent's jaw dropped. "You named your daughter *Inkwell?*" she gasped.

It's not just four-legged creatures that are being used as child replacements. In Japan, with birth rates rapidly declining, the Yumel doll fills a niche. The doll is a 15-inch baby boy, designed for childless people who are unable to care for a pet. The $80 Yumel is brighter than the average infant, with a vocabulary of 1,200 phrases, but no college tuition to pay for later.

OUR CHILDREN, OURSELVES

Children compel us to consider our morality and our mortality. They are the fulfillment of sociobiological imperatives as old as our species; they are, as the song says, our future. Progency is legacy. No wonder nearly every hot-button political, religious, and social issue involves them—from how we handle the tremendous responsibility of bringing them into the world to how we manage their care and instill the right values. Reproductive technology complicates the equation by presenting choices that previous generations did not encounter—be they preventing or aborting pregnancy or catalyzing new life in petri dishes. Information technology and changes in our culture expose our children to a world of outside input before they're even out of diapers—and we

HERE KITTY, KITTY

In the U.S. there are 377.8 million pets versus 290 million people. 77.7 million people own cats, while 65 million people own dogs. Pet spending is booming, as consumers spent $34.3 billion on their pets in 2004. By comparison, posted sales for the candy industry were $25.8 billion, and were $20.7 billion for the toy industry. Approximately 1 million U.S. dog and cat owners purchased health insurance for their pets. According to a survey by Purina and the Healthy Pets 21 Consortium of 2,001 cat and dog owners across the country:

- *Nearly 7-in-10 (68%) pet owners are women.*
- *Six-in-ten do not have children under the age of 18 in the home.*
- *Six in ten pet owners agreed that companionship is the greatest benefit of owning a pet.*
- *Over one quarter of pet owners have given their pets nutritional supplements.*
- *More than 15% consulted with a masseuse about a massage for their pooch.*
- *Pet owners with children in the home are less involved with their pets than those without. While a majority of those without children groom their pet daily (79%), only 21% with children do the same.*

are helpless to protect them completely. We can't un-ring the bells of modernization that have added so many moral challenges, and we'll never be in absolute agreement on what's best for ourselves and our children in every instance.

When we set out to write this book about the emerging consensus among women, many people asked how we could say that women are in agreement when there are such strong differences about abortion, stem-cell research, gay marriage, religion in public schools, and all the other hotly debated issues of the day. Fair question. When we probe beneath the labels and the rhetoric, we consistently find that women share the same goals for their children, even when they have different ideas about how to achieve them. Women will drive this debate, as they have many others, by virtue of their single-minded determination to put children first in our national conversation, to integrate children's needs into workplace constructs, and to incorporate our own hopes and fears, which are embodied in our children, into every public policy discussion. Women are the guardians of our children's futures, as we have always been, and our common will is stronger than any transitional political or cultural tide.

THE NEXT 10 YEARS

With fewer children being born to older parents, our focus in the next decade will be on the care and safety of our children.

- The edge of technology will advance from fertilization to developmental corrections, with improvements in microsurgery allowing in vitro corrections for abnormalities.

- While financially stable single women are becoming mothers by choice in larger numbers, single mothers on the whole represent the largest underclass. Watch for stronger policies to force deadbeat dads to pay up, including property liens and Social Security deductions, and education initiatives that encourage stable parenting models.

- The chief law enforcement issues in local communities will be related to child protection, including heightened prosecution for Internet pedophiles, sexual predators and abductors, and merchants who sell alcohol to teenagers.

- States will adopt significantly more public policies to protect children, often led by female office-holders.

OPEN-COLLAR WORKPLACES

Women are forsaking male models of work life that do not meet their needs and aspirations and inventing a new, more open and satisfying way of work.

Like most working women in America, the authors of this book are constantly searching for the same type of control and flexibility they offer their clients. Kellyanne shuttles between New York and Washington, D.C., with her twin babies, mother, aunt, and handicapped dog in tow. Celinda lives on airplanes. As women who head our own companies, we are acutely aware of the challenges—both complex and exhilarating. We've named our fourth trend Open-Collar Workplaces to denote a major movement, driven by women, toward more flexible work styles.

This trend is not without contradictions—as seen from women who are opting out of the workplace altogether, or among the working poor where options are limited. However, from all the diverse dreams, desires, and realities, we've detected the seeds of a movement. We've taken note of the way **women in every corner of the workplace have shaken up the formula of blue-collar and white-collar in an effort to leave the old models behind and invent a style and philosophy of**

work with more options, greater flexibility, better benefits, and, frankly, deeper fulfillment.

To a great extent this trend has been the handiwork of the women of Generation X (born between 1965 and 1978). Their baby boomer mothers tried to "have it all," all at once, but Gen Xers eschew that stressful mandate for a mellower, more eclectic work style, convinced that success at work and happiness at home are not mutually exclusive, but may require some creative sequencing. It all depends on the way one defines success; increasingly, women are inventing a new rubric that includes both tangible rewards and intangible benefits. In a recent survey in the *Washington Post* about the challenges facing mothers, the authors pointed out that "modern-day mothers have shifted from trying to be the mythical 'Supermom' to a more up-to-date version of the superhero Elastigirl, aka the mom of the hit film *The Incredibles*, whose superhuman talent is the ability to stretch and twist and contort herself into whatever form it takes to keep her family sheltered and safe."

"Having it all is just another way of saying having all the stress and none of the benefits," observed Vera, a 35-year-old legal secretary. "I think women are beginning to realize that the choice isn't all or nothing."

WANTED: TO BE MY OWN BOSS

Anne's first foray into being her own boss grew out of failure and necessity. "I started my own web design business because I couldn't find a job in my field—graphic arts—after college," she said. "I always assumed I'd work for a big advertising agency, but that field is so competitive. At first I was embarrassed to tell people I was self-employed. They'd go, 'Having trouble finding work, huh?' or ask if my parents were supporting me, because they couldn't imagine that I was making a living. I was just getting by, and my parents did a lot for me. One Christmas they gave me six months of gas and electric. It was the best gift I'd ever received."

Priscilla's experience was somewhat different. She was doing well financially, but she was miserable with the work. "I worked for an upscale catering firm for five years," she said. "The karma was lousy. There was a lot of shouting, tremendous pressure, and an atmosphere of fear. Just

THE WORKPLACE

	THEN	NOW
Income	"What do you make?"	"What is your benefits package?"
Success model	Climbing the ladder	Riding the on-and off-ramps
Seniors	Retirement	Protirement
Work style	Hierarchical	Collaborative
Go-getters	Driven to achieve at any cost	Balanced and well-rounded
Mommy mode	Stealth parenting	Taking kids to the office and on business trips
Favorite perk	Golf club membership	On-site day care
Rewards	Money and title	Benefits and happiness

what you don't want when you are creating beautiful meals. I used to dream about what it would be like not to jump every time the phone rang. Finally, when I realized the job was making me physically ill, I decided I had to make a move. My husband helped me get a loan to open up a storefront in our town. We sell ready-made gourmet meals for working mothers and busy families. I have three employees, and this summer I'm adding two more. I am active in the small business association in our area, and I love it. I can walk to work, and the kids come to the store after school. There's a wonderful feeling of old-fashioned values."

Both Anne and Priscilla found a precious commodity—control—when they started their own businesses. They are in good company. Be-

MOM(mom) AND POP(pop) SHOPS

The newest segment of entrepreneurs are junior-seniors. Since 1990 there has been a 23% increase in the number of people age 50 and older who are self-employed. Layoffs and a more competitive job market have driven this group, which will number 118 million by 2020, to consider hanging out their own shingle, giving them the flexibility they desire, which enables them to spend more time with the family.

tween 1997 and 2002, the number of women-owned firms grew by 37%—four times the rate of all employer firms. Today, **women own more than 26% of the nation's 20.8 million companies, generating nearly $2.3 trillion in revenue.** One in every eleven women is a business owner, and they're choosing this route for very different, even opposite, reasons than men.

Studies show that men typically go into business for themselves because an opportunity comes along and they seize it. They value independence, and say the best part of owning a business is being out on their own. Women, in contrast, are more inclined to start their own businesses as a way of integrating various relationships and obligations. They value collaboration and the ability to combine work and family responsibilities. If they've worked in more rigid or closed settings, they are determined to have more openness and ingenuity. Many female self-employed or business owners are escapees from corporate life, where they grew tired of butting their heads against unreasonable bosses, unruly workloads, unregulated hours, and the occasional glass ceiling.

This vigorous trend is surprising even to the businesswomen themselves. More than 25% of women entrepreneurs say they never planned to own a business or considered business ownership a career option; their entry into entrepreneurship came as a result of a life-changing event, such as the death of a spouse, the birth of a child, or getting laid off from a long-held position.

Small businesses account for a growing share of the job market and have become a strong political force in Washington. While larger companies tend to be more pragmatic in their political influence, splitting their electoral and financial support between the two major parties, entrepreneurs are gaining clout by sticking to ideology and backing those who address their needs. For instance, groups like the National Federation of Independent Businesses, Small Business and Entrepreneurship Council, and the American Small Business Association were influential in the passing of the Bush tax cut in 2001, and were a significant factor in the 2004 presidential race. According to National Federation of Small Businesses surveys, women-owned businesses are also shifting the public agenda. Male-owned businesses have tax cuts as their number one agenda item, while women-owned businesses have affordable health care at the top of their lists.

Not so long ago, hanging out a shingle seemed more aspirational than achievable to many women. Now they are becoming more attainable. Fully 20% of women identify themselves as small business owners; of these, 6% are full owners, 4% are partial owners, and 10% are self-employed or earning self-employment income. These numbers are only slightly lower than for men; 10% are owners, 3% partial owners, and 13% self-employed.

According to our survey, women who went into business for themselves did so to gain greater financial security (20%), for flexibility or more time (20%), greater independence (15%), for a change in career (9%), and because it was the "right" time (10%). Their greatest challenges were funding the start-up (27%), fear of failure or the unknown (15%), and going without a regular paycheck and benefits for a period of time (15%).

We asked women who were not currently business owners to share their thoughts and possible aspirations about starting a business. Assuming money were no object, nearly half of them (46%) wanted to start their own business, while 41% eschew entrepreneurship and would stay in their current jobs. Those who were most passionate about starting their own business seemingly had the most to gain, and the most flexibility—younger, lower-income, minority women with less education and no

BY THE NUMBERS

26
The percentage of American businesses owned by women

$2.3 TRILLION
The annual revenues generated by women entrepreneurs

10.1 MILLION
The number of firms at least 50% owned by women

30 MILLION
The number of full-time teleworkers

children. The breakdown was as follows: Women who most aspired to owning their own businesses were African American women (66%), single women (62%), women 18 to 24 years old (61%), women with some college (57%), women who made less than $29,000 a year (56%), and women without children (55%). Furthermore, women who see their current employment as just as job as opposed to a career are more likely than career women to want to venture out on their own (63% to 40%).

Curiously, even those women who did not aspire to actually own a business wanted to work in a woman-owned business. They saw flexibility and time off for family obligations as important lifestyle benefits that were more possible in a woman-owned business: 11% of our survey respondents said flexible hours would be the biggest benefit of working for a woman-owned business, and the same number cited time off for important family obligations. A full 16% said the biggest benefit was that women understand women better, and 13% cited the role model of women's leadership. Men said they wanted to work for women-owned businesses, too, if they had families. Time off for important family obligations was the biggest benefit men saw in working for a woman (13%).

Female small business owners are developing a new culture of work—one that is horizontal rather than vertical. That's good news for the 18 million workers employed by women. Women-owned businesses often aspire to be more flexible, more family-friendly, more technology-reliant, and more creative. Women small business owners also express the desire, when economically feasible, to offer critical benefits, especially health care, to their employees. They'd like to reduce stress and absenteeism with innovative employee constructs, including cross-training, just-in-time work cycles, telecommuting, and bringing kids (and sometimes pets) to work. An Arthur Andersen/Ameritech study suggested that **both men and women would rather work for a woman if their firm were being downsized, believing that their interests would be better protected.**

A study conducted by THE POLLING COMPANY, INC./WomanTrend (TPC/WT) in collaboration with Event Strategies, Inc. (ESI) at the *Northeast Regional Conference on Women Entrepreneurship in the 21st Century*, in August 2002, produced some fascinating data about women small business owners. Analysis of the data derived from the study indicated five overarching concepts:

- Although *"Money"* frequently appears as the issue of greatest concern for WSBO, it is not *the driving force* behind starting a business.

- A woman's desire for professional achievement and longer-term perseverance are *more likely* to lead her to own and operate a small business than the quest for tangibles such as money.

- "Time," not money, *is the most sought-after component* in the lives of women small business owners, and as a true indication of its value and her appreciation for time, women are willing to repay extra hours *in* the workplace with extra hours *away* from the workplace.

- WSBO place the *most value* on employee attributes that pertain more to human nature than acquirable skills, and overall, recognize and appreciate the role employees play in their small business.

- Fostering a family-friendly workplace is of high priority for most WSBO, with 85% "strongly agreeing" with the statement "it is important for me to offer my employees a family-friendly work environment." An additional 8% "somewhat agreed" (net 93% agree). Often times, "family-friendliness" includes allowing employees additional personal time out of the office.

Women entrepreneurs are also among the most philanthropically active businesses. More than 70% of them volunteer in the community at least once a month; over half of them give $25,000 or more a year to charity.

REACH OUT

When Geraldine, 32, was in business school, her teachers often talked about the importance of having a mentor, and she was fortunate to find one in her first boss at an international development firm. Jeffrey was genuinely interested in her advancement. He taught her how to negotiate tough contracts, coached her on presentations, and provided many opportunities for her to network with others in the field. Thanks to Jeffrey, she quickly gained confidence and skill.

There weren't many women executives at the company, and Geraldine was often heralded as a rising star. After she married and had her first child, Jeffrey was supportive, but often at a loss as to how to help her prosper at work while balancing her family life. She wondered if a woman mentor might help her manage these new, more complex issues.

Geraldine's experience is echoed by thousands of women in the workplace. Surveys of women in business show that they often rely on men rather than women to mentor them in business, most likely because there are more men in positions of influence and experience. As long as they follow traditional patterns of career growth, male mentors are very effective. For those women who confront barriers that are uniquely female—matters of style, work-family balance, and bias—and female mentors become invaluable.

A poll by CareerWomen.com found that 64% of women reported that their most important mentors have been male, while 36% reported that women mentors have been the most influential in their careers. There were important differences in the types of mentoring provided. Male mentors helped women by providing general business training, leadership opportunities, coaching feedback, negotiating skills, and networking and advancement opportunities. By contrast, female mentors provided informal fellowship, guidance within the corporation, motivation and encouragement. Women also cite several areas where women mentors were essential, including sharing strategies for women's career success, work-life balance, job share, maternity leave, advice on overcoming gender bias in the workplace, and even style advice.

The results of the survey point to how a mentor's guidance can vary depending on whether the mentor was male or female.

Male mentor

General business training..............................*92%*
Leadership opportunities..............................*95%*
Feedback, coaching, advice *62%*
Networking, advancement opportunities *76%*
Motivation and encouragement.......................*59%*
Guidance within corporation..........................*23%*
Informal fellowship.....................................*21%*

Female mentor

Informal fellowship *79%*
Guidance within corporation *77%*
Motivation and encouragement *41%*
Feedback, coaching, advice *38%*
Networking, advancement opportunities............*24%*
General business training *8%*
Leadership opportunities.................................*5%*

The survey's authors concluded that both male and female mentors were essential for women in business, but to fully prosper over time women needed the advice and support of other women. Recognizing the absence of strong female mentors in the workplace, a number of organizations are filling the gap. Two standouts are the WomentorSM Group and WOMEN Unlimited. The WomentorSM Group is a woman-owned business specializing in educational consulting and training. The WomentorSM Group is able to customize training sessions for organizations interested in gender and leadership and create mentoring programs for organizations and their members. WOMEN Unlimited is a highly visible, successful development program for achievement-oriented women. The company works with top organizations to help attract, retain, and develop emerging, high-potential, and executive women.

In our interviews with women executives, we have found a great eagerness to help other women succeed in business. The idea that women, especially within the same company, will not help each other succeed because they are each fighting for the limited top slots allotted to females is disappearing as women continue to advance. Women tell us that their personal success is linked to the success of women in general. Furthermore, we find that women tend to be far more collaborative than men when it comes to problem solving and sharing credit for projects.

The American business model was built on the idea of personal achievement, emphasizing lone "superheroes" like Ross Perot and Donald Trump as the ideal of success. Women are gradually introducing a different, more egalitarian, model—one that relies on cooperation, team productivity, and a healthy work-life balance. This emerging trend is a powerful demonstration that women do not have to be cutthroat to prosper. They can do it *their* way.

SINGLE IN LIFE AND WORK

According to our survey, single women are much less likely to own their own business than their married counterparts—13% compared to 23% married. They are more likely to aspire to opening their own business, however, with 62% who would open their own business if money were no object, compared to 42% of married women. Funding is an even greater barrier for them in starting their own business than it is to married women—33% name it as the greatest challenge, compared to 28% of married women. However, singles are slightly less worried about the risk of not have a paycheck or benefits: only 11% say it is the biggest challenge, compared to 17% of married women.

If you had the choice, would you prefer to work full-time, part-time, or would you prefer to not work at all?

Total	Men	Women	
41%	**50%**	**32%**	**WORK FULL-TIME**
30%	23%	37%	WORK PART-TIME
26%	24%	28%	NOT WORK AT ALL
1%	1%	1%	DO NOT KNOW (VOLUNTEERED)
1%	1%	1%	REFUSED (VOLUNTEERED)

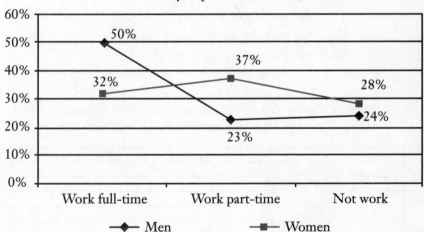

If you had the choice, would you prefer to work full-time, part-time, or would you prefer not to work at all?

THE GOOD LIFE ACCORDING TO WOMEN

Since both men and women spend more of our lives working (including thinking about work and commuting to and from work) than doing nearly anything else, it is not surprising that work issues are at the top of our minds when we discuss women's issues. Whether working for someone else, at her own company, from home, or within the home, women face many challenges in the workforce that are both similar to and completely different from the challenges men face.

Even so, women report the quality of their family and work lives as much better than that of their parents' at their age. **Three-quarters (77%) of women say the quality of their work life is better, with 52% saying it is** *much* **better.**

Would you say the quality of your **work life** *is better or worse than that of your parent's when they were your age?*

Total	Men	Women	
74%	72%	77%	**TOTAL BETTER (NET)**
49%	46%	52%	MUCH BETTER
25%	26%	25%	SOMEWHAT BETTER
15%	17%	11%	**TOTAL WORSE (NET)**
10%	11%	8%	SOMEWHAT WORSE
5%	6%	3%	MUCH WORSE
10%	8%	10%	DO NOT KNOW (VOLUNTEERED)
1%	2%	1%	REFUSED (VOLUNTEERED)

Among Women: Would you say the quality of your work life is better or worse than your parents' when they were your age?

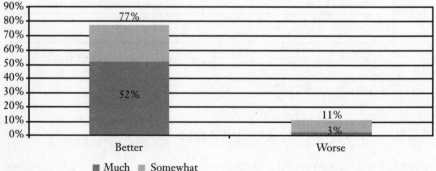

We asked women to tell us what their ideal job and family situation would be. We took note of several themes, as outlined below, along with some of their comments.

The Desire for a "Good Job and a Supportive Family"

- "My ideal would be a job I like and the family to support me."

- "A steady job, a good income, and a loving family."

- "Family: married with kids—two at most. They have good schools, good babysitters, and good friends. They'd be happy, and I'd be happy in my work."

- "My ideal would be to have a work schedule that would not conflict with my family."

- "A stable home and stable finances are important to me."

- "My ideal is a job I really enjoy and that pays well and having a significant other. Good personal and financial relationships."

The Need to Find Work-Family Balance

- "I would be happiest to go to work, have my children in day care, and come home every day to a happy family."

- "I'd like to work in public service and work for someone who would have empathy for my family situation, as my husband is overseas in the military."

- "I'm not sure it exists in the real world, but I'd say ideally, where I can work 40 to 50 hours a week and still have time to do things with my children."

The Desire to Be at Home with Young Children

- "My ideal would be not having to work when my children are young."

- "I want to stay at home with my kids."

- "I would love to stay at home and have babies."

- "Ideally, I would like to be home with my children when they're little, and go back to work when they are 5 years old."

Flexible or Entrepreneurial Job with Family

- "My dream is to work for myself, have my own home, and be financially stable."

- "The ideal would be to work out of my home."

- "I see the possibility that I can have a career at home."

- "I want to be self-employed and have my family around me."

Part-Time Work with Family

- "My ideal would be to work 20 to 25 hours a week, and be there when my kids come home from school."

- "Oh boy! Part-time work with good pay, gives you more time with your family."

PAYCHECK OR PASSION?

Women in our survey were divided over whether their current employment was more of a paycheck or a passion, with 39% calling it their desired career, and 36% viewing it more as a job. In contrast, nearly half of men described it as their true professional calling (49%), with 32% calling it a means to an end.

Would you consider your current employment situation to be more of a job, or your desired career?

Total	Men	Women	
44%	**49%**	**39%**	**MY DESIRED CAREER**
34%	32%	36%	MORE OF A JOB
7%	6%	8%	DO NOT WORK OUTSIDE THE HOME (VOLUNTEERED)
2%	1%	2%	BOTH (VOLUNTEERED)
8%	7%	10%	NEITHER (VOLUNTEERED)
3%	2%	4%	DO NOT KNOW (VOLUNTEERED)
1%	2%	1%	REFUSED (VOLUNTEERED)

African American women are more likely to see their current employment as more of a labor than a true calling (45% to 31%), while white women lean more toward saying it was a desired career more than just a job (40% to 35%).

Where one stands on this question was greatly influenced by where she sits on the economic ladder. Lower-income and less educated women are significantly more likely to see their current employment as more of a job, while higher-income and more educated women say they are in their desired career.

MOTHERS UNITE

Miranda's daughters, Cheryl, 25, and Eve, 28, still remember the way things were when they were young. Miranda was an intensely driven working mother, who did not leave the stresses and strains of her profession at the office. "When Mom was at work, she was off-limits," Eve recalls. "The rule was that we were never to call the office unless there was fire or blood."

"If you were sick," Cheryl adds, "you had to demonstrate it, either with a high fever or by vomiting. It wasn't enough to just feel lousy. Once I wrapped a heating pad around my head for an hour, hoping it would raise my temperature, but I only managed 99 degrees, so off to school I went."

JOB OR CAREER?

JOB	CAREER
Waitress Mom	*Feminist Champion*
Alienated Single	*Alpha Striver*
Multicultural Maverick	*Religious Crusader*
Suburban Caretaker*	

* Suburban Caretakers are split between job and career, but lean slightly toward job.

Miranda, now 57, does not have the best memories of that period, either. "I had gotten a big break, a job as reporter for our local paper, and I was determined to appear just as dedicated and flexible as the men. If the editor called a 6 P.M. work meeting, I didn't flinch. If a volunteer was needed to go after a late story, I was first in line. It's strange now that I think about it, that I never mentioned my daughters or asked for any family time off. I was well aware of the competitive environment, and there was no way I would ever admit that I had to get home to my kids. If the babysitter fell through, I'd lie to my boss and say I had a doctor's appointment or was doing an interview. I didn't want to give him an excuse to think I couldn't do my job because I had children. I kept my kids in the closet for years. It was unhealthy for them and for me—and it certainly didn't advance the cause of women in the workplace."

Miranda's daughters, both mothers with young children, would not dream of putting themselves and their children through such a warped existence. Cheryl plans to stay home with her son, now 2, until he's in the first grade, although she'll do occasional part-time work in her husband's small law office. Eve, a geriatric specialist for a hospital chain, works full-time, but she telecommutes one day a week, usually on Fridays. And if her 3-year-old daughter needs her, she'll make an effort to readjust her schedule. Her boss is a mother, too, and she's an ally.

Miranda's daughters have made different choices about how they'll balance work and family, but they wouldn't suggest that their mother had made a wrong choice. "You have to do what's right for you and your family," Cheryl says.

The women we surveyed agreed by and large that the decision about whether to work or stay home is a distinctly personal one for most women. They weren't critical. Yet there is a pervasive notion that a hostile conflict exists between mothers who choose to stay at home with their children and mothers who work outside the home. **In this somewhat mythical standoff, Working Mom regards Stay-at-Home Mom as a dropout, while Stay-at-Home Mom cites Working Mom for dereliction of duty. Our polling shows that the faceoff isn't necessarily between women. Rather, both groups struggle with cultural expectations. Furthermore, they share the most important value in common—putting kids first, regardless of their social, professional, or economic circumstances. And most women who are at home today expect to be in the workforce when their children are older though still at home.**

As further evidence that the question of work versus home is more nuanced a *Washington Post* poll found that **25% of working mothers work fewer hours than the traditional 40 hour week, while 25% of "stay-at-home moms" currently do some work for pay.** Some women have decided they can have it all, just not at the same time, and certainly with less intensity or absolutism.

In recent decades, the most dramatic increases in labor force participation have been among married women, particularly those with young children. In 1998, 71% of married mothers of children under age 6 did some work for pay during the year. But just 35% worked full-time year-round, which means that nearly two-thirds of married mothers of preschoolers did not work full-time in 1998.

To some extent, **the return of the stay-at-home mom has been glorified by the media**—probably because the idea is so provocative. One myth fueling the tension between working and stay-at-home moms is the idea that two-paycheck families were sacrificing their children's

BY THE NUMBERS

55
The percentage of mothers in the labor force who have infant children

25
The percentage of women age 25–44 who are out of the workforce

22
*The percentage of women with advanced degrees
who are at home with their kids*

11 MILLION
*The number of children under 15
with stay-at-home mothers and working fathers*

well-being so they could buy expensive cars and live in fancier houses. The reality is more pragmatic: **For many families, one paycheck isn't enough to support even the essentials.**

The trend in mothers opting out of the workplace can't be ignored, however. **In the first big decline since 1976, more moms are staying home with the kids, and 7 in 10 working women tell pollsters they would stay home with their kids if they could.** The difference is less family *values* than family *income*. Among many affluent younger moms, staying home with the kids has become the new status symbol. And there is an emerging trend in mothers returning home when their children become teenagers, believing their kids need extra supervision during those vulnerable years. These women are highly educated, financially well-off, and often have had successful careers. They're *choosing* to be home with their children, perhaps with sacrifice, but mostly without guilt. More than 1.1 million of their children are being home-schooled, most often by their mothers.

A generation of former latchkey kids may be the driving force behind this mini-counterrevolution in childrearing. Many of these highly educated, affluent women are choosing to delay or forego careers to raise their children. **One in four mothers ages 25 to 44 is out of the workforce altogether.**

The cultural pendulum has a way of swinging widely from one generation to the next, finally adjusting toward the middle with the third generation. That may be what we're observing with this trend—a more balanced way to integrate work and family. It's about restoring stability, and perhaps sanity. Career commitment doesn't have to mean 80-hour workweeks.

Gen X men are involved in this trend as well. This generation of fathers is far more involved in the lives of their children. A case in point: In 2003, 46% of employees taking parental leave at Ernst & Young were men.

Young couples tend to be more egalitarian when it comes to parenting. **Fathers born between 1965 and 1979 spend almost the same number of hours a day with their children as working mothers— about 3.5 hours.** According to a recent study, 70% of men would take a pay cut to spend more time with their families. Indeed, many workplaces have come a long way since 1991, when the Catalyst Foundation in New York City asked 1,500 chief executives what was a reasonable amount of time for a father to take off upon the birth or adoption of a child. Sixty-three percent said "none."

We asked survey respondents, "In your opinion, what are the biggest challenges facing mothers who work outside the home full-time?" Notably, nearly all respondents voiced concern about family stability, as opposed to fear about job security. Time and child care topped the list, followed by the stress of doing it all. Here, in their own words, are some of their responses:

Time

- "Not spending time with the children"

- "Missing out on too much, and missing a lot of firsts with the children"

- "Problems with making enough time to spend with the children"

- "Lack of time with children, missing out on their growth"

- "Not being completely involved in my child's life"

- "Not enough family time"

- "Balancing time with family and time at work"

Child Care

- "Making sure you have good child care"

- "Finding adequate child care"

- "Child care—it's a hard choice to make, and it's very scary to find a good care person or nanny"

Doing It All

- "Trying to do it all, managing a career and children. Something always is going to suffer; you can't excel at everything all at once."

- "Finding balance to accomplish everything a mother needs to do and have time for herself and time for her spouse."

- "Laundry and keeping up with things and staying in budget."

- "The woman has to accept that she can't do it all. She has to be okay with the fact that something's going to have to give, whether it be not having the house look how she'd like it to look, or spending time with the children."

We also asked respondents, "In your opinion, what are the biggest challenges facing mothers who are at home full-time?" Not surprisingly, they voiced the reverse need—more adult stimulation and companionship. Respondents also stated some trepidation over the way they believed stay-at-home mothers were perceived by others.

Stimulation and Adult Company

- "Perhaps not being able to be with adults or talking with other adults."

- "Remaining sane because of the lack of adult conversation or socialization."

- "Trying to keep your sanity."

- "Keeping your sanity or keeping your individuality."

- "Sanity. Keeping your sanity—jealous husband, kids, having too much to do, being picked on, told to do this or to do that . . . the job never ends and that leads to insanity."

Missed Dreams

- "Isolation, not being able to live up to your potential. If you are educated, to pursue a career you were educated for."

Peer Pressure from Other Moms

- "Facing pressure by society to go out there and work instead of staying at home and raising your children"

- "Peer pressure from working moms"

- "Social pressures from people who think you should have careers"

The clear common ground for these two groups of women is that they are both frustrated by the gulfs between what they want and what they can have. Both want balance. Both feel they are forced to make too many sacrifices—sacrifices that men aren't expected to make. When they think about it, they realize that their argument is not with one another, but with the social structure that forces such sacrificial choices in the first place.

Which brings us back full circle to the motivation for a woman-centered workplace. Having learned through experience that representations of flextime and family-friendly offices rarely gave them balance, but created a lot more fear, many working moms are forging creative alternatives and forcing changes in the workplace that go beyond lip service. On the other side, educated, engaged women, who believe it's essential that they be present for their children for more than a couple of hours a day, crave more integration into an intelligent, adult society. Both groups wonder why the obligation to make things work rests mainly on their heads. (Yes, there are approximately 105,000 dads on duty, hardly enough to make a difference.)

Beverly, a 40-year-old mother of two who works as a representative of a major pharmaceutical company, articulated it well when she said, "Why is it up to me? My bosses are parents. They know what's involved. They are big on family values. But if companies really valued families, they would act as if it's a shared responsibility—something for all of us to figure out."

Not willing to hold their breath for that day, many women are opting out, not of work, but of the workplace *du jour*. That, we believe, is an impetus for the phenomenal trend toward women-owned businesses in this country: If the mousetrap is beyond repair, build your own.

MOMPRENEURS ONLINE

Women have largely overtaken their male counterparts in the income-producing sectors of the Internet. **More than 55% of sellers on eBay are women, accounting for about $1.2 billion in annual sales.** This leap has occurred virtually overnight; eBay may have started out as a fancy garage sale, but women have taken it to another level.

Women eBay entrepreneurs have a role model at the helm in eBay chief Meg Whitman. In 2004 Whitman was selected as *Fortune* magazine's Most Powerful Woman Executive. Whitman, 49, oversees a $62 billion company, with twice the stock value of General Motors.

Whitman is enthusiastic about eBay being a perfect fit for many women. "You can pick the product that you want to sell, and invest as much or as little time as you want," she says. "You can connect with people who share your interests."

It's not a matter of small change, either. Experts estimate that a woman can comfortably earn $50,000 from an eBay business.

BALANCING ACTS

Women have always had to juggle work and family responsibilities. While the 1990s and the turn of the millennium have brought more men into the traditionally female sphere of the home, women still do the majority of the juggling act.

What do you think is the biggest problem facing women at work today?

Total	Men	Women	
36%	34%	37%	**COMBINING WORK AND FAMILY**
15%	12%	17%	RECEIVING EQUAL PAY FOR EQUAL WORK
11%	12%	9%	DISCRIMINATION IN HIRING AND PROMOTIONS
9%	9%	9%	LACK OF AFFORDABLE, QUALITY CHILD CARE
5%	5%	5%	STRESS GENERALLY
4%	6%	3%	SEXUAL HARASSMENT
4%	4%	4%	LOW PAY AND WAGES

(continued on next page)

Total	Men	Women	
2%	1%	2%	NOT ENOUGH OPPORTUNITIES FOR EDUCATION AND TRAINING
2%	2%	1%	LACK OF JOB SECURITY
1%	1%	1%	POOR HEALTH CARE BENEFITS
1%	*	1%	POOR RETIREMENT BENEFITS
4%	4%	4%	OTHER (VOLUNTEERED)
6%	7%	6%	DO NOT KNOW (VOLUNTEERED)
1%	2%	1%	REFUSED (VOLUNTEERED)

Both women and men survey respondents recognize that the biggest problem facing women at work today is combining work and family—37% of women see that as the biggest problem, and 34% of men do. It's a greater obstacle than receiving equal pay for equal work (17% women and 12% men), discrimination in hiring and promotions (9% women and 12% men) and lack of affordable, quality child care (9% for both women and men).

Women with higher incomes and education who are of childbearing age are even more concerned about combining work and family. Those most worried about combining work and family are postgraduates (51%), women who make $70,000 a year or more (50%), Republican women (44%), and women 18–34 and 35–54 (38% and 41%, respectively).

Women see many different avenues toward gaining the openness they desire, though not all of them are options for all women. Part-time work and starting a business seem to be two ways that women could have the flexible schedule they need on the teetering see saw of home and office. Being your own boss and flexibility in work schedule are the two greatest benefits to starting your own business according to both men and women in our survey.

A plurality of women surveyed would prefer to work part-time, ostensibly to free them to focus on their families. Thirty-seven percent of women would prefer working part-time, with 32% preferring to work full-time, and 28% who would rather not work at all.

Not surprisingly, women with children were more likely than women without children to want to work part-time: 39% of mothers would like to work part-time, compared to 30% of women without children; 30% of mothers would rather not work at all, compared to 24% of women without children.

Contrary to stereotypes, women who see their current job as just that are split over whether they would rather work part-time or full-time (35% for each), but women who view present employment as their desired career are more likely to want to work part-time (42% part-time, 34% full-time).

Higher-income women are significantly more likely than others to want to work part-time (50%). Women earning less than $30,000 are the only group that would prefer to work full-time (38% full-time to 33% part-time).

Although they are concerned about work-family balance, it does not keep women from moving up the work ladder. Women have made and are willing to make many sacrifices in order to reach the top of their field. Long hours and weekend work is the biggest sacrifice (20%), followed by assuming more stress and responsibility (15%), and less time spent with family and loved ones (12%). Women are more likely than men to say they have not made any sacrifices to get ahead and would not make them. Thirty-two percent of women wouldn't make any, compared to only 21% of men.

Thinking about your own personal employment experiences, what sacrifices have you made or are willing to make in order to reach the top of your field?

Total	Men	Women	
27%	21%	32%	NONE OF THE ABOVE/I WOULD NOT SACRIFICE ANYTHING
23%	26%	20%	WORK LONG HOURS AND WEEKENDS
14%	13%	15%	HAVE MORE STRESS AND RESPONSIBILITY
12%	11%	12%	SPEND LESS TIME WITH FAMILY AND LOVED ONES
6%	7%	6%	INCREASE WORK TRAVEL
5%	5%	4%	DELAY MARRIAGE
5%	5%	5%	DELAY PARENTHOOD
5%	6%	4%	LOSE TOUCH WITH OLD FRIENDS
3%	4%	6%	OTHER (VOLUNTEERED)
5%	5%	6%	DO NOT KNOW (VOLUNTEERED)
3%	2%	3%	REFUSED (VOLUNTEERED)

Moms were less likely than women without children or men to make sacrifices for their work advancement: 35% of moms have not or would not sacrifice anything, compared to 21% of women without children.

BABY ON BOARD

Today's working mothers aren't hiding the light of their lives under a bushel. Corner offices and computer stations are decorated with colorful Crayloa masterpieces, and bottom drawers may contain toys and art supplies for when the kids come to visit. According to the Travel Industry Association of America, about 10% of business trips taken in 2003 (the last year it tracked the statistic) included children. The explanation: more women in high-profile, upper-echelon jobs. In fact, *40% of all business travelers are women.*

Hotels and resorts are expanding services to cater to business travelers with children, including nanny services and kids' programs.

On the home front, companies are learning to accommodate breastfeeding mothers, offering time and facilities for expressing milk. Many are realizing that it is a simple matter of economics. In a report prepared by a Los Angeles task force called Breastfeeding Works, employers who provided support for breastfeeding mothers experienced a dip in staff turnover and loss of skilled workers after the birth of a child; reduced sick time and personal leave for breastfeeding women and their partners because their infants are more resistant to illness; higher job productivity, employee satisfaction, and morale; additional recruitment incentive for women; and enhanced reputation as a company concerned for the welfare of its employees and their families.

Congress is considering federal bill HR 3531, which would provide the most extensive protection yet to working mothers, including one hour of unpaid leave time; a tax incentive to employers who provide a lactation-friendly environment; and an amendment to the Pregnancy Discrimination Act to clarify that it does apply to breastfeeding mothers.

AND HOW ABOUT THE CHILDLESS UNMARRIEDS?

Childless unmarried women face challenges very different from those faced by married women and married women with children. While balancing work and family is not the difficulty that it is for moms, they have whole other issues, such as being solely responsible for bringing in a paycheck, keeping health insurance and other issues of stability. They do not have a spouse's income to rely on in tough times, nor the options open to many women who have husbands and partners. The desire for financial and job security is even more salient for these women.

Flexibility is less of a concern for childless unmarried women than for their married counterparts, perhaps because they themselves are able to be more open. They are less likely to see flexibility for women with families as the reason there are few women in top management positions.

These women are more willing or able to make sacrifices to reach the top of their field than married women. Only 22% say they have made no sacrifices and are unwilling to do so, compared to 31% of married women. In particular, they are more willing to work long hours and weekends, and to increase their work travel in order to get ahead.

Childless unmarrieds are also less concerned about job security. While more than half of them would still prefer a job that provides security over opportunity for advancement they are more willing than married moms to go out on a limb. When forced to choose between flexibility and security, in fact, childless unmarried women are completely divided: 50% would choose greater security, and 49% would choose greater flexibility. They resemble married men in this response much more than they resemble married moms.

Smudges on the Glass Ceiling

I was in the top third of my law class and was recruited to a good firm. I was one of a handful of women, and I found it very hard to get noticed. I was at the office until 8:00 or 9:00 at night. The guys loved it. They'd work late, then head off to a bar. I felt lonely and cheated. I finally left to take a job with a nonprofit that paid much less. I know some people at my old firm think I was just another girl who couldn't tough it out. I don't care, for myself, but I think we should reevaluate a work culture that requires such back-breaking, alienating schedules.

—MARILYN, 30

As an African American woman in corporate banking, I've had to break two barriers—gender and race. People treat me like a rare object, an oddity. Every time I sit down with new corporate clients, especially if they're men over 50, they feel compelled to tell me about the one African American executive they knew and what a good guy *he* was.

—SAMANTHA, 35

In some places, the glass ceiling is smudged but unbroken, despite the sheer number of women in the workplace, the number of women with bachelor's degrees, and the number of women with even higher professional and academic degrees.

Regardless of your personal experiences, which of the following best describes why there are few women in top management jobs?

Total	Men	Women	
23%	26%	21%	**GENDER DISCRIMINATION IN PROMOTIONS**
21%	17%	24%	MANAGEMENT ROLES PROVIDE LESS FLEXIBILITY FOR WOMEN WITH FAMILIES
17%	17%	17%	EXCLUSION FOR WHAT IS REFERRED TO AS "THE OLD BOYS' NETWORK"
11%	8%	14%	WOMEN ARE THOUGHT TO BE LESS EFFECTIVE IN MANAGEMENT ROLES
11%	13%	9%	MEN ARE MORE AGGRESSIVE IN THEIR CAREER PATHS
4%	4%	4%	WOMEN ARE LESS INTERESTED IN MANAGEMENT ROLES
1%	2%	1%	OTHER (VOLUNTEERED) (SPECIFY) _____

| 9% | 9% | 9% | DO NOT KNOW (VOLUNTEERED) |
| 2% | 3% | 1% | REFUSED (VOLUNTEERED) |

In our survey, women and men describe very different reasons for why there are few women in top management jobs, with women focusing on flexibility. **A quarter of women believe the biggest reason for few women in top positions is the inflexibility that management roles provide for women with families.** Women follow that with sexual discrimination in promotions, which men put as their top reason. Both men and women follow with "the old boys' network" being to blame for failure to promote women. African American women select sexual discrimination in hiring and promotions as the biggest reason for the lack of women in management jobs (27 percent).

What women see as the chief problem correlates to their own experiences in the workforce. African American women are more likely than their white peers to believe discrimination in hiring and promotions is the biggest problem facing women at work today (15% to 8%). Career women are more likely than women who consider their current employment just a job to see combining work and family as a major concern (41% to 33%).

Seventeen percent of women say receiving equal pay for equal work is the biggest problem facing women today, while 9% cite discrimination in hiring and promotions. Men view those two problems as equal at 12 percent for each.

The dramatic leadership trends emerging in small businesses are not yet reflected in corporate America. Although there are more women in management positions, their share at the executive level is actually shrinking. According to the U.S. Census Bureau's Office of Equal Employment Opportunity (EEO), the number of women in management jobs increased by approximately 1 million from 1990 to 2000. Yet, during that time, the number of women in executive management positions dropped 13.1 percentage points, from 31.9 percent in 1990 to 18.8 percent in 2000.

Some barriers are down. **Women make up 51% of enrollment at Columbia and Yale law schools, and 46% of enrollment at Harvard**

BY THE NUMBERS

60
The percentage of workers who believe there aren't enough women in upper management

82
The relative percentage of women's earning to men—the wage gap

300,000
Number of jobs lost by women since March 2001

18.8
Percentage of executive-management positions filled by women

Law. It may take more time for that parity to translate to the career success of making partner. Women account for only 16% of partners at American law firms.

It is a persistent question: Why are women still in so few top management positions? Some suggest that women themselves are less interested in the responsibilities that accompany the top slots—that they are more inclined to "opt out." But a major new study by Catalyst, a research and advisory organization working with businesses and the professions to build inclusive environments and expand opportunities for women at work, suggests otherwise. **The study found that women are just as interested in achieving the top slot—CEO—as men. Furthermore, women with children in the home were just as likely to aspire to the top as those who had no children.**

A more persuasive reason behind women's failure to reach the top was revealed in women's experience of subtle differences between them and their male colleagues. **The majority of women executives reported being excluded from informal networks, left out of the loop of organizational politics, and regularly facing stereotyped beliefs**

about their abilities. Tellingly, women's personal lives were far more deeply affected by their rise through management. While most men in top management positions delegated personal responsibilities to others, including their wives, women tended to handle personal matters on their own.

This overwhelming sense of not fully belonging seems discouraging until you consider that it is inspiring an overhaul of women's ideas about the nature and meaning of the work we do. When women talk about job success, they most often cite values such as satisfaction, relationships, balance, and meaning—as opposed to men, who cite money, advancement, and tangible results. A quest for personal fulfillment is not the surest path to the corner office.

Meanwhile, at the bottom of the ladder, where many female workers reside, the floor is sticky. It's hard to get a leg up when you're living paycheck to paycheck. For most women in blue-collar or service industries, poverty and homelessness are a paycheck or two away. Bread-and-butter issues are front and center for them. Juggling work and family comes second to actually providing for their families.

In this low-wage group, Gen X women are beginning to close the wage gap with their male counterparts. *In 2000 they earned 82% as much as young men, compared to only 68% in 1979.* Gen Xers are also the force behind high-visibility lawsuits—such as the sex discrimination suit filed by women at Merrill Lynch in the 1990s or the one launched by women employees at K-Mart—to keep the pressure on large companies to take equality seriously.

Even though women's pay has been gradually catching up to men's, there is still a gap, which also affects retirement. In a recent survey sponsored by the American Association of University Women, 81% of women (68% strongly) and 69% of men (52% strongly) agree that there is a difference between the wages of women who work full time and the wages of men who work full time.

There was also the interesting survey done by Salary.com for Mother's Day 2005 that said a stay-at-home mom would earn a $131,471 salary based on job titles and an estimated 60 hours a week overtime. Of course women working outside the home are also working

TERMS OF EMPLOYMENT

Grass ceiling: *A set of social, cultural, and discriminatory barriers that prevent women from using golf to conduct business*

Job spill: *Work that carries over into personal time*

Multiskilling: *Being proficient in multiple areas of expertise within a profession*

Silver ceiling: *A set of attitudes and prejudices that prevent older employees from rising to positions of power in the workplace*

a double shift at home and according to Catalyst, in the last 30 years, men have only picked up a few more hours a week of work.

TOP COMPANIES THINK FEMALE

It's official. The hand that rocks the cradle will save your company. A new study demonstrates that **companies with a higher representation of women in senior management positions financially outperform companies with proportionally fewer women at the top.** A study of 353 Fortune 500 companies that remained on the list for four out of five years, found that the companies with the highest representation of women on their senior management teams had a 35% higher ROE (return on equity) and a 34% higher TRS (total return to shareholders) than companies with the lowest women's representation.

Hard-hat Mamas

My father started this moving company in the sixties, and I joined the business after college. That surprised him. If I'd been a son, he would have automatically assumed I'd take over

PERCENTAGE OF WOMEN IN NONTRADITIONAL JOBS

JOB	PERCENTAGE
Clergy	13.9
Taxi driver	13.6
Police officer	12.4
Firefighter	3.5
Carpenter	1.6
Aerospace engineer	11.0
Tractor operator	8.6
Railroad conductor	5.7
Airline pilot	3.4

someday. I had to prove myself in a business comprised mostly of big, strong men doing heavy lifting. I'm five feet two inches in heels, so it wasn't easy. You might say that all of my employees look down on me. But they respect me because I'm fair, I pay them well, and I know what I'm doing.

—CHERYL, 39

Impressive numbers of women are charting new career paths in unconventional settings, such as the construction, transportation, and law enforcement arenas. They're also entering educational venues in pursuit of advanced professional degrees.

The majority of students at law schools, dental schools, and veterinary schools are now women, and by 2005 women will comprise the majority of the nation's veterinarians. Women are joining the military in higher numbers, currently comprising 15% of enlistment. Women are the largest and fastest-growing group of small farm buyers, and they're quickly becoming the majority of farm owners.

A recent study released by the Center for Women's Business Research shows that among the 6.2 million majority-owned, privately held women-owned firms in the United States last year, nontraditional industries such as contracting and construction are the fastest-growing segment. In fact, **from 1997 to 2002 the number of construction firms owned by women grew by 35.5 percent.**

But these are only some of the barriers that have collapsed. They're not falling everywhere. Two significant trends are converging: One is the strong desire by women to pursue occupations that were once closed to them. The other is the growing commitment on the part of many male-dominated industries to harness women's talents and energies.

Thinking about women working or trying to work in fields where women have not been traditionally, which of the following do you think represents the greatest barrier to a woman's success in a non-traditional field?

Total	Men	Women	
24%	26%	22%	STEREOTYPICAL ATTITUDES
15%	14%	16%	LACK OF SUPPORT FROM SUPERIORS
11%	9%	13%	LACK OF SUPPORT FROM COWORKERS
10%	11%	10%	HER OWN FEARS OR SHORTCOMINGS
8%	7%	8%	HABIT/TRADITION
6%	6%	7%	FEELINGS OF ISOLATION OR NOT BELONGING
6%	6%	6%	LACK OF ROLE MODELS
4%	5%	4%	LACK OF SUPPORT FROM CUSTOMERS AND CLIENTS
3%	3%	4%	TOOLS OR EQUIPMENT NOT ADAPTED FOR USE BY A WOMAN
1%	2%	1%	OTHER (VOLUNTEERED)
8%	9%	7%	DO NOT KNOW (VOLUNTEERED)
3%	3%	2%	REFUSED (VOLUNTEERED)

Negative stereotypes of women as workers continue to present barriers to women trying to make it in a nontraditional field, according to our survey respondents. Both women and men see stereotypical attitudes as the greatest barrier to a woman's success in a nontraditional field, with men viewing it slightly more strongly than women—26% of men and 22% of women. Other barriers to entry and achievement perceived by women include lack of support from superiors (16%), lack of support from coworkers (13%), and personal fears or shortcomings (10%).

ENCORE!

Many people are remaining in the workforce well after age 65, the popular and traditional age of retirement. For women, there are myriad reasons for remaining in the workforce, as our survey revealed. These include continued financial stability (30%), followed by wanting to remain active (21%), enjoying what they do (14%), and receiving benefits such as health insurance (13%).

Call it "protirement," or the encore workforce, but the trend is unmistakable: seniors are remaining in or returning to the workplace in droves. As a trend, this one looks like it will blossom into a full lifestyle assimilation. In 2002, 14% of the workforce was age 55 or older, and it is projected that the percentage will climb to 20% within the next decade. **An AARP survey found that 80% of baby boomers planned to work in retirement.** Longevity has a price, and the primary reason for older workers staying in the force is economic necessity. Generational changes have a huge effect on public policy. As people stay active well into their eighties and nineties, they have a new range of concerns about health care, affordable housing, and stresses on the family. Public policies must reflect the dynamics of our population. An aging America must prepare for the challenges facing health and transportation systems, public retirement programs, and a changing workforce.

There is a great deal of angst among women about retirement. A 2004 survey by the Unmarried Women's Project found that unmarried women begin worrying about retirement after age 35, while married women begin worrying at 50. Women increasingly wonder if they will be working until they die. According to Wiserwoman.org, only 18% of women over 65 receive pensions, compared to 31% of men. Ninety percent of older women are Social Security recipients and more than half of them would be living in poverty without these benefits.

The second reason boomers plan to work into retirement is personal happiness. Baby boomers are the first generation that pursued work as fulfillment en masse, and many of them resist retirement. They see it as an effort to put them out to pasture when they're still feeling in their prime. Women are on the front edge of this change. For them, retirement is a positive next stage of life, involving work, continuing education, and activism. They are shifting the emphasis of retirement from being an ending to being a beginning. Rather than wind down and put their papers in order, they are boldly raising the question, "What am I going to do with the next 20 to 30 years of my life?"

In response to the graying of the American workforce, AARP recently announced a new program called the "Workforce Initiative" which is designed to link workers aged 50 and older with jobs at 13 companies who have committed to adding "mature" workers to their payrolls. The Initiative grew from partnership between AARP and Home Depot and now includes such companies as Walgreens, Borders, and Adecco. These older employees have already made significant gains in the job market as workers aged 55 and older accounted for more than half of US job growth in 2004.

Thinking for a moment about women who choose to work after the age of 65, which is a popular age for retirement, what do think is their MAIN reason for doing so?

Total	Men	Women	
28%	25%	30%	**CONTINUED FINANCIAL STABILITY**
22%	23%	21%	WANT TO STAY ACTIVE
14%	14%	14%	ENJOY WHAT THEY DO/NOT READY TO STOP
12%	10%	13%	BENEFITS SUCH AS HEALTH INSURANCE
6%	7%	6%	SOCIAL CONTACT
5%	6%	4%	INTELLECTUAL STIMULATION
3%	4%	2%	DON'T WANT TO FACE AGING AND CHANGE

TREND 4: OPEN-COLLAR WORKPLACES

3%	4%	1%	HABIT/CONSISTENCY
1%	1%	1%	ENTERED A NEW FIELD AFTER RETIREMENT
1%	1%	2%	STARTED A NEW BUSINESS AFTER RETIREMENT
1%	*	2%	OTHER (VOLUNTEERED)
3%	3%	2%	DO NOT KNOW (VOLUNTEERED)
1%	2%	1%	REFUSED (VOLUNTEERED)

Our survey respondents echoed these themes. When asked what they thought was the main reason women chose to continue working beyond age 65, the largest percentage (28%) cited economics. But the second and third reasons carry more weight when combined: "Want to stay active" (22%) and "Enjoy what they do" (14%). Financial realities may motivate them initially, but many women are also glad to have the joy, fulfillment, and stimulation it brings.

Women on the cusp of becoming senior citizens were 10 points more likely than women overall to reason that women work beyond age 65 for continued financial stability (40% vs.30%). Combined with the additional 16% of 55 to 64-year-olds who mentioned that benefits such as health insurance (the third choice for this group overall) were among the top reasons for remaining employed into the golden years, more than half of this population seems to seek more security in later life.

A WORK IN PROGRESS

When some analysts look at the dizzying array of choices and challenges that women face in the world of work, they sometimes come away from the data saying that women are ambivalent about working or even that they wouldn't work if they didn't have to. That has not been our finding. In fact, many women love to work, and they thrive on challenges. **Where they differ from men is in their insistence on bringing their family and work lives together.** Anyone who doubts the force of their collective will need only consider this: 20 years ago, there were smoking areas in every business in America; today, you'd sooner find a breast-pumping room or a day-care center than a single cigarette.

THE NEXT 10 YEARS

Women are lobbying for workplace changes that are inclusive, flexible, and family-friendly. In the next decade, we see this trend advancing.

• We expect a slight increase in women leaving the workplace for longer periods to have children, and the trend will be particularly visible as more women leave the workplace when their kids become teenagers. With this movement will come a more open discussion of who cares for the nation's children. Generation X dads, who have been more aggressive in seeking family-friendly policies for men as well as women, will join their spouses as family advocates in the workplace.

• Women will continue to be on the leading edge of entrepreneurial and small business ventures that will allow them home-work balance. In particular, we look to the growth sectors of information technology and finance, where women have traditionally been absent, to account for the big new trend in women-owned businesses.

• Women have put family and children upfront on the corporate meeting agenda, and they will continue to do so. What was once viewed as a burden to companies is fast becoming a benefit, as the numbers show that the most successful companies have the most women in management. Professional men and women, looking for the best places to work, will choose companies with the highest number of women in executive positions.

• Workplaces will change to be more baby friendly. Smoking rooms will be replaced by lactating rooms.

• Women who are small business owners will finally put health care on the political agenda and make it stick. While health care has been an important item politically for the last 15 years, there is little evidence that either party has suffered from not solving the problem. Women small business owners, who feel the pinch most directly when they try to provide health benefits to their workers and themselves, will increase the pressure on politicians to put their votes where their rhetoric is.

• Women will force a retirement agenda with increased pension and retirement credit for part-time work, universal 401(k) and savings incentives, more involvement in financial planning, and more talk of caregiver credits.

TREND 5

THE ELECTRIC HIVE

The home has emerged as the central nervous system of daily life. There's nothing you can't do at home anymore.

Abigail's two-story ranch house in Wichita, Kansas, is the center of a bustling universe. The garage has been converted to a workshop where she runs a thriving small business making elaborate dried-flower bouquets and wreaths. The kitchen is an open-design family room, with a TV, a laptop computer, and a table large enough to accommodate a Girl Scout troop or her monthly book club.

A man's home may be his castle, but a woman's home is her hive—a place of creation and nurturance. Previous generations viewed the home as a sanctuary, a private place for family, or a showplace—a personal measure of self-worth and pride. Today the home still represents much of this, but the changing dynamics in Americans' relationships and family styles have created significant shifts in what takes place in the home. The gravitational pull of 30-something women is around home and the number of young, single women buying their own homes has boomed recently. And there are significant trends in the way they decorate their home today, and in how they inhabit them.

We've named our fifth trend The Electric Hive, to communicate the way the home has become the central nervous system of modern life. In

THE HOME

	THEN	NOW
Dream	Cocoon	Hive
Buyers	Newlyweds	Single women/ethnics
Entertaining	Elaborate dinner parties	Chips and dip and covered dishes
Home improvement	Hire workers	Take lessons at the local Home Depot
Housekeeping	A woman's work	Delegate!
Grocery shopping	Saturday morning traffic jam at the local supermarket	Online ordering, speciality stores, lifestyle centers
Credo	"A man's home is his castle."	"A woman's home is her central nervous system."
Technology	Appliances	Wireless
Activity	Watch TV, prepare meals	Work/work-out

the long term, we see this trend being fed by the open-collared workplaces that women are pioneering, and the sheer frustration with diversions away from home—traffic, shuttling overscheduled kids, endless errands, and a seemingly daily grind of shopping. Women today are reinventing home space as the vital center of their more expanded lives.

Hiving

When I left my magazine job to write a novel, everyone told me I'd go nuts being home all the time. I think they had this

picture of me in a dark cave. The opposite has happened.
Being at home gives me a center, a way to include more people in my life. My book club meets here. Last month I hosted
a political fund-raiser for a neighbor who's running for family
court judge. My life is less harried and more fulfilling.

—JACQUELINE, 37

In the 1970s, Faith Popcorn coined the term "cocooning" to describe a trend toward viewing one's home as a retreat from the scary, un-
controllable outside world. Today the home as cocoon is turned inside
out, giving way to the home as hive.

As with (busy) bees, a "hive home" represents engagement, interaction, and connection with the outside world. The hive home is a personal community center, the hub for business, entertaining, learning,
artistic endeavors, fitness, and activism. "We have an open-door policy
here. The kids and their friends run in and out. Neighbors stop by to
chat. The TV in the kitchen has e-mail capacity. It's noisy and busy. It's
the life I always dreamed of," said Bailey, 39, who views her home as the
nucleus of her mini-social universe.

**By a margin of two to one, Americans are spending more not
less time in their homes.** Other significant trends feed into this, including the growing numbers of teleworkers and the use of the Internet
as a resource and shopping center.

It was a Victorian notion that "a woman's place is in the home," but
that same expression can mean something liberating when applied to
modern life. The home is a hub of activity, a living homepage, an expression of one's tastes, an amplification of her priorities and passions. She
wants to be home.

CENTRAL NERVOUS SYSTEM

Examples abound of how Americans are using their homes in new, innovative ways. Our studies show that at least one-third of American
women are performing functions at home that were once relegated to
business offices, clinics, clubs, and schools.

Home as Workplace

There are approximately 44.4 million telecommuters in the United States, about half working for companies and half self-employed. They comprise 20% of the workforce.

Home as School

Around 1 million children are being home-schooled, usually by a parent or parents. For adults, the number of those engaged in "distance learning" through enrollment in online courses is rising yearly. In particular, fully accredited universities are creating online universities.

According to the U.S. Department of Education, about 1.1 million chilidren were home-schooled in 2003, and approximately 75% of home-schooled children are white and from two-parent families. About 62% of them have two or more siblings. Although the trend in home-schooling originated primarily in white, middle-class, Christian families, there are signs that the trend may be reaching broader populations.

DID YOU KNOW?

The kitchen is the new high-tech interactive center. Sophisticated appliances meet the needs of tech-savvy families by adding elements that suit their lifestyles. An estimated 15% of broadband users have a PC in their kitchen like the Salton IceBox, a flat screen computer that can be mounted underneath a cabinet. Other popular appliances include refrigerators with built-in televisions, under-the-cabinet flip-down television screens, and islands complete with their own stainless-steel sinks, dishwashers, and cutting board—colander combos. The TMIO Intelligent Oven will start cooking as directed by you via the home computer. High-tech appliances utilize one central wireless network as the center for home operations.

Lavatory as Laboratory

At-home testing and at-home kits are a $3 billion-dollar-a-year business. These include tests for cholesterol, blood pressure, hormone levels, blood sugar, pregnancy, paternity, drug and alcohol, colon cancer, and blood type. Some tests allow the user to see the results instantly; others utilize a mail pouch to send the results to a laboratory. In either case, it's simpler than a trip to the doctor, and perfect for baby boomers and Gen Xers who crave privacy and instantaneous results.

Home as Spa and Fitness Center

More than 50% of Americans own home fitness equipment. Unlike the dust-gathering, clothes hanger machines of old, new exercise equipment is used regularly in 32.3 million homes.

The New (Single) Ownership Society

> Buying this house is the best thing I ever did. It's tiny, but it's mine. Sometimes I sit and look around and think, "I can't believe I own a house!"
>
> —MARY, 34

It used to be that people graduated from college and rented until they got married and started to have children. No longer. Lower interest rates, changing lending practices, and the desire for a stake in the community and investment have created a new class of owners. More and more women, young professionals, and minorities are becoming homeowners, taking a huge step in defining their personal life choices. *Single women are the fastest-growing group of mortgage holders.* In 2003, 54% of single women owned their own homes. In 2003, twice as many single women as single men bought houses. According to the National Association of Realtors, one in five first-time buyers is a single woman, while only one in ten was a single man. That makes single women the second-largest group of home buyers, next to young married couples.

Our survey respondents agreed that single women who buy homes on their own are wise investors not risk-takers.

In your view, which word best describes a single woman who decides to buy a home on her own?

Total	Men	Women	
47%	42%	52%	**A WISE INVESTOR**
25%	24%	25%	FINANCIALLY SECURE
12%	13%	11%	COURAGEOUS
11%	14%	9%	MATURE
1%	2%	1%	NAÏVE
1%	1%	1%	IMMATURE
1%	1%	1%	SELFISH
1%	1%	1%	OTHER (VOLUNTEERED)
1%	1%	1%	DO NOT KNOW (VOLUNTEERED)
*	1%	*	REFUSED (VOLUNTEERED)

Overall, female home ownership has grown by more than 50% in the past ten years. Another big group is divorced or widowed women over 45 who are not remarrying. The array of mortgage options makes home ownership possible where once income, lack of cash for down payment, or even being self-employed would have precluded it.

Second-home ownership is also on the rise. This market is driven by baby boomers—primarily married couples with near-adult children or no children. However, more and more singles are doing this, too. According to the National Association of Realtors, *single women comprise 6% of second-home buyers.*

Delilah, 53, and Lee, 45, are unmarried sisters. Delilah has never been married; Lee was divorced at age 41 after five years of marriage. They bought a small house together near the beach in Cape May, New Jersey, when the market was good because it seemed like a wise investment, and their family had vacationed there for as long as they could remember. It has been a positive experience in every way, increasing family closeness by providing a central place for their brothers and their families to come in the summers. Between them, the two women also have a

FAST FACTS:
HOME BUYERS IN 2004

- *40% were first-time home buyers.*
- *The average first-time home buyer: 32*
- *Nearly one-quarter (24%) of first-timers were minorities.*
- *Single women made up 18% of the buyer market, compared to only 8% of single men.*
- *Sales of second homes reach 36% of the market in 2004, up 16.3% from 2003.*
- *The average second-home buyer is between 47 and 55 years old and has an annual income of $71,000–$85,700.*
- *Hispanic home ownership has risen 8.4% between 1994 and 2004, as 48.7% of Hispanics own their own home.*

large group of friends who are only too happy to join them at the beach on summer weekends. "When we first bought the house, some people were very concerned that it wouldn't work out," Lee said. "It's like they thought you could only do this with a husband. I think we've proved them wrong."

Recent real estate industry trends show it's far easier for single women to qualify for loans than in years past. With zero-down loans, low interest rates, and other creative financing, they have been able to buy a home as not only a place to live but also as a smart investment.

In 2004, for the first time, the median price of a condo exceeded the median price of a single-family home. This is in part due to condos' locations in urban areas, and in building amenities like gyms, concierges and grocery stores such as Whole Foods. However, traditional single-family homes are not being tossed aside. Bigger still seems better, and over-the-top extras remain en vogue. The latest? Elevators and kid's suites (bedroom, bathroom, study/office, and sitting area for entertaining) in separate wings or "towers."

MOVERS AND SHAKERS

About 14% of Americans pulled up stakes and moved in 2004.
Where did they go, and why?

51.3% moved for better housing opportunities

26.3% moved for family-related reasons

15.6% moved for work-related reasons

Where were they going? South and west.
The Northeast lost 100,000 residents, while the South
gained 74,000, and the West gained 125,000.

The increase in home ownership shows a trend toward stability for new populations, but it also signals that the government needs to respond to the challenges and needs of these first-time home buyers by addressing barriers and impediments to success, such as the national acceleration of property taxes.

FUTUREHOME

Imagine this: You are a 40-something working woman with a school-age child and an elderly parent at home. Each morning as you leave for the office, you have confidence that at least the mechanical aspects of your caretaking tasks and housework will be handled while you are away. Your Roomba electronic robot, produced by iRobot, will clean almost as well as a human housekeeper, detecting the best pattern for each room, and spending extra time cleaning high-traffic areas. It doesn't do windows, but that's coming soon.

Roomba's health-care companion will make sure your mother takes her medications on schedule, support her when she goes to the bathroom, and serve her lunch. Thanks to HomeGenie, you'll be able to monitor your mother's care via your home automation system. When the home health aide pays a visit, you can unlock the door to let her in, and make sure that everything's locked tight when she leaves. When your child returns from school, you can check in to be sure he's doing his homework. Your HomeGenie will also monitor security, adding to your peace of mind, and it will alert you if the electricity fails or the basement floods during a storm.

Before you leave the office, you can call your intelligent oven from your cell phone and instruct it to start preparing the dinner you placed in its refrigerated compartment that morning.

Some of these inventions, such as Roomba, HomeGenie, and the intelligent oven, are already available (Roomba retails for less than $200), and each year ushers in new systems and products. No robot or electronic system can replace Mom, of course. But it would be nice to lend her a hand (or a robot).

TRIAL SPIN CYCLE

Most people wouldn't dream of buying a car without test-driving it first. Now Maytag is applying the same marketing logic to its major appliances. If you live in one of 49 U.S. locations that feature Maytag concept stores, you're invited—no, *encouraged*—to bring in your grimiest load of laundry, your dirty dishes, and your homemade cookie dough, and spend an afternoon "test-driving" appliances. Do a load of laundry and run the dishwasher while your cookies bake, and if you're not satisfied, return next week to test different models.

The concept stores are about the size of a department store appliance section (on average 6,000 square feet), but the atmosphere is as cozy as a home. They are located close to venues that a female customer is likely to frequent, such as toy and book stores, and are independently run, in some cases by owners of existing appliance stores who want to expand with a separate Maytag location.

Maytag's innovative sales technique is a prime example of the value of women customers when it comes to making major home improvements and purchases. Appliance manufacturers are also focusing on becoming problem solvers inside the home—essentially asking, "What do women really want and need?" They're responding to the demand for convenience, with refrigerators that can chill wine and make ice in minutes, or thaw meat in half the usual time. They're developing climate control systems that digitally keep foods fresh for more than twice as long. Water filtration systems are built right in to dispense water free of unpleasant odors, chlorine, lead, and sediment. Video LCD displays on microwaves provide recipes and cooking tips. Women respond to technology that makes life easier on a daily basis and buys them time. New appliances also appeal to women's comfort with multitasking by combining multiple functions in one unit. It's not quite the Jetsons—to use baby boomers' favorite childhood model of the future, but it's getting there.

NIX THE KITCHEN PERFORMANCE ANXIETY FOR GOOD

Dream Dinners, Let's Dish, and Super Suppers are among a growing industry of prepared meal services that allow customers to assemble yummy ensembles in store to freeze at home. For a fee of about $200, shoppers are offered a variety of selections, and take home 12 meals that feed 4 to 6 people. According to a national survey conducted by THE POLLING COMPANY, INC. on behalf of Mass Connections, a willing market exists for this service: 71% of Americans say they would be likely to purchase fresh, prepared meals at the grocery store that they can cook or heat at home in little time. For those interested in removing all the work associated with meal preparation, a personal chef might be the way to go. While packages vary, most offer a "five by four," which consists of five full meals for four people, and can cost up to $400 including groceries.

The Do-It-Herselfer

I enjoy breaking the rules. My kitchen is painted shades of
lavender and lime, my bedroom is painted burgundy. It really
says *me*.

—MICAH, 30

I shudder at the thought of someone walking into my house
and saying, "Oh, this is from Pottery Barn." I might as well
have doilies on the furniture or cover everything in plastic.

—LEE, 37

Joanne, 34, is a stay-at-home mother, a new homeowner, and a
Home Depot and Lowe's junkie, an addiction she shares with her 3-
year-old son, Nathan. His obsession with tools, paint swatches, and
power washers gives Joanne an excuse to indulge her pleasure in home
renovation. Some days, instead of joining the sandbox crowd at the park,
they wander the aisles of the Home Depot or Lowe's (Nathan prefers
Lowe's), discussing their home improvement possibilities with the en-
thusiasm of Bob the Builder. Thin, bookish Joanne laughingly admitted
that she never would have predicted this obsession. "When I was growing up, the hammers and nails in our family were strictly the boys' do-
main," she said. "I didn't even know there were different kinds of
screwdrivers. But this house is the first thing I've ever owned, and I'm
proud to be so involved in making it look good. Plus, it's a fun way to
bond with my little builder."

*In the last 10 years, Americans have invested more than $5 trillion
on home improvement.* In 2004 alone, consumers spent $200 billion on
homes and home renovation. For many of them, the expenditure is a
sensible investment that sharply increases home value. Big-ticket reno-
vations include kitchen installations, bathroom and spa installations,
and multiple room additions. Younger female home buyers have energized the home décor and home improvement markets, and as a result
home maintenance and repair spending has increased 14% in the last
two years. A recent survey by *Budget Living* magazine revealed that 77%

of respondents had done a major home renovation project in the prior six months. More and more, the renovation is being executed by women, inspiring major chains like Home Depot and Lowe's to organize their showrooms to be more friendly to women. And their home improvement courses are now geared to them, too.

Americans want what's quick and convenient, and that trend is apparent in home design and décor. Examples: new appliances make housework easier. Self-cleaning windows make the duty bearable. Specialized cleaning tools have replaced all-in-one models, saving time in the long run, as well as money and space. Many of these improvements add tremendous value to a home. According to a Florida State University study of 29,000 home sales, the following improvements added significant value.

Improvement	Value Added
Additional bathroom	24%
Garage	12.9%
Built-in appliances	8.4%
In-ground sprinkler system/landscaping	8%
In-ground pool	7.9%
Family room	7.3%
Separate dining room	6.2%
Security system	5.6%
Kitchen island	5.3%

Home can be a place to get away from work life, or it can be an extension of work life, and décor has become more tailored to the needs of individual consumers. The popularity of television shows like *Trading Spaces*, *Home Again*, and *Extreme Homes* reflects this fascination with space and self-empowerment. It's interesting to note that the audiences for these shows are more blue-collar than upscale.

Once again, Generation X women are on the leading edge of the do-it-herself trend, and there is a marked difference between them and their boomer predecessors. Baby boomers (ages 40–59) are more likely to delegate home-improvement projects, hiring contractors, painters, and decorators, while Generation Xers (ages 26–39) tap into their trademark self-reliance and can-do way of life.

A JANE OF ALL TRADES

Women are taking on major home improvement projects, even when there's a man in the house or they can afford to hire contractors. They are learning to install kitchen cabinets, waterproof the basement, and install drywall and insulation. According to a Sears Roebuck survey, three out of five women homeowners preferred advice from Bob Vila *(This Old House)* to advice from the self-help guru, Dr. Phil.

Be Jane, Inc. is one of several groups responding to the trend. Formed in 2003, Be Jane is the first online community, licensing and media company dedicated to serving the fast-growing population of women DIYs (do-it-yourselfers). Be Jane's website *(www.be-jane.com)* is packed with information and inspiration for women do-it-yourselfers, including strategies, practical advice, and forums to interact with other women. One of Be Jane's most popular features is "Jane of the Month," which highlights one woman and her project. A recent feature applauded Lisa Falleroni, an Alexandria, Virginia, school counselor, who undertook a complex tiling project that involved carpentry, plumbing, and appliance installation. "Tiling floors is my favorite home improvement project," Falleroni said, "because to me it's a 'salt of the earth' type of project. When you 'create' the floor in a room you're also creating the platform on how the rest of the room will feel. I also took to it in such a way that it feels quite natural when doing it. I am so comfortable and things seem to come automatic to me when I'm laying tile—it's a sensation I can't put down in words. The best way to describe it is that it feels like something very familiar; like I did it in a past life."

What's Falleroni's favorite tool? "That would have to be a trowel," she said. "I find carving into the mortar a poetic and sensual experience."

THE *DON'T* WANT TO
DO-IT-HERSELFER

A large part of the population wants to reduce the hassle factor of home maintenance—a fact reflected in the dramatic increase in condominium buyers—over 1 million last year and rising. This trend is being driven by junior seniors (55 to 64) who find that the empty nest isn't so much fun to take care of anymore. This group, whose leisure time was once spent puttering around the garden or reading home décor magazines, now wants freedom to travel or get involved in community activities.

Want low maintenance without selling the family home? That can be arranged, too. We're already seeing a boomlet in home maintenance firms that offer services far beyond the old norm. For a monthly fee, these firms will mow the lawn, trim the hedges, fix the roof, clean up after your dog, and check on your home while you're away.

COOPERATIVE LIVING:
EVERYBODY TOGETHER NOW

Jim and Evelyn have never believed in retirement communities. They know that some of their friends like the idea of living in gated senior communities without children, built around golf courses or walking paths. But as they look toward retirement in the next five years, they know they want to live in a place where there is a mix of families, yet one that caters to the specific needs of seniors. They are considering buying one of 40 homes in a Michigan cohousing development, where independent living and family-style support coexist in just the right mix.

Cohousing, a trend that has been steadily gaining ground over the last 20 years, has become an attractive option for thousands of Americans. It meets the needs of virtually every group—singles, families with young children, and seniors. Cohousing communities balance the traditional advantages of home ownership with the benefits of shared common facilities and ongoing connections with your neighbors. These intergenerational cooperatives are among the most promising solutions to many of today's most challenging social and environmental concerns.

Cohousing communities consist of private, fully equipped dwellings and extensive common amenities, including a common house and recreation areas. They are designed and managed by the residents who have chosen to live in a close-knit neighborhood that seeks a healthy blend of privacy and community.

The physical layout of these communities usually involves clusters of private residences centered around open courtyards, with one building used for common facilities designed for daily use. These are an integral part of the community, and are always supplemental to the private residences. The common house typically includes a common kitchen, dining area, sitting area, children's playroom and laundry, and may also have a workshop, library, exercise room, crafts room, and/or one or two guest rooms. Except on very tight urban sites, cohousing communities often have playground equipment, lawns, and gardens, as well. Since the buildings are clustered, larger sites may retain several or many acres of undeveloped shared open space.

These communities are managed by the residents, who share in common tasks, but an owner can be as involved or uninvolved as he or she likes. According to the Cohousing Association of the United States, there are currently 153 cohousing communities in 29 states, and soon they will be everywhere.

SPACE FOR THE TIMES

All across America, the options we have in where we live and how we organize our homes are expanding to accommodate mixed families, people living longer, singles who want both independence and community, and women who are passionate about integrating their work and home lives. The Homepreneuring trend exists in this vital milieu, and means that in these mobile times people no longer define themselves primarily by the state or region in which they live, but by the type of community that they help to fashion and define. The pioneer-like entrepreneurial grit that inspires many in their chosen work now helps them choose how to live.

THE NEXT 10 YEARS

Trends in work, family, and lifestyle are driving the home-centered movement from sheltered cocoon to buzzing hive. What are the implications for the next decade?

- With single women accounting for a high percentage of new homeowners, we'll see the development of self-contained housing communities for singles, patterned on the model of cohousing.

- New homes will feature structural designs for the "hive" family, with electronically sophisticated home offices, gyms and mini-spas, and "wings" or even detached cottages for elderly parents or adult children.

- The revival of downtown areas that is occurring in virtually every midsize city across America, will bring more people back from the suburbs, reducing the reliance on cars, eliminating school busing, and encouraging the return to mom-and-pop communities.

- Lifestyle centers will find a home on many of these properties. Coffee bars, convenience stores, pharmacies, and sandwich shops will be on-site in large communities, not down the street.

THE MOUSE RACE

Women are overstressed, overwhelmed, and just plain beat. They'd like to dial the rat race down to a slower pace.

Women are too busy—but you knew that. "People always say, 'If you want something done, ask a woman,'" said one overstretched respondent. "Maybe we should retire that saying!" As women fight for control of their lives, our survey also shows that they battle sleepless nights, money crunches, and guilt that creeps in whenever they take a break. They are mindful that the rat race was invented by men; it wasn't their idea, but somehow, what was once the province of corporate America has migrated into the daily grind, with no discrimination as to type of work, annual income, or obligations at home. *Everyone* is stretched.

A recent study by the Families and Work Institute found that:

- 26% of employees were overworked often or very often

- 27% were overwhelmed by how much work they had to do often or very often

- 29% often or very often didn't have time to step back and process or reflect on the work they were doing

TIME & STRESS

	THEN	NOW
The clock	The snooze alarm	24-7
Mental health break	Put the answering machine on and get away from the phone	Nowhere to run, nowhere to hide from the cell phone and instant message
Style	Coffee and newspaper break	TV news in the background while you cook, clean, talk on the phone, or sort laundry
Fantasy	A night of passion	A good night's sleep
Credo	"I only have two hands."	"I can multitask."

The survey also found that *women are more overworked than men.* At first, this finding seemed counterintuitive since men tend to work longer hours at their jobs. But women report that their jobs require more multitasking. One revealing note was the difference between men and women on vacation. Women spend less time than men relaxing (64% of the time versus 72% of the time), and more on meeting family responsibilities.

We call our sixth trend the Mouse Race as a reflection of women's desire to live life on a slower track. **As family and work lives become more complex, many women are pressing the halt button.**

CONTROL IS THE NEW CURRENCY

The search for peace, balance, time, and sleep is ultimately a search for control. The overarching trend among women we have studied is the desire—sometimes even greater than for time or money—to have dominion over the important areas of their lives.

Which area of your life would you say you feel the most control of?

Women		Men	
16%	RELATIONSHIP WITH FAMILY MEMBERS	15%	RELATIONSHIP WITH FAMILY MEMBERS
14%	RELATIONSHIP WITH CHILDREN	15%	RELATIONSHIP WITH SPOUSE OR SIGNIFICANT OTHER
11%	RELATIONSHIP WITH SPOUSE OR SIGNIFICANT OTHER	15%	FINANCES
11%	FINANCES	12%	TIME
9%	CAREER/JOB	8%	CAREER/JOB
8%	TIME	6%	RELATIONSHIP WITH CHILDREN
6%	HEALTH	6%	HEALTH
4%	EDUCATION	4%	RELATIONSHIP WITH FRIENDS
3%	RELATIONSHIP WITH FRIENDS	3%	EDUCATION
12%	ALL OF THE ABOVE (VOL)	13%	ALL OF THE ABOVE (VOL)
3%	NONE OF THE ABOVE (VOL)	1%	NONE OF THE ABOVE (VOL)
1%	DO NOT KNOW (VOL)	1%	DO NOT KNOW (VOL)
*	REFUSED (VOL)	1%	REFUSED (VOL)

It is interesting to see how our eight female archetypes experience the level of control in their lives:

Feminist Champions report having the least control over time and money.

Suburban Caretakers report having the least control over money, followed by time.

Alpha Strivers generally feel the *most* control in all categories, which is what makes them who they are.

Multicultural Mavericks report having the least control over money, although overall they report having a lot of control in their lives.

Religious Crusaders report having the least control over money.

Waitress Moms feel they have the least control over health.

Senior Survivors feel more in control of their lives than most others, with the least control over security and health.

Alienated Singles feel less in control of their lives than all the other groups, with the least control being over money.

Men are very split as to where they feel the most control. Relationship with family members, relationship with spouse or significant other, and finances each garnered 15%. Time was the next runner up with 12%, followed by career/job with 8%, and relationship with children and health each with 6%.

While women feel the most control over their relationship with family members, no single category dominated women's responses with respect to this question about areas of control. The relationship with their children was the area of life 14% of women felt most in control, and trumped both their relationship with their spouse or significant other and finances as the second most popular response.

For married women without children, the relationship she holds with her spouse or significant takes center stage, allowing a central focus on this connection. Additionally, these women were 11-points more likely than married moms to say they felt most in control of their job/career.

The feeling of control among men and women somewhat mimics their traditional places in society as breadwinner and caregiver, respectively. While they agreed on their top choice, (14%) women felt the most control over their relationship with their children, a feeling that was shared by only 6% of men. Over one-in-ten (12%) men said that they felt most control over time, a more elusive area of life for women.

Income affects the overall sense of control women have. Among married women, those with incomes of $29,000 or less say that their relationship with their children is where they are most in charge. Married women with incomes of $70,000 or more say they have most control of their relationship with their spouse or significant other. Unmarried women overall feel *least* in control of their finances, though

Married Women: Which area of your life would
you say you feel the most in control of?

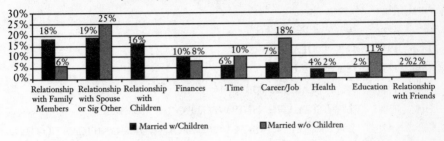

Unmarried Women: Which area of your life would
you say you feel the most in control of?

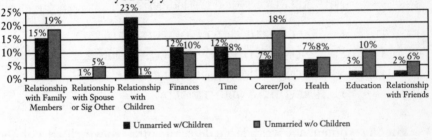

health and time emerge the second and third most difficult-to-handle
areas of life.

Although women overall feel most in control of personal relationships, they feel least in control of finances, followed by health and time.
Men tend to feel more in control as they age and get more education and
income. That is much less true for women.

Married Women: Most Controlled Relationship				
	<$29K	$30–$49K	$50–$69K	$70K+
Relationship with spouse	17%	17%	17%	23%
Relationship with children	24%	15%	13%	12%

Which area of your life would you say you feel the LEAST in control of ?

Total	Men	Women	
25%	**23%**	**26%**	**FINANCES**
18%	19%	17%	HEALTH
16%	17%	16%	TIME
9%	10%	9%	CAREER/ JOB
6%	5%	6%	RELATIONSHIP WITH FAMILY MEMBERS
5%	4%	2%	RELATIONSHIP WITH SPOUSE OR SIGNIFICANT OTHER
3%	4%	2%	EDUCATION
3%	2%	4%	RELATIONSHIP WITH CHILDREN
3%	4%	2%	RELATIONSHIP WITH FRIENDS
1%	1%	2%	ALL OF THE ABOVE (VOLUNTEERED)
7%	8%	6%	NONE OF THE ABOVE (VOLUNTEERED)
4%	4%	4%	DO NOT KNOW (VOLUNTEERED)
1%	1%	1%	REFUSED (VOLUNTEERED)

Among women, age was a large determinant as to which area of life they felt least in control. While young women (18–34) are making history in education and employment, this has not led to a greater sense of financial confidence. Nearly one-third (32%) of women ages 18 to 34 felt least in control of their finances.

Junior senior women (55–64) were evenly split between finances and health as the areas of life about which they felt most powerless. As women age, lack of control over finances seems to lessen, though uncer-

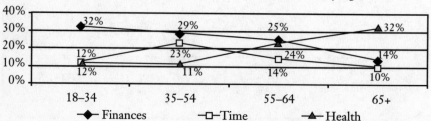

Area of life women feel the least control over (by Age)

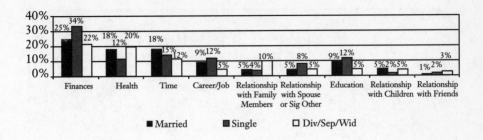

■ Married   ■ Single   □ Div/Sep/Wid

Those who feel *most* in control of finances
(by Sex/Age)

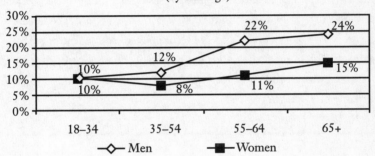

◇ Men   ■ Women

Those who feel *least* in control of finances
(by Sex/Education Level)

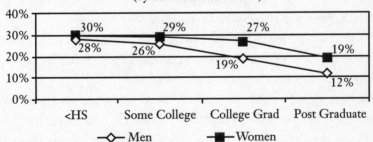

◇ Men   ■ Women

tainties regarding health increase. One in three (32%) women over the age of 65 felt least in control of their health.

While trying to balance career and family, women ages 35 to 54 were more likely than any other age group to feel the least control over their time, though control over finances was their main worry as nearly 3 in 10 (29%) chose this as their top response.

CAN YOU HEAR ME NOW?

"I never realized how much I depended on those six-hour cross-country flights for a break," said a busy executive who travels frequently for her job. "At 30,000 feet, no one could reach me. I could read a book, take a nap, or watch a movie. Now, once we're airborne, my BlackBerry starts ringing." Cell phones, BlackBerries, laptops—all the high-tech gadgets that were supposed to make life so much easier and more efficient—have developed a horrifying downside: there are no longer "unreachable moments." One mom noted, "It's the technological equivalent of your 3-year-old pounding at the bathroom door where you've escaped for one private moment. You can't turn off your kid, and it's getting harder to turn off your BlackBerry."

The impending journey into retirement and uncertain future of Social Security and Medicare most likely has one-quarter of junior-senior women (age 55–64) feeling equal anxiety about managing their finances and health, their top two control concerns.

Married women with incomes of $29,000 or less said they were least in control of their finances, while married women with incomes over $70,000 were least in control of their time.

Married women aged 65 or older were 12 points more likely than their male counterparts to say that they felt least in control of their health.

As men age, comfort with their economic situation becomes more apparent, as control over finances was the most popular response for men aged 65 and older. Among women, there is a less significant distinction, though senior women are more likely than their younger counterparts to feel most in control of their finances. Still, it must be noted that *one of the fastest-growing areas of credit card debt is senior women paying for prescription drugs.*

As education level increases, both men and women feel more secure in their finances, though the difference is sharper among men.

SWEET DREAMS

Women dream of sleep, men dream of sex. That's the simple conclusion of the men and women we surveyed on the question, "Which would you rather have, more sleep or more sex?" Even accounting for the fudge factor (some men not admitting that they'd really rather snooze), it's a conclusive result. Among our survey respondents, two-thirds (66%) of American women said they were in need of more sleep, 24 points higher than the 42% of men who claimed the same. In contrast, 44% of men stated that of the two choices, their preference would be for more sex—more than double the 20% of women who were also looking for additional action between the sheets.

Would you rather have more sleep or more sex? And would you say definitely or probably more sleep/sex?

Total	Men	Women	
55%	42%	66%	**TOTAL MORE SLEEP (NET)**
37%	28%	45%	DEFINITELY MORE SLEEP
18%	14%	21%	PROBABLY MORE SLEEP
31%	44%	20%	**TOTAL MORE SEX (NET)**
10%	14%	7%	PROBABLY MORE SEX
21%	30%	13%	DEFINITELY MORE SEX
7%	7%	8%	DO NOT KNOW (VOLUNTEERED)
7%	6%	7%	REFUSED (VOLUNTEERED)

- While all women dream of more sleep, those never married might be living busier lifestyles as they were 13-points more likely than their wed counterparts to wish for more zzzz's (74%–61%, respectively).

- The sights and sounds, pace and partying in the big city might be causing residents insomnia. Urban dwellers of both sexes were more likely than their suburban and rural neighbors to desire more sleep.

More Sleep (By Sex/Community Type)

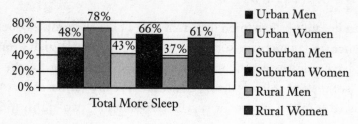

More Sleep/More Sex (By Women/Income)

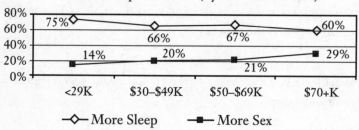

- Men with children were 11 points more likely than men without children to say they would like to have more shut-eye, whereas childless men were 23 points more likely than fathers to say they'd like to have more sex (60% versus 37%).

- Notably, mothers and childless women did not significantly differ in their desire for more sleep (66% and 65%).

- Again, two-thirds (65%) of not-yet-moms would like more sleep, whereas 69% of not-yet-dads were interested in more sex. (Perhaps these women are trying to store up extra "Zs" against the inevitable sleepless nights that come with kids.)

- Among women, as household income increases, the need for more sleep decreases and the desire for more sex increases—in part because upper-income women may be "buying" time with hired help. That said, even women at upper-income levels crave more sleep.

Lack of sleep is no laughing matter. Experts say adults need between 7 and 8 hours of sleep a night, and if they don't get it they become at risk for accidents and illnesses. Sleep is necessary for the proper function of the central nervous system—including memory, physical performance, mental clarity, and mood. Chronic lack of sleep can upset the body's natural rhythms and lead to an excessive release of the stress hormone cortisol, which is implicated in heart disease and cancer.

YOUR MONEY OR YOUR TIME

Given the fact that women seem to be crying out for more time, it's interesting that so many of them are not willing or able to spend more money to get or save it. A chronic money crunch may be the underlying factor in women being overstretched. In our survey, we asked the question, "Would you spend more time to save money or spend more money to save time?" Both married and unmarried women overwhelmingly said they would spend time to save money.

Which of the following describes you more accurately: "I am more willing to spend money to save some time," or "I am more willing to spend time to save some money"?

Total	Men	Women	
56%	54%	59%	**MORE WILLING TO SPEND TIME TO SAVE SOME MONEY**
36%	39%	33%	MORE WILLING TO SPEND MONEY TO SAVE SOME TIME
3%	3%	4%	BOTH (VOLUNTEERED)
2%	2%	1%	NEITHER (VOLUNTEERED)
3%	2%	3%	DO NOT KNOW (VOLUNTEERED)
–	–	–	REFUSED (VOLUNTEERED)

However, it was quite clear that income level had a lot to do with people's willingness or ability to spend money to save time. Spending time to save money was more valuable to lower-income individuals, and spending money to save time was preferred by those who literally could do it, although there was something of a difference between the sexes.

EXAMPLES: SPENDING TIME TO SAVE MONEY

- *Prepare bag lunches instead of eating at restaurants and cafeterias.*
- *Take a bus instead of a taxi.*
- *Shampoo your own carpets and upholstery.*
- *Return your recyclable cans and bottles.*
- *Shop with coupons at more than one store.*

EXAMPLES: SPENDING MONEY TO SAVE TIME

- *Buy prepared foods instead of cooking your own.*
- *Use the services of a housekeeper once a week.*
- *Order merchandise online, even when there is a shipping charge.*
- *Hire a pet walker or a personal shopper.*

Upper-income men ($70K+) were 12 points more likely than their female counterparts to say they were more willing to spend money to save time (64% versus 52%). Could this be the reason men overall are getting more sleep?

Not surprisingly, both men and women from the legendary frugal senior class (65+) were willing to spend time to save money. This World War II generation, accustomed to sacrifice and thrift, has clipped coupons and licked S & H green stamps to stretch dollars during their

DID YOU KNOW?

In a 168-hour week, moms have just 10 hours to themselves

	Married Women				Unmarried Women			
	<$29K	$30–$49K	$50–$69K	$70K+	<$29K	$30–$49K	$50–$69K	$70K+
Spend time to save money	69%	65%	63%	43%	70%	67%	42%	43%
Spend money to save time	25%	27%	29%	54%	20%	25%	53%	47%

working days. Now retired, many of them have free time to do even more to save a buck.

Among married women, only those with annual incomes of $70,000 or higher were more likely to spend money to save time. Unmarried women split at the $50,000 mark: those making less than $50,000 a year were more willing to spend time to save money, while those making more than $50,000 a year were more willing to spend money to save time.

CTRL+ALT+DELETE

To do or not to do, that is her question. Today's time-pressed woman is trying to simply learn how to say "No," in contrast to the "Yes" woman of previous generations of wives, mothers, workers, and managers. That means taking control—first of the automatic impulse to say "yes," and then of everything else. Some women are even hiring one of the booming new crop of personal organizers to help them get a grip. Others are doing it themselves by creating their own ctrl-alt-delete bins—a twist on the computer function that turns your screen blank. It is a liberating exercise.

The struggle to "make a dent" in a person's infinite "to-do" list is nothing new. While many factors have changed over time, including the reprioritization of the items on that list, we developed the following graph, as a short-hand reminder of the large internal filing system that women place their areas of concern.

The **first bin** contains matters of an urgent, essential nature that require the direct, personal involvement. The **second bin** includes items that are important but not urgent, concerns that demand one's direction at least at the beginning and the end of the transaction. These duties can be delegated, without being abdicated. The **third bin** suggests an assortment of items which may be interesting, but are not important at all. It would be nice to do them, have them, be them, but her confident reprioritization assures her that it does not really matter one way or the other. Without guilt, and with a renewed appreciation for the importance of bins one and two, these distractions are confidently shredding within the third bin. **These three bins—"control"/"alt"/"delete" are a short**hand simplification of the complexities unraveled by women.

*Which of the following would you **most** like to have more of in your life?*

Total	Men	Women	
25%	**23%**	**27%**	**PEACE**
16%	18%	13%	TIME
14%	13%	14%	LOVE
12%	14%	11%	MONEY
9%	11%	8%	LAUGHTER
7%	5%	9%	SECURITY
8%	7%	8%	COMBINATION (VOLUNTEERED)
1%	1%	1%	NONE OF THE ABOVE (VOLUNTEERED)
7%	6%	8%	ALL OF THE ABOVE (VOLUNTEERED)
*	1%	*	DON'T KNOW/REFUSED (VOLUNTEERED)

Need for more *peace* (by Sex/Age)

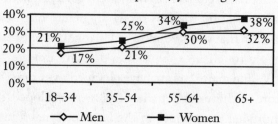

	18–34	35–54	55–64	65+
Men	17%	21%	30%	32%
Women	21%	25%	34%	38%

CNTRL Essential to me	ALT To be delegated	DELETE Abdicated duties
What is essential to me?	*What can I get others to do?*	*What is not important or interesting enough to consume my time?*
(e.g. family, work, health, voting, exercise).	*(e.g. cleaning, car services, dog walking, food prep.)*	*(e.g. chatting on the phone, curling hair, ironing pillowcases.)*

PEACE NOW

Though Americans talk about the need for more time, money, and security, overall what they are truly searching for is the key to a chaos-free life that is full of peace. While peace can connote worldly intentions such as ending violence and terrorism, our respondents may be seeking a more personal sense of calmness, serenity, and control in their daily lives. This sentiment was made clear when we asked survey respondents to choose from a list of six, that which they wanted to have more of in their life:

Peace
Time
Love
Money
Laughter
Security

Peace won. The primary need for more peace in their lives was shared by both men and women (23% and 27%, respectively). Time,

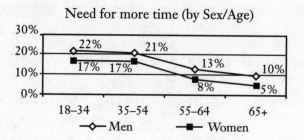

Need for more time (by Sex/Age)

love, and money all occupy subsequent spots, though in varying orders. The peace these respondents crave is not necessarily of the international variety. Rather, they're looking for a personal quiet and serenity.

- Political affiliations matter little in a woman's search for peace. Both self-identified Democrat and Republican women chose this as their top response (28% and 30%, respectively). They may disagree on how to resolve the situation in Iraq, but on the matter of their own personal peace, a bipartisan consensus has emerged.

- High-income married women (30%) were, like women overall, most likely to choose *peace* as what they wanted most in their lives. However, over one-fifth (23%) of these women said *time* would be the greatest gift, which was among the highest of any sub-group of women.

- Black women were 21 points more likely than black men to say they want more peace in their life (33% versus 12%).

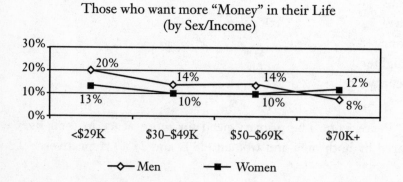

Those who want more "Money" in their Life
(by Sex/Income)

- Fathers, both married and unmarried, are more likely than their childless counterparts to seek more peace.

- Women who reside on the West Coast were twice as likely as women living in all other regions of the country to say they need more time (22% versus 11%).

LESS IS MORE

About a decade ago, Elaine St. James was running a successful real estate investing business and living an incredibly busy, complicated life. One afternoon, sitting in front of a time-management system "roughly the size of Nebraska" that was filled with names of people she needed to call, addresses of places she needed to be, and lists of things she was obligated to do, Elaine had a moment of clarity. As she wrote in Simplify Your Life: 100 Ways to Slow Down and Enjoy the Things That Really Matter, *"Like many others of our generation, my husband, Gibbs, and I had bought into the Bigger Is Better and the More Is Better Yet philosophies of the 1980s. We had the big house, the big car, most of the conveniences, and many of the toys of the typical yuppie lifestyle." St. James and her husband gradually realized all that stuff was complicating rather than simplifying their lives. "We had always known that the Joneses weren't worth keeping up with," she wrote, "but we finally had to face the fact that the only thing we'd ever gotten from a power lunch was indigestion." So she and Gibbs decided to simplify—big time.*

St. James is one of the gurus of the "voluntary simplicity" movement, which is growing, especially among the baby boomer "have-it-all" generation. St. James is quick to say that voluntary simplicity is not asceticism. It doesn't mean giving away all of your possessions and heading for a cabin in the woods. It's more about evaluating the joy-to-stuff ratio in your life, and halting the hyperconsumerism that is creating excess debt, complications, and stress. People who practice voluntary simplicity act

(continued on next page)

consciously to reduce their need for purchased services or goods and, by extension, their need to sell their time for money.

In the past decade, the voluntary simplicity idea has spawned hundreds of organizations, dozens of books, and publications like Real Simple, Everyday Food *and* Quick and Simple.

The voluntary simplicity movement makes some practical sense in light of trends we've highlighted in this book—most notably the desperate need for more peace, time and rest that many women feel. A number of them feel trapped are overwhelmed with the effort to balance job and family but don't have the financial wherewithal to give less time to their jobs. But the question of what you can afford must necessarily be viewed in the context of what you spend and where you place your priorities.

WORKING FOR THE WEEKEND

Family time is considered a top weekend priority for most American adults, though chores and shopping are staples on their compressed, 48-hour "to-do list." A recent survey commissioned by Life magazine examined how America spends the weekend. A full 55% said the agenda is replete with things they must do, rather than want to do during this timeframe. Young adults aged 18–24 said they are often exhausted by Sunday night and 41% admitted feeling depressed as they walk through the office doors come Monday. In contrast, adults aged 55+ finished their weekends feeling recharged, with 61% actually saying they are ready to jump-start their workweek. Nearly one-half (47%) of all respondents said they do most of their grocery shopping on the weekends (which, curiously, means one-half avoid the Saturday squeeze and go during the week). Among households with children, eating dinner at home on a Saturday or Sunday night is ideal. Watching television and exercising were also considered important weekend activities.

MULTITASKING MANIA

In September 2004, the Bureau of Labor Statistics released its first Time-Use Survey, which examined how Americans spend their days. It found that among parents with children under age 6, regardless of employment, women spend more than twice as much time as men providing primary care. The bottom line: **Women's share of the housework hasn't declined in the last 30 years despite a dramatic increase in workforce participation.**

How do they do it? As sources of information, entertainment, and activity around us keep building, women find themselves in a nearly constant flurry of multitasking (doing more than one task simultaneously). They mix dinner with the nightly news, breakfast with the daily commute, and phone calls with Internet browsing.

Women tend to rely more heavily on television as a source for news over other media like newspapers, the Internet, and magazines, mainly because it's a passive way to obtain information while accomplishing other tasks. Some women actually feel guilty if they plop down on the couch to read a newspaper. Instead, they have the TV on as background while they fix dinner, pay bills, fold laundry, do housework, or tend to the kids.

The ability to multitask has been called a distinctly feminine gift, but that is not such a good thing when it increases responsibilities and stress without relief. In a study of viewers, Lifetime Television found that women valued "me time," even when it only amounted to grabbing an hour or two on Sunday to watch a TV movie. It was important to relieve stress by doing nothing every once in a while.

SO MANY CHOICES, SO LITTLE TIME

Welcome to the land of opportunity, where freedom of choice is guaranteed. And each day is chock full of choices. Perhaps too many.

For more information, press 1; to receive computerized instructions, press 2; to listen to an array of choices that will send you reeling, press 3; to complain about the length of time you've been holding, press 4; to get on a different line, press 5; to speak to someone in another country, press 6; to engage in a lengthy and convoluted process of changing your original order, press 7; to speak to a customer representative sometime in the next millenium, press 8; to abandon hope, press 0. And have a nice day!

Want more choices? Which phone company meets your needs? We have Cingular, Covista, Primus, and Quest. Or you can choose Bell-South, MCI, Sprint, Intel, or Talk America. Maybe IT&T, AT&T, or Verizon are better for you. To help you decide, just take a few hours to study the 70 different plans available through these companies. And then repeat the process to pick an Internet service provider and cell phone carrier.

Which health-care provider will best protect you? How about auto, home, and life insurance? Need a vitamin supplement? There are thousands of varieties. Cooking a spaghetti dinner? Decide whether your noodles will be wheat-free, gluten-free, semolina, spelt, quinoa, rice, or spinach.

By the time you're ready to fall into bed at the end of the day, you've made hundreds of choices. And you may not be finished yet. A colleague staying in a New York City hotel recently received a tap on her door just as she was about to retire. It was the housekeeper, handing her an embossed card. "Your pillow menu, Ma'am," she said. She looked down the list. Did she prefer hypoallergenic, down, feather, or buckwheat? Full body, neck support, side sleeper, or standard? Satin, cotton, or silk cover?

"No, thank you," she said, closing the door. She'd sleep better without the stress of one more choice.

The increase in choices seems directly proportional to a loss of control. While choices are a natural byproduct of freedom, they breed disarray and indecision. Many women tell us they seek "controlled chaos"—like a list of 15, not 55 items on a menu. Since 9/11, exerting control means maintaining order, relying on consistency, and occasionally trading in choice for certainty.

Much has been made of women's interest in security since 9/11, but we view the real longer-term trend as women seeking ways to feel more secure, balanced, and in charge of their own environment. While many women welcomed the "slow-down-and-savor-life" ethos in the weeks after 9/11, that quickly gave way to deadlines, appointments, challenges, and the perennial pressure for perfection. The mouse race continues.

THE NEXT 10 YEARS

Will the pace ever slow? Related trends in housing, the workplace, and the increased search for sustainable environments make the rat race less desirable, if not yet less common.

- The best places to work, and the companies with the happiest employees, will be those that offer flexibility, reasonable work hours, and adequate vacation. Burning the midnight oil will no longer be seen as the way to get ahead. Success at work will be measured by how effective workers are at accomplishing the most in the least amount of time, not by how many hours they slave away. Failure to take vacation will earn executives a demotion.

- Since women rely so heavily on communication, interactive media will replace passive sources (newspapers, TV) as a method of getting news and information. The new phone call will be a video chat.

- Women love their cell phones, but this may conflict with the greater desire to have more peace, time, and space in their lives. We suspect that the latter will endure.

- Technology has added ease and efficiency to many, while at the same time increasing demands and expectations. Women will cherry-pick the new technologies, rejecting those that fail to meet their needs for efficiency, control, and convenience, and choosing others, such as online shopping, in greater numbers.

TREND 7

GENERATIONAL COMPRESSION

Longevity, technology, and social constructs blur if not eviscerate the boundaries of age.

For the first time in memory, women across generations have remarkable commonality, expressed in their daily concerns, their values, and even their youthful, optimistic spirits.

Witness three typical moms watching their preschool-age children at the playground. Boomer Mom, 49, is busily making lists for several upcoming events. Her eldest son from her first marriage is graduating from college next month, and she's planning a dinner celebration after the ceremony. Her brother's retirement dinner is scheduled for the following month—a ritual she will face soon. She wonders if she can get a sitter that evening so she can take her 16-year-old shopping for a prom dress.

Across the bench, Gen X Mom, 35, is talking on her cell phone, one eye on her child in the sandbox, the other on the pages of her bulky day timer, stuffed full of notes. Her "work voice" rises and falls around the other women's "mommy voices." It's supposed to be her day off, but there's an emergency at the office, and she finds it impossible to put her BlackBerry down anyway. She wonders if she can get a babysitter so she can dash in for a couple of hours and put out the fire.

Gen Y Mom, 25, seated nearby, closes her legal textbook and takes a swig from a large bottle of vitamin water. She is studying for the bar exam, which she will take the following year. She hopes to start practicing law when her daughter begins first grade. Meanwhile, her husband is supporting the family while she stays home. He is returning from a business trip today. She wonders if she can get a babysitter so they can go out to dinner, just the two of them.

These three women grew up in different eras; indeed, Boomer Mom is old enough to be Gen Y Mom's mother. Yet they are confronting many of the same issues on a daily basis. If they have school-age children, they have more in common with each other than they have differences.

The last four decades have been defined by their culture wars, with

GENERATIONS

	THEN	NOW
Mantra	"Don't trust anyone over 30"	Disappearing generation gap, with new moms at 48 and 28
Women	Sandwich generation	Salad generation
Seniors	Rocking chair	Rock around the clock
Resume	Experience = bucks	Youth = bucks
Gen X	Slackers	Innovators
Young adults	Flying the coop	Fear of flying

different generations vying for center stage. Today, the old wars with their slogans ("Never trust anyone over 30") seem ridiculous. In these times, it appears that a totally unexpected detente may be emerging. There is always generational tension, but our need for one another has trumped the desire to express our differences. Boomers need Gen X and Gen Y to prop up the economy and support their longevity. Gen X and Gen Y need boomers to fund their start in life and stabilize the home and workplace.

We've named our sixth trend Generational Compression, as a way of signifying these remarkable shifts. Generational changes have been rumbling beneath the surface for some time and are finally coming into full bloom. This has a transformational effect on American culture as some women defer, delay, or deny marriage and children, segué in and out of the workforce, and end relationships or start businesses with a flair their mothers would not have embraced. **For the first time in memory, age is no longer a woman's defining characteristic—her stage of life is.** For example, a 50-year-old woman and a 30-year-old woman who have children in elementary school have more in common with each other than they do with their peers who are childless or empty-nesters.

GENERATIONAL SALAD

Depression Baby: 66 to 80+

War Baby: 59 to 65

Baby Boomer: 40 to 58

Gen X: 26 to 39

Gen Y: 5 to 25

Gen Z: 0 to 4

Age ranges are based on common definitions.

The delayed schedules for moving out, getting married, and having children have affected our cultural perceptions of aging. They are creating some conflicts as seniors and juniors vie for a share of the economic pie. But they also have created life-enriching relationships across the generational boundaries.

For the first time, women of different generations are not ideologically and practically separated. Kids are getting older at younger ages, and adults are acting younger at older ages. They're meeting in the middle.

BEANPOLE FAMILIES

In previous eras, the typical family was like a spreading oak, with multiple branches sweeping out from the trunk to form new branches. Extended families were large and layered, with lots of first, second, and third cousins and many aunts and uncles. The bulk of the family settled around two and possibly three generations, with the oldest dying when their grandchildren were young.

Two distinct trends have changed that. Families are having fewer children and people are living longer. Today's family is more like a beanpole—composed of many generations but with fewer members in each. Great-grandparents and even great-great-grandparents are the norm, not the exceptions.

In previous generations, nearly all children were born to young mothers, creating a clear division of the generations: New moms were in their twenties. Grandmothers were in their late forties to early sixties. Roles were delineated. For the baby boomers, though, there were three mommy tracks. The first comprised women who had babies in their early twenties. The second was women who established their careers first and had babies in their thirties and early forties, just as the first group's babies were leaving the nest. In this third cohort were women who had children in their early twenties and also had children later, often because they had divorced and remarried.

This staggered birth picture has created completely different family compositions. Yvonne, 48, is an example of this phenomenon. "My

THE DREAM AGE

The Harris Interactive polls asked: If you could stop time and live forever in good health at one age, what would it be? Verdict: 41.

youngest child is 6," she explained. "She was my midlife baby. Last month my firstborn, who is 22, had her first child. So I'm a mother and a grandmother at the same time, and my 6-year-old daughter is an aunt. The titles don't mean much, do they?" Yvonne's family is a classic beanpole. Her mother is 72 and in good health, and she has two great-aunts (her grandmother's sisters) who are still alive. That's five generations!

Of course, women having their first children in their late thirties and forties will not have as many generations in their families, since their daughters may not have children for another 40 years. But the beanpole will survive as the primary family tree because people will continue to live longer.

BOOM TIMES

One day, Joyce, 55, received a call from a casual friend, Cora, 58. "Some of us women are going to take up kayaking," she said. "Are you interested?"

"It sounds wonderful," Joyce said, "but I have one problem. I can't swim, so I'd be pretty nervous being out on the river like that."

"So, learn to swim," Cora replied.

Conventional wisdom has always held that as people get older, they become more set in their ways and conservative. This isn't always true of female baby boomers—especially the middle group that is roughly between the ages of 41 and 59. Some are trendsetters, and even trailblazers, and will continue to be as they age. They're also at the height of power: the majority of Congress, as well as the last two presidents have been baby boomers. But they're also determined to live fully, even if that makes them take risks that the old guard would never have considered. Gail Sheehy may have been referring to this new picture of midlife when she wrote in *New Passages*, **"Fifty is what 40 used to be; 60 is what 50 used to be."**

Grandboomerang

My grandmother was like a storybook character. She was sweet and plump, and she never yelled. She bought me Nancy Drew books and sewed me little dresses. When she was my age, she was in her final years. I expect to be around for another thirty years or so.

—WYNETTA, 57

By 2006 there will be 80 million grandparents in the United States, nearly half of them baby boomers. They will be the youngest, best educated, wealthiest, most active generation of grandparents in history. Already, **the average age of first-time grandparents is 47!** That's good news and bad news. For one thing, the midlife woman will increasingly face a generational squeeze, especially if she delayed marriage and children. With more than 25% of American families responsible for the care of aging parents, women in their fifties and sixties will become the club sandwich generation—sandwiched between the caretaking demands of growing children and aging parents.

Almost one-quarter of U.S. households (22 million) currently care for a relative or friend who is 50 years old or older. That number will only increase as baby boomers age. Six in ten caregivers are women.

Here's the surprising news: New data suggests that **the burdens of the sandwich generation may be overstated**—indeed, that **grandparents are care*giving* more than they're care*taking*.** The most common pattern in multigenerational households is for children and grandchildren to move into a house that the grandparents own or rent. In 1997, three-fourths of multigenerational households were of this type. In nearly one-third of the grandparent-maintained families, grandparents lived with their grandchildren without the children's parents.

ALL WE ARE SAYING IS
GIVE AGE A CHANCE

The revolution generation is not about to allow itself to be meekly corralled into exile in its prime. When television writers started noticing that being 40 or older was the kiss of death no matter how successful they had been, first they panicked and then they sued.

The panic part was characterized by a furious scramble by older writers to reinvent themselves as younger. Writers whose credits included some of the top-rated television programs of all time—Archie Bunker, M.A.S.H., The Mary Tyler Moore Show—were deleting these once-esteemed credentials from their resumés in order to mask their age. They were teaming up with young writers who served as the team's "face" at story conferences. They were taking on any and every project, at pay scales they wouldn't have considered a decade or two earlier. Finally, when they reached the boiling point, they sued. In an unprecedented legal effort, more than 150 television writers teamed up with AARP to launch 23 class-action lawsuits against the entertainment industry's largest corporations. Their contention was that not just one company but the entire industry had an institutional practice of age discrimination.

The industry's biggest guns brushed off the suits as frivolous and the writers as disgruntled, but it is common knowledge that Hollywood executives, often in their twenties and thirties, don't think older writers have the instincts to appeal to the coveted teen and early twenties market. (One older writer scoffed at this, saying, "Shakespeare wrote Romeo and Juliet, and he wasn't 15.")

In their first courtroom test, the lawsuits hit a roadblock when the cases were dismissed, but the decision was later overturned by a California appeals court. The score: writers 1, industry 0. Stay tuned.

BY THE NUMBERS

80
The average lifespan of an American woman

47
The average age of first-time grandparents

70
The percentage of women over age 65 who live independently

1.5 MILLION
The number of Americans over age 90

6 MILLION
The number of 55- to 74-year-olds with annual incomes over $100,000

Grandparents who own or rent homes that include grandchildren and adult children are younger, healthier, and more likely to be in the labor force than are grandparents who live in a residence owned or rented by their adult children. Grandparents who maintain multigenerational households are also better educated (more likely to have at least a high school education) than grandparents who live in their children's homes.

In another significant trend, **more than 2.5 million grandparents are raising 4.5 million grandchildren.**

Thinking generally about problems facing women, what would you say is the biggest challenge facing older women today?

56%   HEALTH/WELLBEING

16%   MAINTAINING GOOD HEALTH/BEING HEALTHY

11%	GOOD/ACCESSIBLE HEALTH CARE
8%	HEALTH ISSUES (NONSPECIFIC)
5%	HEALTH-RELATED DIFFICULTIES
3%	MENOPAUSE
2%	COST OF HEALTHCARE
2%	OSTEOPOROSIS
2%	PHYSICAL LIMITATIONS
2%	BEING ABLE TO TAKE CARE OF YOURSELF
1%	MEDICAID CUTBACKS
1%	GROWING OLD (NONSPECIFIC)
1%	HIGH COST OF PRESCRIPTIONS
1%	NOT ENOUGH EXERCISE
1%	STAYING SLIM
1%	DIABETES

11%	**MONEY/FINANCES**
6%	LACK OF MONEY
2%	BEING ABLE TO LIVE ON SOCIAL SECURITY
2%	LIVING ON A FIXED INCOME
1%	MONEY (NONSPECIFIC)

6%	**SOCIETY**
4%	TRYING TO SURVIVE IN SOCIETY
2%	AGE DISCRIMINATION

6%	**MISCELLANEOUS**
4%	LONELINESS
1%	FINDING A YOUNGER MAN
1%	AFFORDABLE/AVAILABLE TRANSPORTATION

6%	**EMPLOYMENT**
1%	EMPLOYMENT DIFFICULTIES
1%	KEEPING UP WITH OTHER WOMEN
1%	DON'T GET PAID AS MUCH AS MEN
1%	DISCRIMINATION
1%	GETTING AN EDUCATION
1%	COMPUTER ILLITERATE

4%   **CHILDREN**
2%   WORKING WITH CHILDREN
1%   RAISING CHILDREN ALONE
1%   NOT HAVING CHILDREN AROUND

12%   DON'T KNOW/NO ANSWER

AS LONG AS YOU HAVE YOUR HEALTH . . .

As the largest generation of Americans, the baby boomers, approach retirement, many are doing so more actively and with more zeal than previous "junior seniors." Nonetheless, over half (56%) of women surveyed mentioned some aspect of health or well-being as the number one challenge facing older women. A full 16% of that group specifically stated "maintaining good health/being healthy," while another 11% cited "good/accessible health care." Further responses included "health-related difficulties," "menopause," "cost of health care," and "osteoporosis," among others.

   With longer life spans in the offing, it comes as no surprise that just over 1 in 10 (11%) reported money and finances as problematic for the aging. "Lack of money," "being able to live on Social Security," and "living on a fixed income" were identified among this group.

   Employment troubles and children were seen as less of a concern to older women (6% and 4%, respectively). Likewise, there was relatively little concern about societal influences. "Trying to survive in society" and "age discrimination" were mentioned by 6%, while another 6% stated "loneliness," "finding a younger man," and "affordable/ available transportation."

> • Women aged 18 to 29 were 2.25 times more likely than women aged 65 and over to say that health was the main concern for older women (81% to 36%, respectively). Interestingly, 65% of those approaching senior status (aged 55 to 64) also cited a topic related to health.

- Political moderates were 20 points more likely than conservatives and 23 points more likely than liberals to report some health issue (71%, 51%, and 48%, respectively).

- Women with an annual income of $70,000 or more were 24 points more likely than those who earned less to choose *health* as a major concern for aging women. Investors were 10 points more likely than noninvestors to cite a topic related to health (62% to 52%, respectively).

- Other groups that were more likely overall to mention a health concern include women with some college education, those who attend religious services a few times a week, West Coast residents, and women with blue-collar jobs.

FREE AND WISE

Women see freedom, time, and wisdom as the best things about getting older. "With age comes wisdom." This belief holds true among the one-fifth (20%) of women we surveyed who simply cited "wisdom" as the positive result of aging. More specifically:

- Blacks were 7 points more likely than whites to consider "wisdom" the best thing about getting older (26% to 19%).

- Owners of small businesses were 9 points more likely than those who did not own small businesses to say "wisdom"

DID YOU KNOW?

Having a positive view of aging can add an average of 7.5 years to your life.

when considering the benefits of aging (27% to 18%, respectively).

- Women with annual incomes of $50,000 to $69,000 were more likely than all other income brackets to look forward to both wisdom (24% and 20%, respectively) and retirement (14% and 6%, respectively) as they grow older.

- Childless women (including not-yet-moms) were 5 points more likely than women with children to think age brings wisdom (24% and 19% respectively).

Regardless of your current age, in your opinion, what do you see as the best thing about getting older?

20%	WISDOM
10%	SPEND MORE TIME WITH CHILDREN/GRANDCHILDREN
8%	RETIREMENT/NOT WORKING
8%	HAVE MORE CONFIDENCE/GREATER SELF-ASSURANCE
7%	MORE FREEDOM/FLEXIBILITY
6%	ABILITY TO TRAVEL/VACATION
6%	MORE MONEY/FINANCIAL ASSETS
5%	MORE TIME FOR MYSELF
4%	SPEND MORE TIME ON MY HOBBIES/LEISURE ACTIVITIES
3%	FEWER RESPONSIBILITIES
3%	NO MORE CHILDREN IN THE HOUSE
3%	TRY NEW THINGS
3%	MORE TIME WITH SPOUSE/PARTNER

DID YOU KNOW?

There are more than 51,000 Americans who are 100 or older, among them about 1,400 so-called supercentenarians who top 110.

2%   MORE CHOICES

1%   MEET NEW PEOPLE

1%   EXPAND OR CHANGE CAREER

9%   OTHER (VOLUNTEERED)

8%   DO NOT KNOW (VOLUNTEERED)

1%   REFUSED (VOLUNTEERED)

Increased individual freedoms and choices, purported to be the hall-marks of youth, accounted for a total 29% of responses among *all* women. They specifically mentioned an "increase in self-confidence," "flexibility," "financial assets," and having "fewer responsibilities" as benefits to an empty nest.

Our survey respondents also believe that age begets increased focus on what's most important to individuals as they grow older. More time to spend on oneself, one's family, hobbies, and leisure activities was cited by a combined 28% of respondents.

- Single women were 4 points more likely than married women to claim an increase in self-esteem brought about with age as the best thing about getting older.

- Registered Independents were 10 points more likely than registered Democrats and 8 points more likely that registered Republicans to mention wisdom (27%, 17%, and 19%, respectively). Interestingly, self-identified liberals were 4 points more likely than both self-identified moderates and self-identified conservatives to boast an increase of confidence and self-assurance in aging (12% and 8%, respectively).

- Small business owners were more likely than non-small business owners to say that *wisdom* is the best thing about getting older. Perhaps the freedom of working for one's self provides a comforting and rewarding portal for entry into retirement.

Our results also showed these interesting facts:

- Grandparents say there is "proof in the pudding," and were 6 points more likely than those without grandchildren to declare the best thing about aging is more time with the children and grandchildren (14% and 8%, respectively).

PERMA YOUTH

Despite the complaints about appearance and the billions they spend every year on anti-aging treatments and products, nearly one-half of the women we surveyed (49%) reported feeling younger than their current age. One-third (34%) believed that Father Time and Mother Nature were in sync; they felt their actual age. Just 16% reported feeling older than their years suggesting that perhaps, as has been said, 40 *is* the new 30.

- While women of every race were more likely to report feeling younger than their age, white women were slightly more likely than black women to say they felt younger than their current age (50% to 44%).

- Finding a mate seems to keep women youthful. Single women were twice as likely as their married and divorced or

BOOMIN' INTO RETIREMENT

There are just six years to go until the first boomers hit the age of 65. The 76 million boomers will cause the population of retired persons to double between 2011 and 2029. It's an optimistic group. Only a relative handful tell pollsters they are worried about aging.

Would you say you feel older than your current age, younger than your current age, or about your current age?

16%   OLDER THAN MY CURRENT AGE

49%   YOUNGER THAN MY CURRENT AGE

34%   I FEEL ABOUT MY AGE

 1%   DO NOT KNOW (VOLUNTEERED)

  –   REFUSED (VOLUNTEERED)

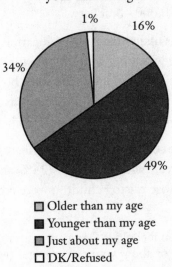

Would you say you feel older
than your current age, younger
than your current age, or about
your current age?

1%   16%

34%

49%

☐ Older than my age
■ Younger than my age
▨ Just about my age
☐ DK/Refused

separated counterparts to report feeling older or about their current age and significantly less likely than the other women to feel younger (even when they actually *were* younger). There was little perceptible difference between married and divorced women.

• The older a respondent was, the younger she felt. The chart demonstrates that as a woman's age increased, so did the

likelihood that she felt younger than her current age. The
big jump was at 40.

- The likelihood of a woman feeling older than her actual age
generally decreased as she became more educated, while the
likelihood of her feeling younger notably increased with
higher education.

- Similarly, women at the lower end of the income spectrum
(those earning less than $30,000 per year) were most apt to
feel older than their age. All women earning more than
$30,000 per year were more likely than most to feel younger
than their years, most notably those in the $30,000 to
$50,000 and $70,000+ brackets.

- A finding that is likely tied to the education and income factors could be seen among women investors (57%) and owners of small businesses (57%), who were both more inclined
to hold onto feelings of youth, while noninvestors (23%) and
non–business owners (17%) each felt old before their time.

- Women without children were more likely than mothers to
feel older or even with their age (24% and 14%, respectively), while those raising children were considerably more

Would you say you feel older than your current age, younger
than your current age, or about your current age? (women respondents)

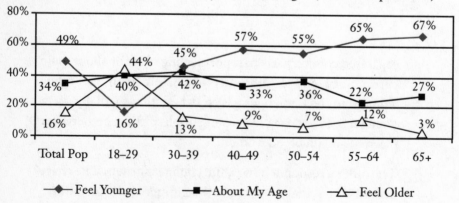

apt to report feeling younger (52% and 35%, respectively). Mothers who were also grandmothers felt the youngest of them all!

- Suburbanites were more likely than their urban or rural counterparts to still feel spry (53%, 46%, and 47%, respectively) and Northeasterners (54%) were more apt than women living in other regions of the country to say the same.

HOT FLASH!

Approximately 43 million women are between ages 40 and 60, and they have a hot news flash for the rest of the population: They're not having a midlife crisis—at least, not in the way it was once defined.

"In a man's world, the midlife crisis was a chance to shirk," said Marci, 51. "Go off white-water rafting. Have a fling with a young woman. Quit your job. That isn't what's going on with me and my women friends. In fact, I wouldn't call it a crisis as much as a reevaluation. We're asking ourselves, are we happy? Where do we want to be in 20 years? What dreams can we fulfill?"

If anything, when women hit midlife, they tend to spend more time with members of the same sex—deepening their reach and broadening their circle of female friends. Growing older becomes less isolating and more intriguing. The question of identity is wide open once again, as their childbearing years end. "Thrill-seeking" has less to do with forbidden affairs than forsaken adventures. Women's ability to metamorphasize in midlife and late life will have positive consequences, not only in mental well-being but in overall health. Reclaiming oneself through new hobbies, friends, interests, and routines halts the rise of negative stress and depression, which have been the leading triggers of health problems in seniors.

BY THE NUMBERS

78 MILLION
Estimated number of baby boomers

49 MILLION
Estimated number of Generation Xers

72 MILLION
Estimated number of Generation Yers

29 MILLION
Estimated number of "Tweens" (8 to 14)*

* Tweens are part of Generation Y.

GENERATIONS X AND Y

According to the 2000 Census, 28% of the entire United States female population is between 20–40 years of age. Popular culture sometimes arbitrarily segregates these cohorts into Generation X (those born between 1965–1975) and Generation Y (those born between 1976–2001). Ironically, research suggests the "X" is an apt descriptor in that there had been no galvanizing issue during their formative years to define them, no Great Depression, World War, Civil Rights debate, or Vietnam War to have impacted their cultural experiences and remain with them as an indelible characteristic, as had been the case with earlier generations.

Still, Gen X is bound by several key attributes that could help to inform the research in this project. Technology is their native tongue, allowing them to maximize efficiency in the workplace and market. The independence and self-reliance they learned early as latch-key kids whose moms were working and whose fathers were often absent from the home altogether (40% of Gen Xers lived in a single-parent household by the age of 16) has been harnessed into entrepreneurial pursuits, or a preference in the workforce to be the supervisor rather than the one supervised.

Much of this is true of Generation Y, which as the most ethnically diverse generation in the history of the United States, is also identified through its multiculturalism. This trend will persist as non-white populations continue to increase rapidly. While a majority of Generation Y are teenagers, their older 20-something counterparts are currently entering or already fully engaged in the nation's workforce. One amazing fact about this generation is that the median age of a Hispanic household is 26.2 compared to the national average age of 35.6.

CARES OF THE YOUNG

When asked, "What would you say is the biggest challenge facing *younger* women today," family- and career-related issues were foremost.

Three in ten (30%) of those surveyed named some combination of familial factors as being the "biggest challenge facing younger women today." Specific responses included "childrearing/raising," "balancing work and family," and the choice of "going to work or raising kids."

Thinking generally about problems facing women, what would you say is the biggest challenge facing **younger** *women today?*

30%	**FAMILY (NET)**
12%	CHILD REARING/RAISING
9%	BALANCING WORK AND FAMILY
3%	GOING TO WORK OR RAISING KIDS
2%	PROVIDING DAYCARE/CHILDCARE
1%	TIME FOR FAMILY
1%	WOMEN BEING BOTH MOTHER AND FATHER
1%	BEING ABLE TO STAY HOME AND RAISE KIDS
1%	YOUNGER WOMEN NOT HAVING FATHER FIGURE

19%   **EMPLOYMENT/CAREER (NET)**

4%   GETTING GOOD JOBS

4%   NOT BEING PAID THE SAME AS MEN

3%   DISCRIMINATION IN THE WORKPLACE

2%   MAKING GOOD CAREER DECISIONS

2%   DECIDING WHAT TO DO WITH THEIR LIVES

1%   LACK OF JOB OPPORTUNITIES FOR WOMEN

1%   WOMEN NOT WORKING

1%   FINDING NON-TRADITIONAL JOBS THAT WOMEN CAN DO

1%   FINDING STABLE WORK WHERE YOU DON'T GET LAID OFF

15%   **PRESSURES/EXPECTATIONS (NET)**

4%   GETTING AN EDUCATION

2%   HAVING A GOOD SELF-IMAGE

2%   MORALS

1%   ACHIEVING OWN GOALS

1%   REALIZING OWN POTENTIAL

1%   ATTITUDES OF OLDER WOMEN

1%   NOT CARING ABOUT WHAT THE FUTURE HOLDS

1%   HAVING SOCIETY'S VERSION OF THE PERFECT BODY

1%   FITTING IN WITH PEERS

1%   EFFECTS OF POLITICAL INCORRECTNESS

9%   **HEALTH/WELLBEING (NET)**

4%   STRESS

2%   DRUG USE

1%   JOINTS GETTING STIFF

1%   HIV

1%   WEIGHT

6%   **MONEY/FINANCES (NET)**

3%   FINANCIAL STABILITY

2%   HAVING TO WORK TO SUPPORT A FAMILY

1%   FINANCIAL ISSUES FOR SINGLE WOMEN

19%   DON'T KNOW/NO ANSWER

GENERATION LINGO

Boomeranger: *An adult child who returns home to live with his or her baby boomer parent.*

Generation 9-11: *The generation of people who were enrolled in high school or university on September 11, 2001.*

Grandboomer: *A grandparent who is part of the baby boomer generation.*

Sea-changer: *A person who retires to a seaside destination.*

Issues involving employment and career choices garnered the attention of nearly one-fifth (19%) of women. "Getting good jobs," "not being paid the same as men," and "discrimination in the workplace" were all among the more specific concerns of young women.

Another 15% of women stated that societal pressures and expectations cause woe and worry for young women. Some motivational factors they specifically mentioned included "getting an education," "achieving own goals," and "realizing own potential," while others cited other influences such as "having a good self-image," "attitudes of older women," and "having society's version of the perfect body."

OH, GROW UP!

Twixters or thresholders are between 18 and 25, just out of college, and feeling betwixt and between. They're somewhat reluctant to cross over the threshold to adulthood. They're also called echo boomers, and in some ways they do echo the era whose slogan was "tune in and drop out."

Why are these bright, well-schooled young people clinging so hard to the nest? It's a complex picture made up of equal parts economic paralysis, comfortable social networks, delayed maturity, dependency, and the quest to "find" themselves in a meaningful way. Unlike their own parents who couldn't wait to break free of the house rules, Twixters are extremely close to their parents and may even share their views on important issues (a sure sign of generational compression). A *Time* magazine poll found that almost 50% of 18 to 29-year-olds talk to their parents every day.

Some parents are thrilled to have their adult children linger. Others are baffled. "Didn't I already raise you?" they might ask. As one mother sighed, "I was all geared up to be devastated by the empty-nest syndrome. Now I'm saying, *'What? You're still here?'* "

Economic factors are the driving force for this trend, and many parents and graduates alike are shocked and disheartened by how little return they're getting on their college investment. Saddled with college loans to pay off and unable to command the anticipated entry-level salaries (much less employment in their fields of study), many young adults remain financially dependent on their parents.

In light of these realities, there is a growing sense among parents and graduates that colleges and universities aren't holding up their end of the bargain, which, they felt, is to prepare students to work and live in the real world. Yet most companies require a college degree for jobs that used to require only high school, leaving little choice. But it's not just the college grads who are lingering. **The number of young adults ages 18 to 24 who are neither working nor going to school has increased 19% since 2000, accounting for 3.8 million people.**

Twixters find themselves in a cultural collision of expectations and reality. The most educated, creative, technologically in-tune, pampered generation in the history of the nation is further putting the brakes on the big moves, such as marriage and motherhood, pushing the average age of new parents even further down the road toward 40.

Already we are seeing economic consequences in the higher average age that people are becoming parents, with less time during their prime earning years to build college funds and bear the costs of raising children while saving for retirement. Delayed parenting also means fewer children to fund Social Security, while delayed employment adds to the problem with fewer dollars going into the system. If this trend continues, it could place a severe strain on the economy, whose health is predicated in part on each generation playing its prescribed role.

THE CLASS OF 9-11 TO THE RESCUE?

And yet. We have seen how world-changing events are capable of shaking trends loose from their trajectories, and the terrorist attack of 9-11 may have such an effect on the slow starters of the twixter generation. In May 2005, the first class to have gone through four years of college after 9-11 graduated. These students had just arrived at colleges across America and were settling into their first courses when 9-11 happened, and there is evidence that the attack on America made such an impact that it changed their direction. A survey, commissioned by the Partnership for Public Service and administered to 805 graduating college seniors, May 2–5, 2005, shows that 83% of the members of the class of 2005 describe themselves as patriotic, and nearly half (43%) of them say that the events of 9-11 made them more so. Twenty percent said they had decided to seek careers in government service as a result—a crucial injection of new blood into the government, which is anticipating the retirement of 1 million federal workers in the next five years.

But it wasn't just the level of patriotism that was different. In interviews with graduating seniors in this survey and others, students said **9-11 jolted them out of their complacency about life in general and made them more serious about making a contribution to society through their work.**

Teach for America, the national corps of recent college graduates of all academic majors who commit two years to teach in urban and rural public schools, received a record 17,000 applications for its 2005 teaching corps. This represented a 29% increase from 2004 in the number of total applicants. Applicants often cited 9-11 as their impetus for service.

It is unclear whether the 9-11-inspired reengagement of college grads represents the beginning of a long-term change. Obviously, the integration of this group and others into the workplace will depend on a healthy economy. "Our research shows that the patriotism surrounding 9-11 did not give the government a free pass in recruiting talent," said Max Stier, president and CEO of the Partnership for Public Service. "We need a new call to public service, one that balances young people's patriotism with two factors that are just as important to them: pay and prestige."

Researchers will follow the class of 9-11 into the future, testing its commitment and altruism as it ages. But as the graduating seniors donned caps and gowns to accept their diplomas in May 2005, it was heartening that so many of them did so with a plan of action not retreat.

THE NEXT 10 YEARS

What are the implications of the further compression of generations?

- Day-care centers will spring up that simultaneously offer assistance for grandpa and junior.

- Support groups, such as Second Time Around Parents, will become commonplace.

- More youthful junior seniors will shift the focus of retirement from retreat to "third age," especially women, who return to school and start new careers after 50 at much higher rates than men.

- Meanwhile, the cost of delayed marriage and childbearing will begin to have economic consequences, as parents face retirement as their kids start college. Watch for families to increase the pressure for affordable higher education.

- For the first time, the issue of benefits and/or tax breaks for family caregivers (who account for up to 25% of health-care services) will appear on political platforms.

- One of the unexpected outcomes of 9-11 is the emergence of a more public service–oriented younger population. Combined with an overstressed military, expect the issue of a required National Service (either civil or military) to be prominent in the public debate.

BEAUTY IN ACTION

Women want integrated lifestyles of health and beauty that help them feel better, look their best, sharpen their minds, and feed their souls.

During the 1970s and 1980s, Rachel went on an average of one major weight-loss diet a year. She tried Atkins, Pritikin, Stillman, food combining, diet shakes, the grapefruit diet, Weight Watchers, macrobiotics, gluten-free, sugar-free, fat-free, and fasting. Whenever there was a new hit diet, she was game. She figures that over the course of 20 years she lost and regained about 1,000 pounds.

Today, at 50, Rachel doesn't diet anymore. The catalyst for her change in attitude was the death of her mother at age 68 from breast cancer. "Suddenly, being thin enough to wear a size zero not only wasn't a priority, I found it vaguely repulsive," Rachel said. "In the year before she died, my mother was so thin, I prayed that she would gain weight. After that, I began to see super skinny people with new eyes. They no longer looked chic to me. They looked sick."

Rachel knew her focus had to be on healthy eating, not just weight loss, and she had to start exercising. Her mother's breast cancer was a strong signal about her own risk factors. As she celebrates the half-century mark, Rachel says she is in better shape than she has been in her life, and healthier, too. "The numbers that really matter to me these days aren't on the scale," she says. "They're cholesterol, triglycerides, and blood pressure." She weighs 145 pounds, which is on the high end for her 5-foot 3-inch frame, but she has a low percentage of body fat. She's in fighting shape. She's also in *living* shape.

When it comes to health and beauty, women really *do* want it all. They are still interested in beauty, but many are not willing to sacrifice being healthy for looking good. Gradually the equation is shifting, making that healthy, spiritually centered glow the new face of beauty. We call our eighth trend Beauty in Action, implying that beauty today *means* something; it isn't a passive look, it's a way of living.

BODY AND MIND

	THEN	NOW
Focus	*Looking good whatever the cost, even to health*	*Aging healthfully*
Dream	*Lose the next 10 pounds*	*Lose the last 10 years*
Wrinkles	*Badge of life lived*	*Botox them*
Makeovers	*A "grown-up" woman's domain*	*Tweens/adolescents getting manicures, pedicures, highlights, waxing, and facials*
Exercise	*Sweat (cardio workouts)*	*Sculpt (yoga, pilates)*
Nourishment	*Deprivation diets*	*"Pfood"—food that combines nutrition and pharmaceuticals*
Spirituality	*New Age*	*LOHAS (lifestyles of health and sustainability)*

LOHAS Nation

My home and garden are living entities. I don't use poisons or
chemicals in my yard, and I don't use them inside my home.
Environmentally friendly cleaning products and an air filtration system get the job done without harm."

—LISA, 33

LOHAS is an acronym that stands for lifestyles of health and
sustainability, and this is a trend led by women. An estimated 68% of
American consumers have joined the health-savvy, organic-loving, eco-
responsive movement, albeit at different levels, spending upwards of
$230 billion for goods and services.

**Women are increasingly buying into lifestyles of health and
inner growth, accepting the mind-body connection to search for
emotional and spiritual "fitness" to complement physical well-
being.** As a result, they are forcing a public discussion of health and sustainability regarding the foods we eat and the environments we inhabit.
Spirituality is no longer relegated to the New Age periphery but suggests a symbiosis of women's many moving parts.

LOHAS consumers are interested in:

Healthy living: Natural, organic and nutritional foods, dietary supplements, and organic personal care products

Alternative healthcare: Homeopathy, naturopathy, holistic disease
prevention, and complementary health care

Personal development: Mind, body, and spirit products: CDs, books,
tapes and seminars, yoga, fitness and weight loss, and spirituality

Ecological lifestyles: Biodegradeable home and office products,
organic/recycled fiber products, environmentally friendly appliances, and ecotourism and travel

Sustainable economy: Green building and industrial goods, renewable
energy, resource-efficient products, socially responsible investing,
alternative transportation, and environmental management

DID YOU KNOW?

According to the Population Research Center and the University of Texas in Austin, those who attend church more than once a week have a life expectancy seven years greater than those who never attend.

WOMEN-CENTERED FITNESS

A common complaint of women is that they don't have time to exercise. Finally, someone listened. Curves, a women-only fitness chain with 1,500 locations, is the fastest growing franchise in the United States. Its name suggests what it is *not* selling—stick-thin bodies. Its circuit of exercises can be completed in 30 minutes. Others are following suit. Women's demand for quick and simple fitness, integrated into their lifestyles, has led airlines and airports, among others, to offer fitness options, including sports shoes and T-shirts for workouts.

Mainstreaming Makeovers

> It's interesting. In most ways I'm less consumer-oriented, less materialist than I was 10 years ago. I spend less money on clothes and makeup. I want a simpler life. On the other hand, I plan to have a face lift in three or four years. I want always to look as good as I can.
>
> —JERI, 46

In 2003, 86% of women regularly got some form of beauty treatment, from highlights to teeth whitening, to Botox (43% more Botox treatments were performed in 2003 than in 2001). **The number of women undergoing cosmetic surgery has increased dramatically—**

WE DO HOUSE CALLS

A small but growing number of physicians is opting out of the HMO mess and offering VIP health care to those who can afford the heavy price tag. These so-called concierge physicians charge annual fees to special care, ranging from more time with patients, more complete tests, same-day appointments, and house calls. Pay-to-play health care is a boon for the well-heeled, but on the other end of the spectrum 45 million Americans don't even have basic health insurance.

For the tech-able who can't afford the high price of specialty care, medical information, advice, and treatments are now just a click away. Two-thirds of Internet users report searching the web for information on a specific medical problem and just under one-third say they have researched doctors and hospitals online. Some patients now e-mail descriptions of their ailments, symptoms, and questions directly to the physician. Doctors reply with diagnoses and recommendations. The approach not only cuts down on unnecessary office visits and phone calls, but it allows doctors to be more productive and focused on the patients who do need to be seen in person. Perhaps the best feature of this new kind of house call is that health insurance providers such as Blue Cross, Cigna, and Harvard-Pilgrim are increasingly footing the bill.

to the tune of nearly $10 billion a year and rising. There were nearly 8.3 million surgical and nonsurgical cosmetic procedures performed in 2003, a 20% increase over 2002. Women had nearly 7.2 million cosmetic procedures, 87 percent of the total.

The top five surgical cosmetic procedures in 2003 were liposuction (384,626, up 3% from 2002); breast augmentation (280,401, up 12%); eyelid surgery (267,627, up 17%); rhinoplasty (172,420, up 10%); and breast reduction (147, 173, up 17%).

The top five nonsurgical cosmetic procedures in 2003 were Botox injection (2,272,080, up 37% from 2002); laser hair removal (923,200, up 25%); microdermabrasion (858,312, down 17%); chemical peel (722,248, up 46%); and collagen injection (620,476, down 21%).

Cosmetic surgery is no longer viewed as a simple matter of vanity; for some, it is a symbol of social standing and economic wherewithal. Once the exclusive province of the white and wealthy, cosmetic surgery is becoming more accessible, and more mainstream. Women pay for "tweaking" procedures, such as Botox and other fillers, with credit cards, bonuses, or loans. **The number of women of color seeking facial**

Beauty In	Beauty Out
Japanese-style hair straightening: Lengthy, expensive thermal straightening have replaced flat irons as the best and most enduring way to get rid of those curls.	*Curly is back: There is a surge in procedures designed to keep curls silky.*
Detoxifying baths: Salts, oils, and seaweeds, as agents to remove impurities from the body.	*Fortifying baths: Nutrients added to the tub are absorbed by the skin, giving a vitamin-rich glow.*
Hand treatments: Anti-aging extended to the hands, as doctors employed the same techniques used on the face to reduce the lines in hands.	*Hand cream: Topical creams are replacing more expensive injections to restore firmness and fullness to the hands.*
Lip service: Lip tints provide lasting color and bare comfort.	*Lip pink: Vitamin hydrators used on lips boost the natural color, and results are typically seen in four weeks.*

reconstructive surgery rose from 71,000 in 1999 to 488,000 in 2003.

People age 35 to 50 had the most procedures—3.7 million (45% of the total). People aged 19 to 34 underwent 24% of procedures; those aged 51 to 64 had 23%; those aged 65 and over had 5%; and those aged 18 and younger had less than 3%. Racial and ethnic minorities had 20% of all cosmetic procedures.

Traditional cosmetic companies are also featuring more ethnically diverse women in their advertising and creating product lines for women with deeper skin tones. Spokeswomen like Halle Berry, Jennifer Lopez, and Penelope Cruz are prominent in advertising.

Beauty is not just about cosmetics. A new interest in good health practices is attempting on the inside what plastic surgery is achieving on the outside. More than 60% of women credit diet, nutrition, and positive health practices for making them feel younger, and health club membership among people age 55-plus has quintupled since 1997.

This trend is a vivid example of the feminization of America. Cosmetic surgery, spa treatments, facials, and diet consciousness are happening beyond the ladies room.

MIRROR, MIRROR ON THE WALL

In spite of a significant trend toward healthy diets, our survey confirmed that weight still matters. Weight issues dominate women's wish list for what they would change about themselves. When asked, in an open-ended question, to identify the one thing they would change about their appearance, 39% identified some aspect of weight management, particularly weight loss (30%). Every single group of women put weight loss first, and were twelve times more likely to say they needed to lose weight than to gain it. Another one-in-five (19%) cited some other aspect of their body when focusing on desired change. A relative handful mentioned those "trouble areas" that seem easier to control and mend quickly—hair and wrinkles.

The big news, however, may be that a full 22% said they would change *nothing* about their appearance!

What one thing about your appearance would you change?

39%   WEIGHT MANAGEMENT (NET)

30%   LOSE WEIGHT

1%   LOSE 20 LBS

2%   LOSE 10 LBS

3%   WEIGHT CONTROL

3%   GAIN WEIGHT

19%   BODY/APPEARANCE (NET)

3%   BE TALLER

2%   NEED FACE LIFT

2%   TEETH

1%   BETTER MIDSECTION

1%   REDUCE MY STOMACH

1%   HEIGHT NONSPECIFIC

1%   BE SHORTER

1%   FIX MY NOSE

1%   IMPROVE SKIN TONE

1%   TONING MY BODY

GOD AND MANNA

The diet industry has gone to God, with the bestselling book, The Maker's Diet, *by Jordan S. Rubin, N.M.D., Ph.D. Rubin's premise: If people ate the way God intended they would be healthier, happier, and more spiritually alive. Another diet to hit the God-and-manna theme is the* Hallelujah Diet, *by the Reverend George Malkums, a preacher-turned-diet-adviser. He promotes a simple diet of fruits, vegetables, and nuts—the natural fare God provided in the garden of Eden. "The Last Exodus," part of the Weigh Down Workshop, Inc., is an 8-week program of prayer, lectures, motivational speakers, and Bible study.*

1%	POSTURE
*	MY TEMPLE
*	CLEAR UP SKIN
*	GETTING FIT
*	THINNER LIPS
*	FIGURE
*	FACIAL ISSUES (NON-SPECIFIC)
*	SCARRING
*	GET RID OF STRETCH MARKS

4%	**HAIR (NET)**
1%	NEW HAIR STYLE
1%	STOP LOSING HAIR
1%	SHAPE OF HAIR
1%	GRAY HAIR
*	CUT HAIR SHORT

2%	**WRINKLES (NET)**
1%	AGE LINES
*	REMOVE WRINKLES AROUND EYES
*	LESS WRINKLES IN NECK
8%	DON'T KNOW

| **22%** | **NOTHING/SATISFIED WITH** |

AGE BEFORE BEAUTY?

Here's a tough choice. Would women rather look thinner or younger? We posed this question to our survey-takers, and a majority of women (53%) reported they would opt for fewer pounds over fewer wrinkles. Interestingly, younger women (18–34) and women 55 to 64 are the most concerned about appearing slimmer. The desire to look younger does not differ much by age.

If given the choice, would you agree to shave a year off your life if you could be your ideal weight for the rest of your life?

Total	Men	Women	
32%	30%	33%	YES
63%	**64%**	**63%**	**NO**
5%	6%	4%	DO NOT KNOW)
1%	*	1%	REFUSED (VOLUNTEERED)

If given the choice, would you agree to shave off a year
of your life if you could be your ideal weight the rest of your life?

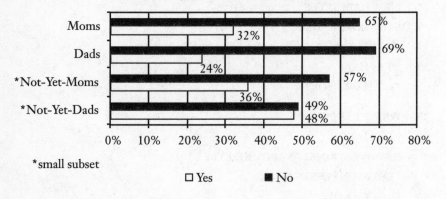

* small subset

□ Yes   ■ No

*If given the choice, would you rather **look** younger or thinner?*

Total	Men	Women	
47%	**40%**	**53%**	**THINNER**
36%	41%	31%	YOUNGER
11%	12%	9%	NEITHER (VOLUNTEERED)
4%	4%	5%	BOTH (VOLUNTEERED)
1%	2%	1%	DO NOT KNOW (VOLUNTEERED)
1%	1%	1%	REFUSED (VOLUNTEERED)

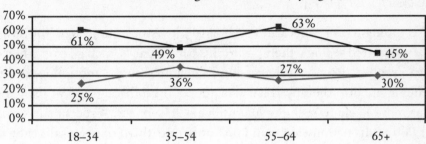

Women: Younger vs. Thinner (By Age)

• Single women were nearly twice as likely as single men to say they'd prefer to appear thinner (54% to 28%).

• Hispanic women were 10 points more likely Black and white women to say they'd want to look younger (40%, 30%, and 30%).

• Women aged 55 to 64 were 10 points more likely to say they would rather look younger than thinner (63% to 53%).

Even though women want to look thinner, they're not willing to chop off a year of their lives to get there. We asked the question, "If given the choice, would you agree to shave a year off your life if you could be your ideal weight for the rest of your life?"

A notable 63% of respondents said no. They want that extra year. Moms and not-yet-moms (who plan to be parents someday), not surprisingly, were the least willing to make this trade-off, while singles without children were the most willing.

In this discussion, the proof is most definitely in the pocketbook. The anti-aging industry is projected to reach $41.9 billion by 2005. And people spend $70 billion annually on medicines prescribed to offset aging-related diseases.

LIGHTEN UP!

According to the American Psychoanalytic Association, when Tony Soprano started seeing a therapist for his panic attacks, men all over America dropped their typical aversion to being "shrunk" and followed the tough guy into therapy. That was quite a breakthrough, as women are far more likely to seek out and utilize help services. A recent survey of 1,000 adults nationwide found that **only one-third of men said they'd discussed depression with their doctor, while more than two-thirds of women had.** Half of all men still believe that there is a stigma attached to being treated for depression.

Women are the guardians of the nation's emotional health, and while they're prodding their men to lighten up, they're also pushing for a kinder, gentler entry into life for their children. Colleges and universities have become more intent on offering support for students' emotional growth and well-being, at last responding to the growing rates of depression and bipolar disorders among adolescents and young adults. They've introduced workshops for coping with homesickness and perfectionism, yoga classes and free massages to destress, and even animal therapy during exam weeks.

Some may scoff at the touchy-feely trend, but the integration of mind and body is at the core of beauty in action.

THE NEXT 10 YEARS

As the alliance of beauty with health, fitness, and wellness becomes more ingrained in the public mind, women will be aggressive in pushing for these things.

- Expect more pressure to be exerted on health insurance companies to cover proven alternative treatments, such as acupuncture, massage, meditation and stress reduction therapies, and approved supplements.

- Women will encourage the community (schools, grocery stores, restaurants, and manufacturers) to be part of the

MESSAGE TO BARBIE: EAT SOMETHING!

Everyone was pretty excited when Barbie, America's favorite dollfriend, had a makeover. Since 1959, she'd been walking around on tippy-toes (ouch), trying to balance an oversized chest above tiny little hips. So when Mattel announced that Barbie was going to become more realistic (breast reduction, flat feet, more curvaceous hips), moms cheered, hoping the new Barbie would be a healthier role model for their weight-obsessed young girls. But in the end, the curves never made it off the drawing board. Although the flat feet were a godsend, the reduced breasts only made Barbie look like the skinny girl ideal. Not an ounce of fat and as perky as ever.

Barbie is the leader of the body image band. By the time a girl is 17 years old, she has received more than 250,000 commercial messages through the media that sing the praises of skinny. In a recent survey by **Teen People** *magazine, 27% of girls affirmed that the media pressure them to have a perfect body; 68% of girls in a study of Stanford undergraduates and graduate students felt worse about their own appearance after looking through women's magazines. The number one wish for girls 11 to 17 is to be thinner. Girls as young as age 5 have expressed fears of getting fat. **In a survey of elementary school students, girls commented that they would prefer to live through a nuclear holocaust, lose both of their parents, or get sick with cancer than be fat.** Fully 80% of 10-year-olds have been on diets. Of these, less than 20% are actually overweight. More than 8 million girls and young women struggle with eating disorders. Untreated, they are at risk of severe health complications and even death. Studies also show that women have a lot more influence than they think to help their daughters develop healthy body images.*

Now that Barbie has dumped Ken, chances are good she'll be back in the gym, trying to lose that extra millimeter of fat. Tell your daughter she doesn't have to go along.

campaign to teach children healthy eating and exercise habits.

• Beauty is always on the front burner for women, but they will become less inclined to take drastic measures. For example, the emphasis in cosmetic dermatology will be away from surgical facelifts and toward less invasive, drive-through fixes such as injectable laser treatments and small-scale liposuction.

• Mental health coverage will become part of mandated health coverage.

• A self-reliant population of medical consumers will increasingly log-on for information about health, treatments, and specific medical conditions. Visits to the doctor will occur in cyberspace, where everyone has access.

PURSE-STRING POWER

Women control $5 trillion in consumer spending and are the primary purchasers of cars, computers, electronics, appliances, insurance, and other high-ticket items.

There was a time, not all that long ago, when men didn't discuss money matters in front of women because they didn't want to trouble their delicate sensibilities. Besides, the logic followed that women wouldn't understand the complexities of mortgages, insurance annuities, and taxes. "Don't you worry your pretty little head about it," was the prevailing attitude. As recently as the late 1980s, it was not uncommon for an older widow to admit that she had never balanced a checkbook, never knew how much her husband made, and had no idea whether they had investments or insurance. It was also standard operating procedure for banks and car dealers to ask women to bring their husbands in as co-signers on loans. Today, 9 out of 10 women identify themselves as the primary shopper for their household, and 80% of all personal checks are signed by women. That means they essentially set the agenda for the American economy by deciding what they will or will not invest their hard-earned dollars to buy. Women have surpassed men in purchasing and using technology—including laptops, palm pilots, cell phones, DVD players, digital cameras, and computers. Of $96 billion spent on electronics, $55 billion was spent by women.

Our ninth trend, Purse-String Power, demonstrates how women have taken over the decision making about how money is spent in America. This trend is not, in the first instance, about the haves and have-nots, for, while there is a disparity in income and asset power in America, there is tremendous similarity in behaviors when it comes to deciding what to purchase. A woman will rarely commit her time, money, or passion unless something has real meaning for her. She wants to know, "Do I like it?" and "Is it like me?" These questions express a uniquely female need to identify with her choices, to feel right about them, to own them. Marketers who want to capture the minds and money of women must reach them at this core level.

MONEY

	THEN	NOW
Control	Men controlled big ticket purchases like cars, computers, and electronics.	Women control most of the spending, even on big-ticket items
Motivation	Does everyone else have it?	Will it make my life better and easier? Do I get something extra?
Where	Drive to the mall and supermarket	Go online and around the corner
Products	Target white customers	Target African American, Hispanic, Asian customers
Kids	Allowance pays for candy bar and comic book	10- to 18-year-olds influence $170 billion in annual discretionary spending.

FINANCIAL WIZARDS

Women aren't just good at spending. Increasingly, **they're taking on the job of portfolio managers for themselves and their families.** A study of more than 1,000 baby boomer women by Prudential Financial found that 95% of them were either solely or jointly responsible for IRAs, compared with 61% in 2000; 80% were solely or jointly responsible for 401(k)s compared with 59% in 2000; and 94% were solely or jointly responsible for savings accounts, as opposed to 85% in 2000.

Money is an issue for single women, who need a financial plan that will see them through life on their own; for widows and divorcees who face an uncertain retirement; for young mothers who want to make sure their kids have healthy college funds; and for all women raised to understand that they have a stake in their family's financial security.

The trend is evident in the way financial firms are finally fancying women. Merrill Lynch has created a Women's Business Development division, Charles Schwab has developed a group of advisers who cater to women's desire for more personal interaction, Citigroup has established Women & Co., offering a variety of financial services and educational opportunities to women. They see the future, and it's in the hands of women.

MULTI-CULTURAL BOOM

The rapid rise in Hispanic households means more pocketbook power for women. From a consumer decision making perspective, these are matriarchal households: if you engage the average Latina woman, you reach an extended family. There are currently 39.9 million Hispanics living in the United States, and one in seven Americans is of Hispanic origin. **Hispanic spending power in the United States reached $700 billion for 2004.** In some categories, Hispanic consumers spend more than other groups. The average Hispanic family spends $117 a week on groceries, compared to the national average of $87. **The spending power of Hispanic and Asian Americans will total more than $1.3 trillion by 2007.** According to a study by People en Espanol, 56% of

TOO RICH OR TOO THIN?

College students place greater importance on their credit rating than on their pants size. Fully 79% of undergraduates surveyed would rather be 20 pounds overweight than $20,000 in debt.

U.S. Hispanics agreed that "I love to shop," compared to 39% of the general population.

Black families also tend to be matriarchal. Almost half (46%) of Black households (family and nonfamily) are headed by women, compared to only 25% of white households. Currently, **13 million African American women age 18 and over influence more than $260 billion in spending a year.** The spending power of Black women will increase 32% to $342 billion by 2006.

THE HAVES AND HAVE-NOTS

When we evaluated the financial status of different groups of women who participated in our surveys, we found the following:

Feminist Champions: These women have a mixed financial picture—with the highest in the $90,000+ income category, but the median in the midrange of $40,000 to $50,000. Still, they are the most educated of all the groups, making their long-term earning power and financial outlook full of possibility.

Suburban Caretakers: They tend to be middle-income, in the $40,000 to $50,000 range. However, these women are likely to be married and have family investments and retirement plans to help secure their future.

Alpha Strivers: These women have the highest median income, in the $60,000 to $70,000 range, and they are the most likely of all women to have investments.

Multicultural Mavericks: While they tend to have a relatively low median income—between $25,000 and $30,000—this status is offset by several factors. They may live with or be partially supported by parents, or attend school full- or part-time. They have a relatively high level of education. They are primarily childless, giving them fewer financial obligations. Low income is not a status quo for them, but typically a temporary state for them.

Religious Crusaders: These women have the second highest median income—between $50,000 and $60,000—in part because they are married. More than 13% of them have incomes exceeding $90,000. They are the most likely to own their own businesses, and most have investments.

Waitress Moms: These women have a median income around $40,000, but they are unlikely to have investments or stable retirement plans. Most of them have no formal education beyond high school, giving them limited opportunities for financial growth.

Senior Survivors: Although they have a low median income—$25,000 to $30,000—most of these aged 65+ women are retired and living off pensions and Social Security income. Housing is a major factor in their overall financial status. Many have paid off their homes or live with adult children, reducing the strain on their pocketbooks.

Alienated Singles: These women are the least financially stable of all the groups, with a median income of $30,000 to $40,000. It isn't just their paychecks that place them in the economically marginal category. They are also the least likely to be high school graduates and the most likely to be single parents—a combination that places them at high risk for poverty.

MONEY TALK: OUT OF THE CLOSET

"My parents never talked about money." We have repeatedly heard that assertion from women, especially those born before 1980. There has been a longstanding taboo against discussing money, especially in front of children. "My parents really struggled to raise seven kids on my father's paycheck from a cardboard factory," said Ellen, 46. "We kids knew enough not to ask for much, and we all had jobs during school, but we never heard any discussion between our parents about how they managed. We didn't know what Dad's paycheck was, how much debt they had, or what kind of insurance. Consequently, when I was struggling to budget for my family in lean times, I didn't have a clue."

Yvonne, 37, was raised in a more prosperous household than Ellen, but she was equally ignorant financially. "If someone were to have asked me where money came from, I probably would have said, 'My mother's purse.' In many ways, my consciousness was clouded by the fact that we always seemed to have plenty of money. I didn't have to think for myself. Later, I learned that we weren't really rich. My parents had a lot of debt. They took out a loan to pay my college tuition, and another to pay for my wedding."

Most people would probably agree that financial savvy doesn't come naturally; it has to be taught and learned. How, then, to explain the reluctance of parents (and even most schools) to teach their children solid financial skills? The Jump$tart Coalition for Personal Financial Literacy, founded in 1995, determined that the average high school graduate lacks basic skills in the management of personal financial affairs. Many are unable to balance a checkbook and most simply have no insight into the basic survival principles involved with earning, spending, saving, and investing. Many young people fail in the management of their first consumer credit experience, establish bad financial management habits, and stumble through their lives learning by trial and error. The Coalition's direct objective is to encourage curriculum enrichment to ensure that basic personal financial management skills are attained during the K through 12 educational experience. In 2005 the coalition sponsored resolutions in the House and Senate, declaring April as Financial Literacy for Youth Month.

While we hail women's increasing financial influence, it is clear that this upward trend also places extra pressure on women to become educated spenders, savers, *and* investors. There are troubling notes in the financial picture. American consumer credit debt continues to increase, and reached a level of in excess of $2.1 trillion in 2004, of which $791 billion is revolving consumer credit. The average debt is $8,000. Meanwhile, Americans still aren't taking saving seriously. In 2004, personal savings as a percentage of income was at one of the lowest levels in history—just 2%, a decline from 7.5 percent in the early 1980s.

CHARITY BEGINS WITH WOMEN

Single women are big donors, according to a major ongoing study of 4,000 households by the Center of Philanthropy at Indiana University. They are 37% more likely to be charitable donors than are single men. In addition, single women, those who are divorced, widowed, or never married, give on average about $600 more than single men.

According to Cheryl Altinkemer, a board member of the Women's Philanthropy Institute, the results were surprising. "We didn't know that women would be more philanthropic," she said. "Women are sometimes under the radar screen because they tend to volunteer and they tend to give anonymously at a higher level—older women especially."

Who are the women philanthropists? They are business owners with new wealth, widows and other women with inherited wealth, and even middle-class women who consider charitable giving a moral and civic responsibility. They are also women who, when previously belonging to a lower economic group, were generous with their time. Volunteerism begets philanthropy. As women control more of the nation's wealth, philanthropic organizations are hoping their natural altruism and community mindedness will pay off.

HOLD THE TESTOSTERONE

We all know about car guys, cowboys of the interstate, the romancers of the off-road. Men talk about their cars with the reverence they usually reserve for discussions of sex—and many analysts suggest that men see their cars as extensions of their sexuality.

But a funny thing has happened on the way to the dealership. While men continue to wax romantic about horsepower and valves per cylinder, women are actually influencing the interiors and—get this— *buying* the cars. For the first time ever, women car buyers have surpassed men, and the car-purchase gap is pretty impressive. Today, more than 65% of all car purchases are made directly by women, and that's not even the most dramatic statistic. Industry experts estimate that up to 90% of all car purchases are influenced by women who either buy them or have the final veto over the choice. **Indeed, women have a disproportionate influence over big-ticket items like the family car. They do the bulk of the research, and they have already made the top three choices by the time the man in the family even gets involved.**

Here's more news. The cars that women are choosing to buy are overwhelmingly 4-wheel-drive vehicles and compact SUVs, such as the Toyota Highlander and the Toyota RAV4. **Over 50% of SUV sales are made to women. Women are also purchasing 42% of all light trucks.** Old stereotypes no longer apply. Unfortunately, the news hasn't leaked down to the local car dealer.

There are certain places women have traditionally feared to tread, and the car dealership is one of them. They see patronizing, smirking sales reps hovering around them with ill-intentioned zeal. The shark mentality of the typical car dealership seems wildly at odds with the predominance of women making automobile purchases.

Women know it's perilous to enter a car dealership without a man in tow. They're notoriously poor hagglers who despise the macho rituals of sticker-price negotiation that men claim to relish. Women buying cars on their own are apt to pay up to $2,000 more. Not surprisingly, there's a big trust gap between women and car dealers.

Instead of dragging along an obligatory male to the dealership, or trying to convince car companies to be more responsive to them at the dealer level, women are simply taking their business elsewhere.

We see this reflected in two trends:

1. Among the top five vehicles preferred by women, three are GM Saturn models, and women account for more than 60% of all Saturn purchases. Women Saturn purchasers overwhelmingly say that Saturn's no-haggle policy is one of the primary reasons they favor the manufacturer. Maybe Saturn's high percentage of female executives has something to do with the company's savvy in

marketing to women. At 40%, the percentage is unprecedented in the automobile industry.

2. Women are single-handedly driving the trend in online car buying, or at least browsing, and steering clear of the dealership's confrontational, haggle-rich environment. Instead, they're immersing themselves in an information-rich environment where they can choose the design of their car to fit their preferences.

The domestic automobile industry has been slow to recognize the need to change the way it markets to women. Sadly, many American car manufacturers have resisted these new trends. Instead of finding ways to better relate to the people who are actually buying cars—women!—they are openly courting a target market that has been steadily declining—young men. The bulk of television ad buys is made around sporting events, especially football and Nascar.

Domestic automobile manufacturers continue to market to the testosterone crowd at their own peril. Some foreign competitors are getting serious about women and what they care about. It was a European company, not an American manufacturer, that designed the first pregnant crash-test dummy.

MULTITASKING ON WHEELS

As car companies stretch their imaginations to figure out what women really want, they're designing concept cars that bring the housework on the road. One manufacturer is hyping its minivan equipped with microwave, minifridge, and even a washing machine: the perfect car for getting kids from one soccer game to another. Some carpooling moms might balk at the all-housework-all-the-time model, and rightfully ask, "Was this a man's idea?"

IF YOU BUILD IT, THEY WILL BUY . . .

The 2004 Geneva Motor Show featured the first concept car built by women for women. Volvo's YCC was designed and engineered by a group of women to meet the criteria women say they want in a car. With a sweeping roof, large alloy wheels, a wraparound bumper, and squat, sturdy dimensions, the YCC looks like a rugged sports coupe. Among its features: no hood, no gas cap, easy-clean paint, head restraints with room for ponytails, numerous exchangeable seat covers of various colors and materials (linen, leather, felt, etc.), compartments for handbags, gull-wing doors that make it easier to load and unload larger items and children, computerized assistance for parallel parking, and improved sight lines. At the point of purchase, retailers can conduct a body scan of the driver measuring height and length of arms and legs. The data is stored in the vehicle's key, and the car recommends a seat position for the driver that provides her or him an optimal line of vision and reach. The car also electronically notifies the owner's chosen service center when maintenance is due, and the service technician contacts the owner to book the appointment.

UNTANGLING THE WEB

When Joyce's husband Ben bought his first home computer in 1989, he strutted in front of the massive unit like a peacock, predicting that it would revolutionize their home. One of the first pieces of software he purchased was a check-writing program, and he assured Joyce that writing checks on the computer and printing them out was an excellent way of simplifying the family finances. Frankly, Joyce didn't get his excitement. What could be simpler than grabbing the checkbook from the drawer in the kitchen, scribbling in the amount, and stuffing it into an envelope? "No, no," Ben assured her. "Trust me. It's better."

The opportunity to find out came that very day when the paper boy arrived for his monthly collection. "Hold on," Ben said, hurrying into the family room to generate the computerized check. Joyce invited the boy in for a cold drink, and they sat and waited as Ben powered up the computer (two minutes), opened the program and selected a blank check (one minute), typed in the details (one minute), entered the check number, date, purpose, and amount into the record (two minutes), turned on the printer and waited for it to warm up (one minute), inserted the special check paper and printed the check (two minutes), tore the check at the perforation, and signed it (one minute), and in a mere 10 minutes presented it to the paper boy, now on his second glass of lemonade.

"That was fast," Joyce remarked to her beaming husband, who was too thrilled by the wonders of technology to hear the irony in her voice.

Joyce told us this story during a discussion of the way women use the Internet, and it seemed to symbolize the key difference between men and women when it comes to computer use. "For Ben, the thrill was the novelty," Joyce said. "He was saying, 'Look what we can do.' But I found it annoying. It felt like he was trying to solve a problem that didn't exist, and in the process complicating something that was simple."

It went on like that for a few years. Ben used the computer to "organize"—or, in Joyce's opinion, complicate—their home life. Joyce went on as before. She didn't really start using the computer until the advent of the Internet. "We were redecorating our kitchen, and I found I could go online and look at every refrigerator model, every oven. It was thrilling," she said. "I could do the research, comparison-shop, and feel as if I really knew what was what before I ever walked into a store."

Like the automobile, the computer has evolved from a toy to a tool, due in no small part to the fact that women comprise 51% of Internet users, compared to 49% of men, and their numbers are increasing. The fastest-growing segment of all Internet users is women over the age of 55!

DID YOU KNOW?

Women spend about $55 billion on electronics each year, and most of the purchases are for themselves.

MEN ZONE OUT, WOMEN TUNE IN

What we see repeatedly is women taking over technology, not because they're geeks, or because they're seduced by the bells and whistles, but because they have found practical applications that make their lives better.

Bulky animation, fancy sound clips, clever pop-ups, and the latest games may appeal to men, but women want their Internet browsing straight and to the point. They prefer uncluttered sites, accessible pull-down menus, one-stop shopping venues, and relevant links. Web designers should pay heed: **While women may love to browse in stores, they expect to find what they want quickly online.**

Online browsing is not a leisure activity for women, or something they do in their spare time. It's an integral part of their lives. Considering that they make up to 80% of all online purchases, companies selling on the Web will have to do it *their* way if they hope to be successful. **It is estimated that women will spend $123 billion online in the coming**

WOMEN'S FAVORITE TOOL: TECHNOLOGY

3.3
Average number of hours women spend online every day

65
Percentage of women who, offered one source for news, information, and entertainment, would choose the Internet

43
Percentage of women who make regular online purchases

58
Percentage of women who prefer the Internet because it's convenient

year. To gain a share of that market they must heed the lessons they've already learned about selling to women. Even when they're shopping online, women want to relate to the company and product. They prefer to see a product in use and in context. When they don't feel it, they point and click out of there.

Marketers can also address women's concerns about aftercare, support services, warranties, and the ease of returns. While women may relish the time-saving aspects of shopping online, and delight in the greater variety of products, they'll drop it cold if it fails to deliver on the important features of quality and service.

WORD OF MOUSE

Women of all ages use the Internet to strengthen connections. Here's an example of how one mother and daughter, located at opposite ends of the country, use their computers on an average day.

Amy, 42, married and the mother of a 2-year-old, works in an office three days a week and telecommutes one day a week.	*Janet, 71, is a retired widow, with three children and five grandchildren. Her daughter Amy lives across the country, a second daughter lives in her city, and a son lives overseas.*
Orders a case of wine from an online wine store for an upcoming party	*Researches cataract surgery for a friend*
Visits an online department store and orders a pair of shoes	*Listens to the* Morning Edition *of public radio in the background*
Sends flowers for Mother's Day	*Writes a long letter to her son overseas*

(continued on next page)

Checks live-cam traffic report before leaving for work

Purchases airline tickets for an upcoming visit to her daughter, Amy

Writes marketing study for upcoming meeting, and puts it on a PowerPoint presentation

Browses Amazon and purchases a new book by her favorite author

Sends latest pictures of son Max to Mom

Prints the photo of her grandson and frames it

Researches vacation destinations

Sends a reminder note to her children that their great-aunt's ninety-first birthday is coming up

Checks in to her favorite political blog, and forwards an interesting article to her sister

Writes a chatty note to a friend

CARE OF THE POCKETBOOK

Ivy Baker Priest, the thirtieth Treasurer of the United States, who served during the Eisenhower administration, once quipped, "We women don't care too much about getting our pictures on money as long as we can get our hands on it." Her remark is reflective of the central truth about women and money: our passions are primarily practical, focused on control more than on ego. Susan B. Anthony is no doubt laughing in her grave that while the dollar coin bearing her visage was a bomb, the contribution she made to women's equality as a suffragist helped assure they had the power to spend the currency of the day.

Women's role as caregivers gives them a prominent role in a myriad of purchases that support home, family, and community. Their once-passive financial role is now one of leadership. The American economy in the coming years will be influenced greatly by the decisions women make about how to spend their own and the nation's money.

THE NEXT 10 YEARS

- Women are the spenders driving the economy, but the next 10 years could witness an increase in the number of women, especially singles, who are savers and investors.

- As our nation becomes increasingly multicultural and bilingual, beyond urban centers, successful merchandising will depend on the ability to individualize mass-produced products. An example: Netflix, the movie-by-mail service, offers a language menu at the start of its films; just click and hear dialogue in your native tongue.

- Just as with bottled water in the 1980s, or soy products in the 1990s, women will likely be the catalysts in taking new technology and communications devices and services, currently on the fringe, into the mainstream—as technologies increase the ability to stay in touch with children and family. Examples: videophones, videocams, and hand-held PDAs like the BlackBerry.

JUST-IN-TIME POLITICS

Traditional women's issues have been expanded. Today, women are driving the national security and Social Security debates. If it's a critical issue right now, women are behind it, no matter what their party.

One dramatic change in American politics over the past decade is the decreasing influence of region as a bright-line distinction. For all the talk about "blue states" and "red states," many women are comfortably "purple"—mixing and matching their political positions based on issues as much as ideology.

The decline of region as a key determinant of women's voting behavior is in part due to the fact that people are much more mobile than they used to be. It used to be that your region was your permanent stake. It was where you grew up, or where you went to college, or where you held your first job, or where the military base was located. Today, Americans move around—especially those in their twenties and early thirties. They are less likely to identify themselves by their region or state. Far more significant is the type of neighborhood they live in—whether they're urban, suburban, or rural. While the media likes to present current political life as a Hatfield-McCoy battle between the coasts and the heartland, the true picture is much more homogenous. And while

women are not a monolithic group, we've found that on important issues and attitudes they share a remarkable agreement.

We call our tenth and final trend, Just-in-Time Politics, to communicate the fluid state of political life, as women go about quietly erasing
the barriers that separate us.

THE HERS AGENDA

Most American women don't wake up in the morning thinking, "I'm a
Republican" or "I'm a Democrat." They wake up thinking, "I'm late for
work . . . Jenny has soccer practice at 3:00 . . . there's a sale at Kmart . . .
I've got to pick up Mom's prescription." When they *do* think about politics, it's because an important area of their lives is influenced by public
policy. They've lost their job, there is a health crisis, a family member in
the military is being shipped overseas. Politics is personal. That's a fact
of being human, and it's a facet of being female.

POLITICS

	THEN	NOW
Image	*Soccer mom*	*Security mom*
Agenda	*Kids and kitchen*	*Guns and butter*
Affiliation	*Party*	*Issue*
Influence	*Grass roots activism*	*Grass–tops control*
Identity	*Region of the country*	*Neighborhood or community*
Debate	*Right vs. left*	*Right vs. wrong*
Woman president	*"Not in my lifetime."*	*"Any day now."*

THE FACTS ABOUT
WOMEN VOTERS

- *More women make their voting decisions late in the game. Seven percent of women solidified their 2004 presidential choice in the week before the election.*
- *Women are not single-issue voters.*
- *Her family status has a strong influence on the way a woman votes.*
- *Women tend to be pro-incumbent.*

It used to be that what was deemed personal fell into the category of "soft" issues that related to personal health, home, and hearth. The big news is that women are becoming the policy makers in areas typically reserved for men. While it is not surprising to find women taking the lead in education and health-care decisions, they have now also assumed control on policy regarding retirement and national security as well. **The HERS agenda—health, education, retirement, and security—is the primary agenda for both major parties.**

To most women, affordable, comprehensive health care is an essential, not a perk of employment. **Women are health-care voters;** 89% of them agree that the system needs a fundamental overhaul. They outnumber men as the leading consumers of health-care services, and are the family's gatekeepers, focused on prostate cancer screenings, blood pressure and cholesterol measurements, and prescription drugs oversight for everyone. They also comprise a greater proportion of employees in the health-related fields. They view this issue through both a personal and a professional lens, noting how it affects their families and employees. Small-business women cite access to health coverage as even more important than access to capital or clients.

When it comes to education, research consistently shows that women are more focused on education issues than men. They are more likely to vote in school-bond elections, and to take education issues into account when voting in national, state, and local elections. They are also more likely to tell the men in their lives how to vote. This is true even if they don't have children in the schools. By a wide margin, women re-elect candidates who support early childhood education and who vote to reduce school size.

The retirement agenda, once the province of male breadwinners, has become a women's issue. Women are particularly supportive of changes in policy, such as portable pensions; retirement benefits for homemakers, caregivers, and part-time workers; and expanding retire-ment benefits for small businesses. According to a 2000 survey, **72% of women cited retirement benefits that can be moved from job to job as one of the most important issues to them personally.** These eco-nomic concerns start even younger among unmarried women, who are worrying about retirement as early as age 30; among married women re-tirement concerns tend to hit around age 45.

In a dramatic reversal, significantly more women than men have been concerned about national security and feel more personally threat-ened by terrorism. Shortly before the Persian Gulf War in January 1991, men were much more likely than women to favor sending ground troops into Iraq. CNN/Gallup archives show there was a 22-point gap then, with 67 percent of men and 45 percent of women favoring such action. But, since 9/11 a seismic gender shift on matters of war has appeared. The move from soccer moms to security moms is an example of how women personalize big-ticket issues. They're saying, "The war on ter-ror means something to *me*." Today, **43% of women say a member of their family could be the victim of a terrorist attack, compared to only 18% of men.** They have emerged as security voters, extremely vig-ilant about protecting the lives, freedom, and future of their families and loved ones.

Women's broad support of the HERS agenda creates a niche market for politicians. Speak to women in their language, and they may follow you to the ballot box.

Our polls and interviews with women reinforced the shift away from abortion politics to a broader spectrum of issues that control voting be-havior. Only 5% of respondents said abortion was the most important issue in the 2004 election. This finding can seem contradictory given the rising heat from the right and left over this issue. For strongly pro-choice and pro-life advocates, abortion symbolizes a line in the sand behind which other, larger issues of freedom, government intervention, and morality rest. However, our survey respondents reflect a truth about American women: While Feminist Champions on the left, and Religious Crusaders on the right, may be abortion voters—and they tend to be the loudest voices heard—the vast majority of women ultimately make their voting decisions on the economy, health care, the war, and national security. The other groups of women relayed these views.

Suburban Caretaker: Generally identifies herself as pro-life—not surprising since she tends to be religious. However, her top issue is the economy, and she is the least likely of all the groups to feel that job opportunities are better today than in her parents' generation.

Alpha Striver: Generally identifies herself as pro-choice, but abortion does not rank high on her list of most important issues. She is most concerned about the war in Iraq and national security, followed by the economy.

Multicultural Maverick: Generally identifies herself as pro-choice, and believes that abortion should be legal for any reason. However, she tends not to feel motivated by abortion rhetoric in election seasons. Her primary issues are jobs and education.

Waitress Mom: She is a moderate on abortion; in fact, equal numbers of Waitress Moms self-identified as pro-choice and pro-life, and she straddles the line between Republican and Democrat. Her top issues are jobs, retirement, health care, and homeland security.

Senior Survivor: Although she is generally pro-life, she is not particularly religious, and abortion registers fairly low on her list of key issues. She is often, however, a single-issue voter of a different kind, on Social Security and Medicare.

Alienated Single: She leans pro-life when asked, but supports Democrat and Republican candidates equally—that is, when she votes. Among our respondents in this group, 86.4% did not vote in the last election.

WHAT DO WOMEN CARE ABOUT?

We asked women which issue was the most important in deciding who to vote for in 2004.

13%	JOBS AND THE ECONOMY
13%	IRAQ
11%	MORAL VALUES
10%	SOCIAL SECURITY AND MEDICARE
8%	HOMELAND SECURITY AND TERRORISM
8%	EDUCATION
7%	HEALTH CARE AND PRESCRIPTION DRUGS
5%	ABORTION
3%	NATIONAL DEFENSE AND VETERANS ISSUES
3%	TAXES
3%	FEDERAL BUDGET DEFICIT
3%	GAY AND LESBIAN RIGHTS ISSUES
5%	OTHER
9%	DO NOT KNOW

GRASS-TOPS CITIZENRY

Who is the woman-as-citizen? Although she was only granted the right to vote 85 years ago, she is busy making up for lost time. Her influence is extensive, although she is not always certain how to exert it, or convinced that it is worth the bother. She may be some years, or even decades, away from calling the White House her primary residence, but she's a reliable foot soldier at the grass roots who's beginning to sprout in stature as a "grass-tops" community leader. The woman citizen has long viewed her role as negotiator and consensus-builder—the one who plants flowers in the scorched earth of political life.

WE THE PEOPLE . . .

Huppie: *A Hispanic urban professional*

Luppie: *A lesbian urban professional*

Nascar dad: *A white, working-class father*

NOPE (not on planet earth): *A person or attitude that opposes all real estate development or other projects that would harm the environment or reduce property values*

Purple state: *An American state in which Democrats and Republicans have roughly equal support*

Seabiscuit candidate: *A political contender who comes from behind to win an election*

Security mom: *A woman with children who believes the most important issue of the day is national security, particularly the fight against terrorism*

Theocon: *A conservative who believes that religion should play a major role in forming and implementing public policy*

Tripartisanship: *The involvement, support, or cooperation of the three major political parties (Republican, Democrat, Independent)*

Volvo Democrat: *A white, well-educated, moderately affluent, liberal, suburban professional*

Waitress mom: *A woman who is married, has children, works in a low-income job, and has little formal education*

The engaged activist woman is somewhat nameless and faceless; she doesn't get a lot of "hot" media coverage, but she knows how to organize. In every town in America, women are organized around community issues—roads, taxes, school boards, safety—and you might find them working together without even knowing one another's party affiliations. Furthermore, they outvote men in every election—by almost 8 million in 2000, 4.3 million in 2002, and 10 million in 2004.

A Place at the Table

I can remember sitting with my mother and her friends at these long tables, stuffing envelopes for hours for some mediocre guy who was running for the legislature or the city council. Occasionally, he'd stop by to say hello, and all of the ladies treated him like he was a rock star. Even as a kid I thought it was stupid. I knew a lot of women like my mother who slaved in the party for years, and I never heard anyone suggest that they could run for office.

—CELINE, 48

It's funny, because I used to be one of those voters who always picked the woman on a ticket, no matter what her party was. But I haven't done that in the last couple of elections because, frankly, there's too much at stake. I am much more serious about casting my vote on the issues, not on the politician's sex. Let me say, though, that it's discouraging more women are not serving in Congress.

—RHONDA, 40

The power that women exert in shaping the national agenda is not the result of more women being elected to higher office; women are still poorly represented on the federal political stage. However, it is clear that the old models of sexual politics no longer apply. For one thing, the common assumption that women will vote for a female candidate over a male candidate is not true. **Women have proved themselves to be**

more agenda-conscious than gender-conscious, and all women are not alike. The sex of the candidates matters, but not as much as it once did, and only as it relates to a plethora of other candidates, issues, and policy positions. When asked, "If one candidate were a man and one were a woman, for whom would you vote?" both women and men ally slightly with the candidate who shares their sex, but the most popular response is an unaided, "It depends/No difference/Need to know more about them." In addition, female candidates who run on traditional women's issues no longer attract women voters. The White House Project, an organization dedicated to improving the numbers of women in politics, recently released a study that examined voters' views toward female candidates for governor. The results demonstrate that when it comes to the issues, female voters want women candidates to go beyond traditional "kitchen table" issues of education and health care, and sound tough and resolute when they discuss the economy, taxes, the war, and crime.

These shifts in voter attitudes can be uncomfortable for those operating out of a static feminist model, but confirm the larger, more positive trend: Women are serious about policy. They are not willing to be relegated to the margins of public debate or expend their power on single issues.

So, why aren't more women achieving grass-tops visibility in public life? Although women still find it more difficult to get elected than men, it may be partially a function of deliberate choice rather than dismal circumstances. **Only 7% of voters say they would vote against a qualified woman for president (as opposed to 64% just 50 years ago),** and while that remains to be seen, the numbers reflect an increased comfort level with women in high office. The explanation may have more to do with the way women choose to exert their influence. As political veteran Madeleine Kunin has observed, "It is not lack of polling data or campaign contributions which keeps many women from ascending higher on the political ladder. It is fear and loathing for the political system itself." Many savvy women have made a calculated risk-reward analysis and determined that they can make a difference closer to home. Those women who do seek elective office often prefer to serve on school boards, town councils, and state legislatures rather than uproot their families and move to Washington, D.C. However, watch for this interesting generational trend: While a handful of young mothers and single women serve in the Senate and the House of Representatives, more women in national politics are mature empty-nesters, seasoned at the local level.

When we asked our survey respondents about the importance of electing more women to public office, women were more than twice as likely as men to say this was "extremely important" (22% to 10%). An equal 13% of men and women said this was "a little important," while a surprising 1 in 10 (11%) said electing more women to public office was "not at all important"; 5% of women shared that sentiment.

How important is it to you personally to have more women in elected public office in the United States—very important, somewhat important, not very important or not at all important?

Total	Men	Women	
89%	85%	93%	**TOTAL IMPORTANT(NET)**
16%	10%	22%	EXTREMELY IMPORTANT
28%	25%	31%	VERY IMPORTANT
32%	37%	27%	SOMEWHAT IMPORTANT
13%	13%	13%	A LITTLE IMPORTANT
8%	11%	5%	NOT AT ALL IMPORTANT
2%	4%	1%	DO NOT KNOW (VOLUNTEERED)
*	1%	*	REFUSED (VOLUNTEERED)

- Single women were significantly more likely than their married or once-married counterparts (34%, 18%, and 21% respectively) to feel that more women elected public office was an extremely important accomplishment.

DID YOU KNOW?

Only 3% of American moms want their child (male or female) to grow up to be president of the United States.

MADAME PRESIDENT?

How likely is it that a woman will be elected president in the near future, and how do we feel about that? When provided with a list of seven possible feelings/reactions, a plurality of men and women in our survey (35% and 33%, respectively) stated that they would be "hopeful" if a woman was elected president of the United States in their lifetime. Nearly 3 in 10 women (29%) said they'd be "enthusiastic" if such an event occurred, compared with only 17% of men. Twice as many men as women (20% to 10%) said they would feel "indifferent" should a women enter the White House.

Which of the following words would best describe how you feel if a woman president were elected in your lifetime: enthusiastic, hopeful, confident, indifferent, uncertain, disgusted, worried?

Total	Men	Women	
34%	35%	33%	HOPEFUL
23%	17%	29%	ENTHUSIASTIC
14%	20%	10%	INDIFFERENT
7%	7%	7%	UNCERTAIN
5%	5%	6%	SKEPTICAL
5%	3%	6%	TRIUMPHANT
5%	5%	5%	WORRIED
2%	3%	1%	OTHER (VOLUNTEERED)
3%	4%	3%	DO NOT KNOW (VOLUNTEERED)
1%	1%	*	REFUSED (VOLUNTEERED)

- Four in ten (41%) liberal women would feel enthusiastic if a woman became president of the United States, compared with 22% of their conservative counterparts.

- Women aged 18 to 34 were more "enthusiastic" than their older counterparts about the possibility they would see a female president in their lifetime.

As the level of education increased for women, so did their propensity to use the word "enthusiastic" when describing how they would feel should a woman be elected president of the United States in their lifetime.

- Men aged 18 to 34 were more "indifferent" than their older counterparts towards electing Ms. President.

THE POWER OF ONE

The importance of voting resonates across the sexes, as 54% of men and 57% of women stated with great intensity that voting was "extremely important" to them personally, followed by another 27% of men and 28% of women who said that it was "very important." But an analysis of the numbers shows that women are much more committed voters than men.

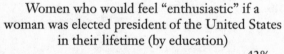

Women who would feel "enthusiastic" if a
woman was elected president of the United States
in their lifetime (by education)

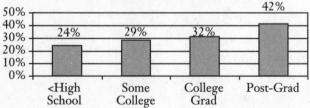

How important is voting to you personally—extremely important, very important, somewhat important, a little important, or not important at all?

Total	Men	Women	
97%	**94%**	**97%**	**TOTAL IMPORTANT(NET)**
56%	54%	7%	EXTREMELY IMPORTANT
28%	27%	28%	VERY IMPORTANT
10%	10%	9%	SOMEWHAT IMPORTANT
3%	3%	3%	A LITTLE IMPORTANT
4%	5%	3%	NOT AT ALL IMPORTANT
*	*	*	DO NOT KNOW (VOLUNTEERED)
–	–	–	REFUSED (VOLUNTEERED)

- Women with postgraduate degrees were much more likely than women with a high school education or less to believe that this right is extremely important (71% to 44%).

- Single women were 9 points more likely than single men to say that voting was extremely important, but are 11 points less likely than married women to express this sentiment.

- Rural women were 9 points more likely than urban women to agree that the right to vote is extremely important (61% to 52%).

- Among women, the higher the annual income, the more likely she was to say that voting was extremely important.

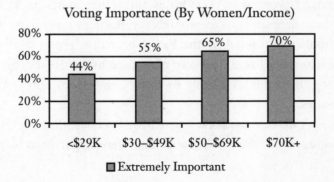

Voting Importance (By Women/Income)

Extremely Important

- Republican women place more importance than Democratic women on voting (64% "extremely important," versus 57%).

- Women aged 65 and older were 11 points more likely than their younger counterparts (those 18 to 34) to see the importance in exercising this right (59% to 48%).

Generation "Why?"

My generation takes it for granted that we can do anything we want. We were raised on the "Free to Be You and Me" track. It's frustrating to see so many of us taking it all for granted and not voting.

—MELISSA, 28

One of the more unsettling political trends is the declining participation of younger voters—in particular, women under 30. Young women are a generation reared to be assertive—to go after rewarding careers and demand fulfillment in their relationships—but when it comes to choosing their elected officials they are Generation "Why?" They want a more compelling reason to go to the polls than the catch-all value of the political process. They are involved in volunteer activities in record numbers, but often do not feel that politics contributes to their lives or to changing the world. Half of the young women who volunteer do not vote. They seem happy to hand the reins over to men or to their moms; indeed, women in their fifties and sixties are twice as likely to vote as their daughters. A new study by Rutgers University and two other schools and funded by the Pew Charitable Trusts confirms that alarming situation: Just 22 percent of women under 30 are regular voters, making them the least likely to vote of any group of women in the United States.

This isn't exactly the legacy that baby boomer moms intended for their daughters, but their political passion may be partly to blame. Gen

Xers and Yers were taught to distrust the government by their baby boomer parents, and their more recent experiences, such as Monica Lewinsky, Congressional deadlock, and the WMD imbroglio, have reinforced their cynicism. Shortage of female role models in elected positions fuels the impression that electoral politics has nothing to do with them. The political process has become disconnected from ordinary life. The average American spends five minutes a week thinking about politics.

The scorched-earth style of recent campaigns is alienating young voters, who tend to favor solitude to slugfests—including in politics. In withholding their votes, they are saying in effect, "This process is not like me, and I don't like it." They are refusing to participate until politicians begin to relate to them.

The political blog is emerging as a key entry point into the political process for young people. According to the *Wall Street Journal*, about 8 million Americans now publish blogs and 32 million people read them regularly. Internet-based participation is difficult to track at this stage in its development. Blogs have only been around since the late 1990s, and the political blogging movement has only spiked in the last two years. But it stands to reason that the best way to reach young people is to find them where they are, and where they are is on the Internet.

Soul Proprietors

Our nation was founded "under God," so I would say religion is extremely important—the principles more so than the affiliation.

—RUTH, 63

Religion has become increasingly significant in defining voter trends and consumer behaviors, a trend driven by women. Women are the guardians of the soul. In a recent Gallup poll, when asked to rate the importance of religion, 83% of women over 50 and 65% of women under 50 rated it extremely important—compared to only 59% of men

over 50 and 56% of men under 50. This trend transcends religious affiliation, although most of those who consider religion important are affiliated with a church, synagogue, or other community of worship.
Forty-three percent of women voters in 2004 attended religious services
a few times a week or more.

Issues of integrity and morality are essential to women when choosing a candidate. **More than 65% of women across party lines say the
integrity of a candidate is more important than his or her intelli-
gence or abilities.**

In recent elections, including 2004, we have seen the emergence of a
strong religious vote, which breaks along party lines, but on the whole
the nation's true feelings about the secular-religious coalescence are in
flux. We are in the process of defining the relationship between matters
of the soul and matters of the state, and women will be the ultimate ar-
biters of the debate.

THE NEXT CAMPAIGN

Traditionally, women have tended toward Democratic candidates more
than Republicans. However, as recent elections have demonstrated,
they're not averse to switching parties or mixing their votes to support
individual candidates or issues. As the 2006 election nears, all eyes will
remain fixed on the women's vote. She wants and deserves to have as
much information as possible to make an educated choice, and to make
sure the candidates hear her voice.

THE NEXT 10 YEARS

- National security will share a place at the top of the political
  agenda with personal security concerns—especially retirement issues of health and housing, including long-term
  care.

- Expect to hear a new phrase—"the Mother Agenda"—in
  upcoming elections.

- The debate about moral values will not abate, but will shift course, away from issues that are abstract to most Americans and intractable to the hard core, and back to practical life-and-death issues such as the death penalty, the right to die, and stem-cell research. Watch for an emerging consensus.

- Women will continue to be the guardians of faith and spirituality, in word and action, forcing a renewal of a "we" generation of social responsibility, volunteering, and aid to the poor. This trend is already being seen in evangelical circles.

- A woman will be on the presidential ticket, and her chance of getting elected will be equal to her male rival.

CONCLUSION:

WHAT DO WOMEN REALLY WANT?

Where do these 10 vigorous trends take us as we look ahead? Let's step back and envision an eclectic bouquet of implications for family, the workplace, politics, and the culture.

IN THE FAMILY . . .

- As the cost of delayed marriage and childbearing begin to have economic consequences, with parents juggling retirement needs with their children's college funds, watch for families to increase the pressure for affordable higher education.

- Commitment ceremonies and registries for singles will become big business, as women demand acknowledgment for their choices and help in outfitting their homes.

- Committed partners, both gay and heterosexual, will achieve more domestic benefits—if not by law, then as a corporate recruiting tool.

- Reproductive technologies will be applied not just to make babies, but to make *healthier* babies.

- Women will exert their role as family warriors in the courts, pressing for tighter laws to protect communities against pedophiles, lobbying for a cleaner environment, and insisting that public schools feed their children healthful foods.

IN THE WORKPLACE . . .

- Expect more businesses to get in line behind flexible workplaces, including shared hours, family leave, and other family-first policies. The best places to work will be those that achieve this.

- Women's entrepreneurial edge will be in the growth sectors of information technology and finance, where women have traditionally been less prominent, to account for the fastest growth in women-owned businesses, along with the service industry.

- Success at work will be measured by how task-oriented workers are—how effectively they accomplish the most in the least amount of time, not by how many hours they slave away. Failure to take vacation or staying wired to the office during vacation, will be viewed as pathetic, not committed.

- The best places to work will also be those that give domestic partner benefits to a diverse group of "families" and allow portability of benefits.

- College graduates, both male and female, looking for the best places to work, will consider intangible factors, such as rates of divorce or attrition, and take note of how many women are in executive positions.

IN POLITICS . . .

- "Moms Mobilization" will be one of the most potent forms of grass-roots activism.

- Small-business women, who feel the pinch most directly when they try to provide health benefits to their workers and themselves, will increase the pressure on politicians to produce parity with larger companies and with the benefits enjoyed by the politicians themselves.

- For the first time, the issue of benefits and/or tax breaks for family caregivers (who account for up to 25% of health-care services) will appear on political platforms.

- Unmarried women will be the number one "get" for candidates in upcoming elections, in the way that soccer moms were in 1996 and Nascar dads were in 2004.

- A woman will be on the presidential ticket.

IN THE CULTURE . . .

- More youthful junior seniors will shift the focus of retirement from retreat to "third age," especially women, who return to school and start new careers after 50 at much higher rates than men.

- Women will reclaim face-time in their families, workplaces, and communities, pushing for techno-etiquette (no ipods at the dinner table, no cell phones at cocktail parties and weddings, no BlackBerries on vacation).

- "Just say no" will become the mantra of overscheduled, guilt-trapped yeah-sayers, as women who chronically *do* choose to *do-not*. The question of the day will no longer be:

"How much can I squeeze in?" but rather, "Which relationships, activities, obligations and possessions are excess baggage, and which are luggage to carry on life's travels?"

• In higher education, spiraling costs, murky job prospects, and technological learning alternatives will force a long overdue reassessment of the Ivy League versus practical, flexible, affordable training environments. We'll see more quality career programs and online courses that are linked to jobs. The focus will be on life and work skills, not amorphous life experience, and the top schools will be those with the most graduates placed in their chosen jobs.

• Women will shatter the mystique of the White Coats (doctors), the Black Robes (judges), and the Men in Blue (law enforcement), and become their own advocates in the vital areas of their lives. No longer willing to put authorities on pedestals from which they make unilateral proclamations, women will assume responsibility and demand the right to participate in decisions related to their health, freedom, and security.

In every area of our lives we can anticipate a positive outcome. Indeed, it's already happening. In our polls, women told us, "It's a great time to be a woman." **When asked if they agree or disagree with the statement, "There has never been a better time to be a woman in the United States," using a scale of 1 to 10, an overwhelming majority of women (72%) agreed, giving the statement a 7 or higher. Nearly 3 women in 10 (29%) gave it a 10.**

Do you agree or disagree with the following statement; "There has never been a better time to be woman in the United States of America."

Total	Men	Women	
67%	64%	72%	**TOTAL AGREE (NET)**
12%	11%	14%	7
20%	19%	22%	8

6%	5%	7%	9
29%	29%	29%	10 "STRONGLY AGREE"
4%	8%	2%	DO NOT KNOW (VOLUNTEERED)
*	1%	*	REFUSED (VOLUNTEERED)
7%	**6%**	**7%**	**TOTAL NOT AGREE (NET)**
4%	3%	4%	1 "NOT AT ALL AGREE"
1%	1%	1%	2
2%	2%	2%	3
19%	**19%**	**18%**	**TOTAL NEUTRAL (NET)**
2%	1%	2%	4
10%	11%	10%	5
7%	7%	6%	6

What is especially intriguing about this result is that it didn't track in seemingly obvious ways. For example, low-income women (income <$29K) were more likely than high-income women (income $70K+) to strongly agree that there is no better time to be a woman in America. (33% versus 25%); and rural women were 4 points more likely than urban women to claim the same (31% versus 27%). Once again, single women revealed their optimism by strongly agreeing that this is the best time to be a woman.

In the financially and socially marginal categories—especially Waitress Moms and Alienated Singles—this optimism will only be justified by motivating factors in public policy that help lift the underclass—including access to education, health care, pension benefits, and affordable housing. Political and social efforts to engage Alienated Singles, who are more likely to disappear from the safety net, can give them a hand up in becoming part of the social contract.

As we have surveyed the nation's women to discover what they really want, we have repeatedly come away with a coalescing sense of optimism, and even excitement about being female in the early years of the twenty-first century. Sure, women are struggling with a balancing act between job and family, are concerned about their financial futures, and aren't too sure that their long-held personal dreams are achievable amidst the daily grind and larger chaos. But they are energized by their options, and recognize that for the first time in history they have a voice that is louder, clearer, more confident, and less ignored. When we say that women exert a unified power to make change in our culture and commerce, we aren't implying that they somehow get together and take a vote about it. However, in virtually every arena where women affect a sea change, the catalyst is their inability to get what they want and need by traditional means, and their decision to do something about it.

This new reality represents a dramatic shift in the way women have learned to use their power. Gone are the days of pounding on closed doors and demanding equal access. Today's women are simply bypassing settings that ignore their needs, creating parallel circuits which, in turn, immensely impact the old standards. This trend is vividly apparent in the big-ticket commerce of cars and computers.

We noticed a striking absence of the sense of victimization that has characterized past generations of women; their mantra seems to be, "If you want it, go out and get it." What women really *want* is the opportunity to do just that.

Women have long been a physical majority, but in this new revolution they are no longer a silent, dutiful majority. They are reforming this country in their own image. They are at last assuming their rightful place.

POLLING METHODOLOGY AND RESULTS

The What Women Really Want polls were conducted on two separate occasions, at a computer-assisted telephone interviewing (CATI) phone facility using live callers. The sample was drawn utilizing a random digit dial (RDD), where phone numbers were generated by a computer to ensure that every household in the nation had an equal chance to be surveyed.

The first survey was fielded over three nights (February 17–20, 2005). Nine questions specific to our book were added to a national omnibus survey of women, which also included demographic queries. Of the questions, six were open-ended and three were closed. The survey size was 800 women. Only 200 women were asked the survey in its entirety; the remainder were asked close-ended questions and demographics. Sampling controls were used to ensure that a proportional and representative number of female adults were interviewed from such demographic groups as age, race, and ethnicity and geographic region. The margin of error is calculated at +/- 3.5% at the 95% confidence level, meaning that in 19 out of 20 cases, the results obtained would differ by no more than 3 percentage points in either direction if the entire female population nationwide were to be surveyed.

The second survey was fielded over six nights (March 23–29, 2005). Sampling controls were used to ensure that a proportional and representative number of female adults were interviewed from such demographic groups as age, race, and ethnicity and geographic region. The margin of error is calculated at +/- 3.5% for total men and women; +/- 3.9% for women; and +/4.9 for men at the 95% confidence level, meaning that in 19 out of 20 cases, the results obtained would differ by no more than the percentage points listed for each group in either direction if the entire population nationwide were to be surveyed.

POLL # 1

National Survey of 804 Women for What Women Really Want
For the polling company, inc. and Lake, Snell, Perry, Mermin and Associates

TOPLINE DATA
February 21, 2005
Margin of Error: 3.0
Field Dates: February 17–20, 2005
N = *804*

A. Are you 18 years of age or older?

   100%   **YES**

B. Is there someone in the household I could speak with who is 18 or older?

   100%   **YES**

1. Generally speaking, what would you say is the biggest challenge facing women today? (OPEN END) (N=201)

   22%   WORK (NET)
   10%   GETTING EQUAL PAY AS MEN FOR SAME JOB

3% QUALITY IN WORKPLACE

3% JOBS/WORK (NONSPECIFIC)

1% WORKING CONDITIONS

1% QUALITY OF JOBS

1% NOT ENOUGH JOBS

1% WORKING OUTSIDE THE HOME TO PROVIDE FOR FAMILY

1% CAREER CHOICES

* GETTING AHEAD IN BUSINESS WORLD

* ANYTHING CAREER-RELATED

16% TIME BIND (NET)

15% BALANCING CAREER AND FAMILY

1% TOO MUCH TO DO IN TOO LITTLE TIME

16% HEALTH (NET)

4% STAYING IN GOOD HEALTH

3% COST OF HEALTH INSURANCE

3% WEIGHT

2% BREAST CANCER

1% HEALTH CARE

1% STRESS

1% TRYING TO STAY YOUNG

* SINGLE MOMS GETTING HEALTH CARE FOR THEIR KIDS

* DR. NOT PAYING AS MUCH ATTENTION TO WOMEN'S HEALTH
ISSUES

* REMAINING INDEPENDENT

13% SOCIETAL STRESSES (NET)

4% SEXISM/EQUAL RIGHTS

2% APPEARANCE

2% DON'T GET ENOUGH RESPECT/RECOGNITION WE DESERVE

1% ABORTIONS (MANY WOMEN HAVING ABORTIONS)

1% GOOD EDUCATION

1% DIVORCE RATE

1% BETTER AT DOING THINGS THAN MEN ARE

* NO POWER

* ABILITY TO GROW OLD GRACEFULLY

9%	**FAMILY (NET)**
4%	RESPONSIBILITY FOR RAISING CHILDREN
1%	BEING A SINGLE MOTHER
1%	BEING BOTH MOTHER AND FATHER HURTS FAMILIES
1%	TOO MUCH RESPONSIBILITY
*	TEACHING CHILDREN MORALS
*	TAKING CARE OF AGING MEMBERS OF THE FAMILY
9%	**MONEY/FINANCES (NET)**
3%	MAKING ENOUGH MONEY
2%	FINANCES (NONSPECIFIC)
2%	FINANCIAL SECURITY AFTER YOU CAN'T WORK
1%	NOT HAVING A RETIREMENT PLAN
1%	SOCIAL SECURITY
13%	DON'T KNOW

[SPLIT SAMPLE—HALF ASKED QUESTION 2A AND HALF 2B]

*2a. Thinking generally about problems facing women, what would you say is the biggest challenge facing **younger** women today? (OPEN END) (N = 103)*

30%	**FAMILY (NET)**
12%	CHILDREARING/RAISING
9%	BALANCING WORK AND FAMILY
3%	GOING TO WORK OR RAISING KIDS
2%	PROVIDING DAY CARE/CHILD CARE
1%	TIME FOR FAMILY
1%	WOMEN BEING BOTH MOTHER AND FATHER
1%	BEING ABLE TO STAY HOME AND RAISE KIDS
1%	YOUNGER WOMEN NOT HAVING FATHER FIGURE
19%	**EMPLOYMENT/CAREER (NET)**
4%	GETTING GOOD JOBS
4%	NOT BEING PAID THE SAME AS MEN
3%	DISCRIMINATION IN THE WORKPLACE
2%	MAKING GOOD CAREER DECISIONS

2%   DECIDING WHAT TO DO WITH THEIR LIVES

1%   LACK OF JOB OPPORTUNITIES FOR WOMEN

1%   WOMEN NOT WORKING

1%   FINDING NONTRADITIONAL JOBS THAT WOMEN CAN DO

1%   FINDING STABLE WORK WHERE YOU DON'T GET LAID OFF

15% PRESSURES/EXPECTATIONS (NET)

4%   GETTING AN EDUCATION

2%   HAVING A GOOD SELF-IMAGE

2%   MORALS

1%   ACHIEVING OWN GOALS

1%   REALIZING OWN POTENTIAL

1%   ATTITUDES OF OLDER WOMEN

1%   NOT CARING ABOUT WHAT THE FUTURE HOLDS

1%   HAVING SOCIETY'S VERSION OF THE PERFECT BODY

1%   FITTING IN WITH PEERS

1%   EFFECTS OF POLITICAL INCORRECTNESS

9%   HEALTH/WELL-BEING (NET)

4%   STRESS

2%   DRUG USE

1%   JOINTS GETTING STIFF

1%   HIV

1%   WEIGHT

6%   MONEY/FINANCES (NET)

3%   FINANCIAL STABILITY

2%   HAVING TO WORK TO SUPPORT A FAMILY

1%   FINANCIAL ISSUES FOR SINGLE WOMEN

19% DON'T KNOW/NO ANSWER

*2b. Thinking generally about problems facing women, what would you say is the biggest challenge facing **older** women today? (OPEN END) (N=98)*

56% HEALTH/WELL-BEING (NET)

16% MAINTAINING GOOD HEALTH/BEING HEALTHY

11% GOOD/ACCESSIBLE HEALTHCARE

8%   HEALTH ISSUES (NONSPECIFIC)

5%   HEALTH RELATED DIFFICULTIES

3%   MENOPAUSE

2%   COST OF HEALTH CARE

2%   OSTEOPOROSIS

2%   PHYSICAL LIMITATIONS

2%   BEING ABLE TO TAKE CARE OF YOURSELF

1%   MEDICAID CUTBACKS

1%   GROWING OLD (NONSPECIFIC)

1%   HIGH COST OF PRESCRIPTIONS

1%   NOT ENOUGH EXERCISE

1%   STAYING SLIM

1%   DIABETES

11%   MONEY/FINANCES (NET)

6%   LACK OF MONEY

2%   BEING ABLE TO LIVE ON SOCIAL SECURITY

2%   LIVING ON A FIXED INCOME

1%   MONEY (NONSPECIFIC)

6%   SOCIETY (NET)

4%   TRYING TO SURVIVE IN SOCIETY

2%   AGE DISCRIMINATION

6%   MISCELLANEOUS (NET)

4%   LONELINESS

1%   FINDING A YOUNGER MAN

1%   AFFORDABLE/AVAILABLE TRANSPORTATION

5%   EMPLOYMENT (NET)

1%   EMPLOYMENT DIFFICULTIES

1%   KEEPING UP WITH OTHER WOMEN

1%   DON'T GET PAID AS MUCH AS MEN

1%   DISCRIMINATION

1%   GETTING AN EDUCATION

1%   COMPUTER ILLITERATE

4%   **CHILDREN (NET)**

2%   WORKING WITH CHILDREN

1%   RAISING CHILDREN ALONE

1%   NOT HAVING CHILDREN AROUND

12%   DON'T KNOW/NO ANSWER

3. Regardless of your current age, in your opinion, what do you see as the best thing about getting older? (OPEN-ENDED, PRECODED)

20%   WISDOM

10%   SPEND MORE TIME WITH CHILDREN/GRANDCHILDREN

8%   RETIREMENT/NOT WORKING

8%   HAVE MORE CONFIDENCE/GREATER SELF-ASSURANCE

7%   MORE FREEDOM/FLEXIBILITY

6%   ABILITY TO TRAVEL/VACATION

6%   MORE MONEY/FINANCIAL ASSETS

5%   MORE TIME FOR MYSELF

4%   SPEND MORE TIME ON MY HOBBIES/LEISURE ACTIVITIES

3%   FEWER RESPONSIBILITIES

3%   NO MORE CHILDREN IN THE HOUSE

3%   TRY NEW THINGS

3%   MORE TIME WITH SPOUSE/PARTNER

2%   MORE CHOICES

1%   MEET NEW PEOPLE

1%   EXPAND OR CHANGE CAREER

9%   OTHER (VOLUNTEERED)

8%   DO NOT KNOW (VOLUNTEERED)

1%   REFUSED (VOLUNTEERED)

4. What one thing about your appearance would you change? (OPEN END) (N=201)

39%   **WEIGHT MANAGEMENT (NET)**

30%   LOSE WEIGHT

1%   LOSE 20 LBS

2%   LOSE 10 LBS

3%   WEIGHT CONTROL

3%   GAIN WEIGHT

19% BODY/APPEARANCE (NET)

3%   BE TALLER

2%   NEED FACE LIFT

2%   TEETH

1%   BETTER MID SECTION

1%   REDUCE MY STOMACH

1%   FIX MY NOSE

1%   HEIGHT (NONSPECIFIC)

1%   BE SHORTER

1%   IMPROVE SKIN TONE

1%   TONING MY BODY

1%   POSTURE

*   MY TEMPLE

*   CLEAR UP SKIN

*   GETTING FIT

*   THINNER LIPS

*   FIGURE

*   FACIAL ISSUES (NONSPECIFIC)

*   SCARRING

*   GET RID OF STRETCH MARKS

4%   HAIR (NET)

1%   NEW HAIR STYLE

1%   STOP LOSING HAIR

1%   SHAPE OF HAIR

1%   GRAY HAIR

*   CUT HAIR SHORT

2%   WRINKLES (NET)

1%   AGE LINES

*   REMOVE WRINKLES AROUND EYES

*   LESS WRINKLES IN NECK

2%   MISCELLANEOUS (NET)

1%   MY WHOLE SELF/EVERYTHING

1%   LOOK BETTER (NONSPECIFIC)

22%   NOTHING/SATISFIED WITH APPEARANCE

8%   DON'T KNOW

5. Would you say you feel older than your current age, younger than your current age, or about your current age? (ROTATE RESPONSES)

16%   OLDER THAN MY CURRENT AGE

49%   YOUNGER THAN MY CURRENT AGE

34%   I FEEL ABOUT MY AGE

1%   DO NOT KNOW (VOLUNTEERED)

–   REFUSED (VOLUNTEERED)

6. In your opinion, do you think has most contributed to women being able to look younger today? (OPEN END) (N=201)

31%   HEALTH/WELLNESS (NET)

11%   EXERCISE

5%   TAKING CARE OF YOURSELF

5%   PROPER DIET/EATING HEALTHY

3%   LESS STRESS

2%   ENOUGH REST/SLEEP

1%   ENERGY/BEING ACTIVE

1%   GENES HEREDITY

1%   WEIGHT LOSS

*   NOT SMOKING

*   VITAMINS/MINERALS

*   DON'T HAVE TO WORK AS HARD

*   INCREASED AWARENESS OF THINGS YOU SHOULDN'T DO

11%   COSMETICS/SKIN CARE (NET)

6%   NEW/DIFFERENT TYPE OF COSMETICS

3%   BETTER SKIN CARE PRODUCTS

1%   DIFFERENT AGE/WRINKLE CREAMS

1%   PUTTING ON MAKEUP

7%	**SURGERY (NET)**
7%	PLASTIC/COSMETIC SURGERY
*	BEING MORE LIKELY TO HAVE A FACE LIFT

2%	**PRESENTATION/STYLE (NET)**
1%	HAIR/HAIR STYLE
1%	CLOTHES/STYLE/WAY I DRESS

1%	**ATITTUDE (NET)**
*	A YOUNG ATTITUDE
*	A POSITIVE ATTITUDE
*	HAPPY WITH LOVE IN MY LIFE

54%   DON'T KNOW

7. Which of the following represents the greatest challenge for older women as they try to achieve new goals? (READ LIST, ROTATE RESPONSES)

20%	HEALTH
18%	FINANCIAL STATUS
16%	FAMILY RESPONSIBILITIES
14%	FEAR OF UNKNOWN
8%	AGE
8%	EMPLOYMENT STATUS
7%	DOING SOMETHING DIFFERENT
3%	OTHER (RECORD VERBATIM)
5%	DO NOT KNOW (VOLUNTEERED)
*	REFUSED (VOLUNTEERED)

I would now like to talk to you about parenting and motherhood.

8. In your own opinion, what is the biggest challenge facing new mothers? (OPEN END) (N=201)

34%	**CHILDREARING/CARE (NET)**
7%	LACK OF EXPERIENCE RAISING CHILDREN
4%	LEARNING TO BE RESPONSIBLE
3%	GENERAL CARE

3%   DISCIPLINING CHILDREN

2%   BALANCING BETWEEN KIDS AND HUSBAND

2%   RAISING KIDS PROPERLY

2%   SAFETY OF CHILDREN

2%   FEAR OF UNKNOWN

2%   DEMANDS OF A NEWBORN

2%   FINDING GOOD CHILD CARE

1%   THE TERRIBLE TWO'S

1%   PROPER EDUCATION

1%   KNOWING WHAT TO DO WHEN YOU CHILD IS SICK

*   ALLOWING CHILDREN TO GROW AT OWN PACE

*   FEAR OF KIDNAPPING

*   PROVIDING A GOOD HOME

*   BALANCING EVERYTHING

*   NOT TAKING CARE OF CHILDREN

23%   WORK/FAMILY TIME BIND (NET)

8%   BALANCING CAREER AND FAMILY

4%   SPENDING ENOUGH TIME WITH KIDS

3%   TIME MANAGEMENT

3%   NOT SPENDING TIME WITH CHILDREN BECAUSE OF WORK

2%   RETURNING TO WORK AFTER A CHILD

2%   HAVING TO WORK

1%   BEING HOUSEWIFE AND MOTHER

*   INDEPENDENCE/TIME FOR SELF

11%   SOCIETAL STRESSES (NET)

2%   DECIDING BETWEEN CAREER AND FAMILY

2%   TEACHING KIDS TO BE GOOD PEOPLE

1%   WOMEN HAVING BABIES YOUNG

1%   HOW THE WORLD IS CHANGING FOR THE WORST

1%   CHILDREN HAVING ACCESS TO GUNS

1%   KEEPING KIDS OFF DRUGS

1%   PEER PRESSURE

*   NO ONE ACCEPTS RESPONSIBILITY FOR WHAT THEY DO

*   THE WAY SOCIETY IS

* KIDS THAT ARE OUT OF CONTROL
* RATE AT WHICH KIDS MATURE

10% MONEY (NET)
7%   DEALING WITH THE EXPENSE
2%   SECURITY/EMPLOYMENT
1%   BEING FINANCIALLY ABLE TO STAY HOME
*   MEDICAL EXPENSES/HEALTH INSURANCE

8% SUPPORT/HELP (NET)
3%   BEING A SINGLE PARENT/NO FATHER
4%   HAVING A SUPPORT NETWORK
1%   BEING SELFLESS
*   FAMILY COHESIVENESS

2% HEALTH (NET)
1%   DIET
*   DISEASE
*   GETTING ENOUGH SLEEP

8%   DON'T KNOW

9. Regardless of your current situation, please describe to me your ideal *career and family situation. (OPEN END) (N=201)*

GOOD JOB AND FAMILY

"The job I like and the family to support you.

To have a steady job with a future, and a supportive family."

"I work 1 day/week with great staff and have two kids and have a great husband."

"My ideal career is to be a coach, and if my family has more understanding for each other."

"A white-collar job behind a desk with children."

"Steady job, steady income, and good money."

"Family: married with kids—two at most. They have good schools, good babysitters, and good friends."

"To be a lobbyist and to create a schedule that will not conflict with the family."

"Good job and a supportive family."

"To be a child psychologist and have a stable home and stable finances."

"Being an expeditor with a husband and two kids—a boy and a girl."

"A job I really enjoy and that pays well and having a significant other. Good personal and financial relationships."

"An ideal career is to have a job you enjoy and be able to be there for your family, having them near is very important."

"My ideal career would be my current job at more pay, and partnered with one child."

"To be a teacher and remarry."

"I'd like to be a Noble Prize scientist/inventor.

My ideal family situation would be one in which everyone in my family was happy and knew how much I loved and respected them.

"I want to be a cosmologist: have a husband, two kids, a cat and a bird."

"Dental hygienist and having a close family life."

"Being a nurse and having a family"

"I always wanted to be a singer or own a restaurant or café and then I could give my children everything I didn't have."

"A mother and father who get along well and raise their children together, and have a medically related career, which I love."

"Being a nurse, and have my kids all grown up and happy."

"Be a doctor, have a family and children."

"Be married, have kids, and a better-paying job."

"To be a nursing assistant/no problems with inlaws or family."

"To be married, professional, and middle-class."

"It would have job security; both parents are in the home, both employed, they own a vehicle and their home. It's a job I enjoy."

"For everybody in the family to get along, and not have to worry about finding a job."

"Happily married with no children and not a hospital worker."

"Something working with animal care or rescue if it paid enough to be married with two children."

"Be a social worker, and have a son who is grown-up and happy."

BALANCE WORK AND FAMILY

"To go to work, have my children in day care, and come home to see my family."

"It would definitely be a career working with the public. I'd never be happy just sitting at a desk.

And working with someone who would have empathy for my family situation; my husband is in the military and I have to adjust to his situation."

"That doesn't exist in the real world, but I'd say ideally, where I can work 40–50 hours a week and still have time to do things with my children."

"Secretarial work and taking care of my daughter."

"9 to 5 Monday through Friday and remarry someday and have another child"

"Working three times a week and then spending the rest of the time at home with my children."

"Working part-time and being able to stay home with your family."

"Having a 9–5 position and affordable child care nearby or in the place of work."

"Staying at home while my husband worked, then when children were grown, went back to work."

"One parent should work while the other parent will stay home with the children."

"Both my husband and I could work the same time to be home together with the kids."

"I would have liked to be an x-ray technician, but not have children and work at the same time."

IDEAL CAREER

"Being a teacher, being happy"

"Teaching."

"Bookkeeping to have a supportive spouse and have your children learn in school."

"My ideal situation would be me having my independence working in the hospitality field."

"To become a teacher, married with two+ kids."

"Career in helping other people such as making

Medicare better for them."

"A job in the medical field."

"Just a job that I like."

"Nursing."

"Entertainment for a career . . . well-rounded performer."

"To become a director of a facility for nonviolent female offenders and their children."

"To work in corporate America."

"Supervisor in the hospital, and my husband was a doctor."

"A good job with good health care"

"A train conductor assistant/Amtrak"

"I would be a dental assistant, have a nice house and be able to have dinner with the whole family every night."

"To teach art."

"Help people who are handicapped."

"A successful freelance writer."

"A health career (don't know which one), and I don't have a family so I can't say."

"Teacher is my ideal career and I like my family life as is."

"Head of a corporation being paid what I'm worth."

"Being artistic and creative."

LIVE CLOSER TO FAMILY

"I would love to live with my grandchildren in Illinois."

"I would love to be an archivist or researcher in a museum. As for family, I would love it if all my family lived near each other."

"Living near my whole family and seeing the grandchildren on a regular basis."

"To be strong, communicate, and being closer to family."

BE STAY-AT-HOME MOM

"Working part-time while kids are in school, being a stay-at-home mom with two children."

"A situation where women stay at home and the men work."

"Not having to work when my children are young."

"Staying at home with the kids."

"Work hours should be from 8–4 P.M. and men should work while women should stay home and care for the kids."

"Taking care of the children, while the father goes to work."

"I would love to stay home and have babies."

"The ideal situation is staying home and raising your children."

"The women would not have to work and they could stay home and care for their children."

"To stay home with my kids."

"To stay at home."

"Ideally, I would like to be home when they are in school age and then work when they are about 5 years old."

"Stay at home mom with two kids."

"Stay at home and take care of my family."

"I want to be married with kids, and not have to work so I can stay home with them at least when they're little."

"Being a mother, being supported by a spouse, and being able to stay home."

"To stay at home and not have to worry about money."

"My ideal career and family situation is a stay-at-home mom, being married and having a newborn."

"The father supports the family and the mother raises the children with morals."

"Being a stay-at-home mom."

"The ideal is to stay home and raise your children."

"Homemaker and having a family always around."

"Being a stay-at-home mom."

"Being able to stay home with my children and not have not work outside the home."

MARRIAGE

"I would like to be married for a very long time."

"Being a working female and live in a married household."

MOTHERHOOD

"Being a mother."

"To be a great mom."

"I wish my two kids were healthy."

OWNING A HOME

"A house, a yard, and a car."

"I would love to own my own home and be a massage therapist."

WORK AT HOME/ENTREPRENEUR

"Working for myself, have own home, and financially stable."

"Being self-supported, having my family home"

"Mother could stay home and work out of her home."

"Entrepreneurship as her career."

"Working from home. A profession where I'd be working with people and being able to stay home with the children."

"A career at home."

"Self-employed and having more family around me."

WORK PART-TIME

"Being able to work part-time, 20–25 hours a week"

"Work part-time."

"Working part-time outside of home."

"Oh boy! Part-time work, full-time pay, gives you more time with your family."

"The woman does volunteer work or part-time work so she can be home with her family when she wants."

MORE TIME FOR FAMILY

"I'd have worked only one job and spent more time with my kids."

"Family should be first."

"I have no desire to have a career. I would like to spend more time with my family, and my husband. He works a lot. I would like to have a minimal job for five to six hours a week. Answering phones and getting out meeting people."

"Teaching, but more time with my kids."

"To have a relationship with the kids."

"Back when I worked in the government, it was hard to find time for my child. So spending more time with them would have been ideal."

"To me, ideal would be a two-parent household who are devoted to each
other, worship together and believe in God."

"Ideally, work less hours. As for the family situation—need to spend more
time at home."

FINANCIAL STABILITY

"If I had a chance to do it again, I would be a doctor—I would like to have had
more money to educate my children."

"Not having to work due to financial need, and having a happy, healthy family."

"Office work and a roof over your head."

"Making more money and having everyone at home at dinner time."

"Husbands would make enough money."

"I'd have somebody to be a fun and financially stable person to have a relationship with—to have fun and travel, someone to enjoy life with."

"An executive of some type and being able to retire with money."

"When there is plenty of money and time with your family."

"Both parents being in the home, and having enough money to live reasonably
well."

"Being settled and living comfortable."

"Being able to work part-time and still having money to live off of while traveling. In regard to my family situation I'd like to keep my domestic partner who could work decent hours with better pay."

"Ideal—independently wealthy; my family situation is fine."

"Being able to go on vacation three times and kids in private school."

"Making more money."

"I would like to be financially stable and have three children."

"Being rich! Not having to worry about anything. She would also like to have a
ton of grandchildren (near her she says not necessarily living with her),
and to be able to travel."

CURRENT SITUATION IS ALREADY IDEAL

"Well, I work for the government and it is a promising career and I have two
daughters that are good helpers around the house."

"I like what I'm doing now, being a nurse."

"I have an ideal career"

"I'm happy now."

"Family has grown, careerwise is stable."

"My financial situation is perfectly fine."

"My ideal career is what I am doing right now as a therapist. My husband is currently deceased."

"I'm a stay-at-home mom."

"My family situation is fine and I'm satisfied with my status."

"I don't have an ideal career, an ideal family situation now is taking care of my grandchild 17 months old."

"I enjoy being a housewife and just being retired. My husband is deceased."

"I worked in a credit union—the owner died—I liked the work and would have liked to remain in that career. I'm very happy with my family—now married 50 years and have five grown children."

"My ideal is what I do now which is being a teacher."

"I teach and I love it and I am happily married to my husband for the last 30-odd years."

"I don't know what that means, I thought I had it. Being a public school teacher and getting the summers off. I guess any job that allows you to make money and still be a good mother."

"I am a geologist and it was my ideal career—my ideal family situation would be to be with my husband who died."

"Exactly what I am doing. I make my own hours. I am a practice manager in a medical office."

"My own career as a domestic goddess and a mother of three is ideal career and family situation. The food is cooked, the house is clean, the kids are cared for, and husband doesn't make the world of money but he is content."

"My job working for the government."

MISCELLANEOUS

"Having a college education allows for higher-paying jobs and you can certainly afford a nanny then."

"Well, since I was married in 1943 I did not work outside the home. I am a good dancer and dance every week. I am also an excellent tailor and seamstress."

"Going to work and having a clean house"

"Just being happy."

"I guess we need to have good values."

"Life should be fulfilling and they should have fun with each other, feel responsibility toward one another."

"That everything would run smoothly for one day."

"Balance work with school."

"Everybody respects everybody and communicates."

"To be healthy."

"Wish I could have followed through with what I wanted to do."

"To be able to get up and do what I want to do."

"Actually I want to go back to school, I have a degree in accounting."

4%	RETIRED
15%	DON'T KNOW

Demographics:
Now I have a few more questions for statistical purposes.

10. What is your age, please? (CODE RESPONSE)

13%	18–24
8%	25–29
8%	30–34
10%	35–39
9%	40–44
10%	45–49
10%	50–54
10%	55–60
5%	61–64
9%	65–74
8%	75+
1%	REFUSED (VOLUNTEERED)

11. Are you currently registered to vote as a Republican, Democrat, Independent, or are you not registered at all?

13%   POSTGRADUATE
1%   DON'T KNOW/REFUSED (VOLUNTEER)

15. *Which of the following media sources do you consider your primary source of news and information? Would it be . . . ?*

23%   A LOCAL NEWSPAPER
3%   A NATIONAL NEWSPAPER SUCH AS *USA TODAY*
29%   YOUR LOCAL EVENING TV NEWS
15%   CABLE TELEVISION NEWS CHANNELS
8%   NATIONAL NETWORK EVENING NEWS
8%   RADIO
7%   INTERNET
5%   ALL (VOLUNTEERED)
1%   NONE (VOLUNTEERED)
*   DON'T KNOW (VOLUNTEERED)
1%   REFUSED (VOLUNTEERED)

16. *Do you have any children?*

78%   TOTAL WITH CHILDREN (NET)
18%   YES, 1
27%   YES, 2
33%   YES, 3 OR MORE
21%   NO
1%   REFUSED (VOLUNTEERED)

17A. *(ASKED ONLY TO RESPONDENTS WITH CHILDREN) And, what is the age of your youngest child? (OPEN END)*

24%   AGE 5 AND UNDER
1%   8 WEEKS
1%   3 MONTHS
2%   7 MONTHS
1%   10 MONTHS
1%   15 MONTHS

32%   REPUBLICAN

34%   DEMOCRAT

17%   INDEPENDENT/UNAFFILIATED

11%   NOT REGISTERED

1%   OTHER (RECORD VERBATIM, VOLUNTEERED)

5%   DON'T KNOW (VOLUNTEERED)

12. *Thinking for a moment about your social, economic, and political i you generally consider yourself to be conservative or liberal?*

42%   TOTAL CONSERVATIVE (NET)

19%   VERY CONSERVATIVE

23%   SOMEWHAT CONSERVATIVE

21%   MODERATE

28%   TOTAL LIBERAL (NET)

17%   SOMEWHAT LIBERAL

11%   VERY LIBERAL

*   OTHER (VOLUNTEERED)

6%   DON'T KNOW (VOLUNTEERED)

1%   REFUSED (VOLUNTEERED)

13. *Are you currently . . .*

58%   MARRIED

20%   SINGLE

10%   DIVORCED

2%   SEPARATED

9%   WIDOWED

1%   REFUSED (VOLUNTEERED)

14. *What is the last grade of formal education you completed?*

7%   LESS THAN HIGH SCHOOL

28%   HIGH SCHOOL GRADUATE

28%   SOME COLLEGE/VOCATIONAL SCHOOL

24%   COLLEGE GRADUATE

2%	22 MONTHS
4%	1
4%	2
4%	3
2%	4
2%	5

10%	**AGE 6–10**
5%	6
2%	7
1%	8
2%	9

10%	**AGE 11–15**
2%	11
3%	12
2%	13
1%	14
2%	15

6%	**AGE 16–18**
2%	16
2%	17
2%	18

14%	**AGE 19–24**
1%	19
2%	20
4%	21
1%	22
5%	23
1%	24

14%	**AGE 25–35**
1%	25
2%	26
2%	27

2%	28
2%	29
1%	31
2%	32
1%	34
1%	35
17%	**AGE 35 AND HIGHER**
1%	36
1%	37
2%	38
2%	39
3%	40
1%	41
1%	42
1%	43
1%	45
1%	47
1%	52
1%	54
1%	57
5%	REFUSED

17B. (ASKED ONLY TO THOSE RESPONDENTS WITHOUT CHILDREN)
How likely are you to have children in the next five years? (N=179)

36%	**TOTAL LIKELY NOT YET MOMS (NET)**
15%	VERY LIKELY
21%	SOMEWHAT LIKELY
50%	**TOTAL NOT LIKELY NOT YET MOMS (NET)**
7%	JUST A LITTLE BIT LIKELY
43%	NOT AT ALL LIKELY
7%	DON'T KNOW ((VOLUNTEERED)
6%	REFUSED ((VOLUNTEERED)

18. What type of school do your children currently attend or what type of school did they attend when they were younger? (N=625)

71%   PUBLIC

10%   PRIVATE

6%   RELIGIOUS

1%   HOME-SCHOOLED

3%   OTHER (RECORD VERBATIM) (VOLUNTEERED)

13%   DO NOT ATTEND SCHOOL (VOLUNTEERED)

1%   DON'T KNOW (VOLUNTEERED)

1%   REFUSED (VOLUNTEERED)

19. Do you have any grandchildren? (IF YES: HOW MANY?)

37%   TOTAL HAVE GRANDCHILDREN (NET)

6%   YES, 1

6%   YES, 2

25%   YES, 3 OR MORE

62%   NO

1%   REFUSED (VOLUNTEERED)

20. Would you describe your racial or ethnic background as:

76%   WHITE/CAUCASIAN

12%   BLACK/AFRICAN AMERICAN

5%   HISPANIC/LATINO

1%   ASIAN MIDDLE EASTERN

2%   NATIVE AMERICAN

2%   OTHER (VOLUNTEERED)

2%   DON'T KNOW/REFUSED (VOLUNTEERED)

21. Are you . . . ? (READ CATEGORIES)

24%   CATHOLIC

46%   PROTESTANT

2%   JEWISH

3%   AGNOSTIC/ATHEIST

*   MUSLIM

2%   MORMON

10%   OTHER (SPECIFY) (VOLUNTEERED)

9%   NONE/UNAFFILIATED (VOLUNTEERED)

3%   REFUSED (VOLUNTEERED)

22. How often do you attend religious services?

2%   EVERY DAY

31%   A FEW TIMES PER WEEK

27%   A FEW TIMES PER MONTH

13%   A FEW TIMES PER YEAR

23%   SELDOM/NEVER

3%   DON'T KNOW/REFUSED (VOLUNTEERED)

23. How would you describe the community in which you live?

25%   URBAN

37%   SUBURBAN

33%   RURAL

3%   DON'T KNOW (VOLUNTEERED)

2%   REFUSED (VOLUNTEERED)

24. Which of the following best describes your current work status or occupation?

23%   PROFESSIONAL/EXECUTIVE/OWNER

12%   WHITE-COLLAR/ADMINISTRATIVE/CLERICAL

8%   BLUE-COLLAR/SERVICE/MANUFACTURING

11%   PART-TIME WORK OUTSIDE OF THE HOME

13%   STAY-AT-HOME/DO NOT WORK

5%   UNEMPLOYED

5%   STUDENT

18%   RETIRED

4%   OTHER (VOLUNTEERED)

*   NOT SURE (VOLUNTEERED)

2%   REFUSED (VOLUNTEERED)

25. Do you own or are you a partial owner of a small business, or are you self-employed or earn self-employment income? (READ LIST)

18%   **TOTAL SMALL BUSINESS OWNER (NET)**

8%   YES, OWNER

3%   YES, PARTIAL OWNER

7%   YES, SELF-EMPLOYED OR SELF-EMPLOYMENT INCOME

81%   NO

2%   DON'T KNOW/REFUSED (VOLUNTEERED)

26. Do you, or does anyone in your household, belong to a labor union or teachers' association? [IF YES] And do they work in the PUBLIC SECTOR or the PRIVATE SECTOR?

17%   **TOTAL UNION MEMBER (NET)**

13%   YES, PUBLIC-SECTOR UNION

4%   YES, PRIVATE-SECTOR UNION

68%   NOT A MEMBER OF A LABOR UNION

13%   DON'T KNOW ((VOLUNTEERED)

2%   REFUSED ((VOLUNTEERED)

27. And regarding your family's annual income, please tell me which of the following categories best describes your family's total annual household income before taxes.

18%   LESS THAN $25,000

8% $25,000 TO $29,999

11% $30,000 TO $39,999

9% $40,000 TO $49,999

8% $50,000 TO $59,999

5% $60,000 TO $69,999

5% $70,000 TO $79,999

3% $80,000 TO $89,999

11% $90,000 OR HIGHER

5%   DO NOT KNOW (VOLUNTEERED)

17%   REFUSED (VOLUNTEERED)

28. Do you currently hold any investments in stocks or stock mutual funds either directly or through a 401(k) or pension plan?

    47%   YES

    45%   NO

     8%   DON'T KNOW/REFUSED (VOLUNTEERED)

29. Region

    17%   **TOTAL NORTHEAST (NET)**

     4%   NEW ENGLAND

    13%   MIDATLANTIC

    36%   **TOTAL SOUTH (NET)**

    18%   SOUTH ATLANTIC

     7%   EAST SOUTH CENTRAL

    11%   WEST SOUTH CENTRAL

    26%   **TOTAL NORTH CENTRAL (NET)**

    18%   EAST NORTH CENTRAL

     8%   WEST NORTH CENTRAL

    20%   **TOTAL WEST (NET)**

     5%   MOUNTAIN

    15%   PACIFIC

POLL # 2

March 2005

National Survey of 800 Women and 400 Men for What Women Really Want

the polling company, inc./WomanTrend and Lake Snell Perry Mermin and Associates

March 23–29, 2005

Margin of Error: +/– 3.5%

Women N = 801

Margin of Error: +/– 3.5%

Men N = 401

Margin of Error: +/– 4.9%

A. Are you 18 years of age or older?

 100%   YES   (CONTINUE)

B. Is there someone in the household I could speak with who is 18 or older?

 100%   YES   (CONTINUE)

1. Are you currently registered to vote as a Republican, Democrat, Independent or are you not registered at all?

Total	Men	Women	
28%	27%	28%	REPUBLICAN
32%	31%	33%	DEMOCRAT
22%	24%	21%	INDEPENDENT/UNAFFILIATED
12%	14%	11%	NOT REGISTERED
*	—	%	OTHER (RECORD VERBATIM, VOLUNTEERED)
2%	2%	2%	DON'T KNOW (VOLUNTEERED)
4%	3%	4%	REFUSED (VOLUNTEERED)

Natividad and Associates

N1 Many people did not get a chance to vote in the November 2004 election for U.S. president, and other offices. How about you? Were you able to vote in the election or, like many people, did you not get a chance to vote?

(If YES, Did you vote in person, by mail, or by absentee ballot?)

Total	Men	Women	
81%	81%	81%	**TOTAL VOTED (NET)**
71%	72%	71%	YES, VOTED ON ELECTION DAY IN PERSON
5%	4%	5%	YES, VOTED ON ELECTION DAY BY MAIL/ABSENTEE BALLOT
3%	3%	3%	YES, VOTED EARLY IN PERSON
2%	2%	2%	YES, VOTED EARLY BY MAIL/ABSENTEE BALLOT
18%	20%	18%	NO, DID NOT VOTE
*	—	*	NOT SURE (VOLUNTEERED)

N2 *In the election for U.S. president, did you vote for the (ROTATE) Democrat John Kerry, the Republican George W. Bush, Independent Ralph Nader, or someone else?*

(IF RESPONDENT DECLINES TO SAY HOW HE OR SHE VOTED, SAY:) *This survey is being done for research purposes only. Your willingness to discuss your vote is really important for assuring the accuracy of our research, and we promise that we will always maintain the privacy and confidentiality of your responses.*

Total	Men	Women	
38%	39%	37%	GEORGE W. BUSH
34%	33%	35%	JOHN KERRY
1%	1%	1%	RALPH NADER
*	1%	*%	OTHER CANDIDATE (VOLUNTEERED)
17%	18%	15%	DID NOT VOTE IN PRESIDENTIAL RACE
2%	1%	2%	DO NOT KNOW (VOLUNTEERED)
8%	7%	9%	REFUSED (VOLUNTEERED)

N3 *I am going to read you a list of issues that may have come up during the election. Regardless of what you may think is important now, thinking back to last November and Election Day, please tell me which one of these was most important to you in deciding who to vote for. (READ AND ROTATE, ACCEPT ONE RESPONSE ONLY)*

Total	Men	Women	
14%	14%	13%	JOBS AND THE ECONOMY
14%	15%	13%	IRAQ
10%	9%	10%	SOCIAL SECURITY AND MEDICARE
10%	9%	11%	MORAL VALUES
10%	13%	8%	HOMELAND SECURITY AND TERRORISM
7%	6%	8%	EDUCATION
6%	6%	7%	HEALTH CARE AND PRESCRIPTION DRUGS
4%	5%	3%	NATIONAL DEFENSE AND VETERANS' ISSUES
4%	4%	3%	TAXES
3%	4%	3%	FEDERAL BUDGET DEFICIT

3%	1%	5%	ABORTION
2%	1%	3%	GAY AND LESBIAN MARRIAGE/RIGHTS ISSUES
5%	5%	5%	OTHER (VOLUNTEERED)
9%	9%	9%	DO NOT KNOW (VOLUNTEERED)

N4   *Now turning to the elections in 2006. Honestly, how likely are you to vote in the upcoming election in November 2006—very likely, somewhat likely, not very likely, or not likely at all?*

Total	Men	Women	
90%	91%	89%	**TOTAL LIKELY (NET)**
80%	80%	80%	VERY LIKELY
10%	11%	9%	SOMEWHAT LIKELY
8%	7%	7%	**TOTAL NOT LIKELY (NET)**
2%	1%	2%	NOT VERY LIKELY
6%	6%	5%	NOT LIKELY AT ALL
2%	2%	3%	DO NOT KNOW (VOLUNTEERED)
*	—	*	REFUSED (VOLUNTEERED)

N5   *I am going to read you a list of concerns people have. Please tell me which of the following worries you the most personally.*

Total	Men	Women	
30%	33%	28%	**JOBS AND ECONOMIC SECURITY**
22%	23%	21%	HOMELAND SECURITY AND TERRORISM
22%	21%	22%	HEALTH CARE SECURITY
14%	13%	15%	RETIREMENT SECURITY
5%	4%	6%	CRIME AND PERSONAL SECURITY
3%	2%	4%	OTHER (VOLUNTEERED) (SPECIFY) _____
2%	3%	1%	NONE OF THE ABOVE (VOLUNTEERED)
2%	1%	2%	DO NOT KNOW (VOLUNTEERED)

1. Do you agree or disagree with the following statement; "There has never been a better time to be woman in the United States of America." Please use a 1–10 scale, with 1 being "NOT AT ALL AGREE" and 10 being "STRONGLY AGREE."

Total	Men	Women	
7%	**6%**	**7%**	**TOTAL NOT AGREE (NET)**
4%	3%	4%	1 "NOT AT ALL AGREE"
1%	1%	1%	2
2%	2%	2%	3
19%	**19%**	**18%**	**TOTAL NEUTRAL (NET)**
2%	1%	2%	4
10%	11%	10%	5
7%	7%	6%	6
67%	**64%**	**72%**	**TOTAL AGREE (NET)**
12%	11%	14%	7
20%	19%	22%	8
6%	5%	7%	9
29%	29%	29%	10 "STRONGLY AGREE"
4%	8%	2%	DO NOT KNOW (VOLUNTEERED)
*	1%	*	REFUSED (VOLUNTEERED)

Political/Community Involvement

Of all the things that are important to you,

2. How important is voting to you personally—extremely important, very important, somewhat important, a little important, or not important at all?

Total	Men	Women	
97%	**94%**	**97%**	**TOTAL IMPORTANT (NET)**
56%	54%	57%	EXTREMELY IMPORTANT
28%	27%	28%	VERY IMPORTANT
10%	10%	9%	SOMEWHAT IMPORTANT
3%	3%	3%	A LITTLE IMPORTANT
4%	5%	3%	NOT AT ALL IMPORTANT
*	*	*	DO NOT KNOW (VOLUNTEERED)
–	–	–	REFUSED (VOLUNTEERED)

3. *How important is it to you personally to have more women in elected public office in the United States—very important, somewhat important, not very important or not at all important?*

Total	Men	Women	
89%	**85%**	**93%**	**TOTAL IMPORTANT (NET)**
16%	10%	22%	EXTREMELY IMPORTANT
28%	25%	31%	VERY IMPORTANT
32%	37%	27%	SOMEWHAT IMPORTANT
13%	13%	13%	A LITTLE IMPORTANT
8%	11%	5%	NOT AT ALL IMPORTANT
2%	4%	1%	DO NOT KNOW (VOLUNTEERED)
*	1%	*	REFUSED (VOLUNTEERED)

4. *Which of the following words would best describe how you felt if a woman president were elected in your lifetime: (READ AND ROTATE AND ACCEPT ONE ONLY) enthusiastic, hopeful, confident, indifferent, uncertain, disgusted, worried?*

Total	Men	Women	
34%	**35%**	**33%**	**HOPEFUL**
23%	17%	29%	ENTHUSIASTIC
14%	20%	10%	INDIFFERENT
7%	7%	7%	UNCERTAIN
5%	5%	6%	SKEPTICAL
5%	3%	6%	TRIUMPHANT
5%	5%	5%	WORRIED
2%	3%	1%	OTHER (VOLUNTEERED)
3%	4%	3%	DO NOT KNOW (VOLUNTEERED)
1%	1%	*	REFUSED (VOLUNTEERED)

5. *Please complete the following statement, "The main hesitation I have in voting for a woman for president is . . ." (OPEN END)*

Total	Men	Women	
15%	**15%**	**14%**	**QUALIFICATIONS (NET)**
6%	5%	6%	QUALIFICATIONS (NONSPECIFIC)

3%	3%	3%	CREDIBLE
2%	2%	2%	CAPABLE
2%	3%	1%	EXPERIENCE
2%	1%	3%	ABILITY
1%	1%	*	KNOWS ISSUES
*	*	*	EDUCATION
8%	**8%**	**8%**	**CONCERNS WITH ATTRIBUTES (NET)**
4%	3%	4%	EMOTIONAL
2%	2%	2%	IS SHE STRONG ENOUGH
1%	1%	1%	HANDLING PRESSURE
*	*	*	INTIMIDATED BY MEN
*	1%	*	IS SHE LEVEL HEADED
*	1%	*	PROBLEMS WITH POWER
5%	**3%**	**5%**	**BIAS OF OTHERS**
2%	1%	2%	WORLD LEADERS
1%	*	1%	WOMEN ARE BIASED
1%	—	1%	MEN
1%	1%	1%	AMERICAN BIAS
*	*	1%	COLLEAGUE INCOOPERATION
*	—	*	AMERICA NOT READY
*	—	*	OTHER COUNTRIES
*	—	*	WOULD NOT BE TREATED EQUALLY AS A MAN
*	—	*	LACK OF RESPECT
4%	**5%**	**4%**	**POLITICAL (NET)**
1%	*	1%	PARTY AFFILIATION - REP
1%	2%	1%	UNPRECEDENTED
1%	1%	1%	COULDN'T WIN THE GENERAL ELECTION
*	*	—	UNKNOWN
*	—	*	PARTY AFFILIATION GENERAL
*	*	*	PRIORITIES
*	*	—	OUTCOME OF ELECTION
*	*	*	PARTY AFFILIATION - DEM
3%	**3%**	**3%**	**GENDER ROLE (NET)**
2%	1%	2%	IT'S A MAN'S JOB

*	1%	*	GENERAL RESERVATION
*	*	*	WOMEN BELONG AT HOME
*	*	*	A WOMAN COULD NOT SURVIVE
*	*	*	CARE FOR FAMILY
*	*	—	NURTURERS NOT LEADERS
*	—	*	BIBLICAL REFERENCE AGAINST
*	—	*	SAFER THAN A MAN
3%	**4%**	**2%**	**ISSUES (NET)**
*	—	*	PRESERVATION OF RIGHTS
*	—	*	ABORTION
1%	1%	1%	INTERNATIONAL RELATIONS
1%	2%	*	MILITARY ISSUES
*	*	*	TERRORISM/SECURITY
*	—	*	LOYALTY TO WOMEN'S GROUPS
2%	**2%**	**2%**	**HILLARY CLINTON (NET)**
2%	2%	2%	HER POLICIES
*	*	*	HER POLITICS
*	*	*	HER POSITIONS
1%	**1%**	**1%**	**QUALITY OF INDIVIDUAL (NET)**
*	*	*	HONESTY/DON'T TRUST THEM
*	*	*	LEADERSHIP
*	—	*	VALUES
8%	**6%**	**8%**	**MISCELLANEOUS (NET)**
3%	4%	3%	DEPENDS ON THE WOMAN
1%	1%	1%	MONTHLY CYCLE/PMS
1%	*	1%	WOULD NEVER VOTE FOR A WOMAN
1%	1%	*	NOT MANY QUALIFIED CANDIDATES
1%	—	1%	HER OWN SAFETY
*	*	*	NONE ARE RUNNING
*	—	*	ASSASSINATION
*	—	*	CONDOLEEZA RICE
*	—	*	CAN SHE DO THE JOB?
*	—	*	LACK OF TIME

44%	**46%**	**43%**	**NO HESITATION**
13%	13%	13%	DON'T KNOW

6. We hear a lot of talk about security in today's culture. What does it mean to you personally? What does it mean to you to have "security" or be "secure"? (OPEN END) (RECORD VERBATIM) (PROBE, Anything else?)

Total	Men	Women	
17%	**17%**	**18%**	**ECONOMIC (NET)**
13%	12%	13%	FINANCIAL SECURITY
3%	3%	3%	EMPLOYMENT
1%	1%	1%	RETIREDMENT
1%	1%	1%	SOCIAL SECURITY
*	*	*	ECONOMY (NONSPECIFIC)
16%	**13%**	**18%**	**SAFETY (NET)**
8%	7%	9%	FEEL SAFE
7%	6%	8%	SAFETY (NONSPECIFIC)
1%	—	1%	EVERYONE SAFE
1%	1%	1%	WHEN TRAVELING
*	*	1%	AT AIRPORTS
14%	**11%**	**16%**	**NEED/IMPORTANCE (NET)**
14%	11%	15%	IMPORTANT
*	—	*	I NEED IT
*	*	1%	MORE IMPORTANT THAN EVER
*	*	*	NEED TO DO MORE
*	*	*	NECESSITY
12%	**11%**	**12%**	**HOME AND FAMILY (NET)**
4%	5%	4%	FAMILY IS SAFE
3%	2%	4%	HOME IS SECURE
2%	2%	2%	CONFIDENT I CAN TAKE CARE OF MY FAMILY
2%	2%	3%	CHILDREN ARE SAFE
*	1%	—	NOT LOCK FRONT DOOR
*	*	*	SCHOOLS ARE SAFE
*	*	*	FAMILY VALUES

11%	**13%**	**10%**	**GOVERNMENT ACTION (NET)**
4%	5%	4%	ELIMINATE TERRORISM
2%	2%	2%	HOMELAND SECURITY
1%	*	1%	MORE NATIONAL SECURITY
1%	2%	1%	SECURE THE BORDERS
1%	*	1%	STOP IMMIGRATION
1%	1%	1%	POSTAL SECURITY
*	1%	*	STRONG MILITARY
*	1%	*	SUPPORT OUR TROOPS
*	1%	*	NO REAL PROGRESS
*	1%	*	FEDERAL GOV'T DOING WELL
*	*	*	9/11
*	—	*	ALERT CODES
*	*	*	HOPE WE'RE DOING ENOUGH
11%	**12%**	**10%**	**QUALITY OF LIFE (NET)**
6%	7%	5%	FREEDOM FROM FEAR/WORRY
1%	1%	2%	ENJOYING LIFE
1%	1%	1%	BELIEF IN THE FUTURE
1%	1%	1%	PEACE OF MIND
1%	1%	*	HAPPY
*	*	*	SLEEP AT NIGHT
*	*	*	FEELING CALM
*	*	*	HOPE
*	1%	*	COMMUNITY
*	1%	*	OVERALL WELLBEING
*	—	*	A GOOD FEELING
6%	**9%**	**5%**	**FREEDOM (NET)**
4%	5%	3%	FREEDOM (NONSPECIFIC)
1%	1%	*	PRIVACY
1%	1%	*	NOT LOSING RIGHTS FOR SECURITY
1%	1%	1%	RIGHT TO BEAR ARMS
*	*	1%	THE BILL OF RIGHTS
*	1%	*	PROTECTION FROM THE LAW/GOV'T

*	1%	*	LESS GOV'T
*	—	*	CAN WE TRUST OUR LEADERS?
5%	**5%**	**5%**	**PROTECTION (NET)**
3%	3%	2%	FROM CRIME
2%	1%	2%	PROTECTION (NONSPECIFIC)
1%	*	1%	FEEL PROTECTED
2%	**3%**	**1%**	**LESS EMPHASIS (NET)**
1%	1%	1%	I DO FEEL SECURE
1%	*	1%	NO SUCH THING
*	1%	*	WE'RE TAKING THINGS TOO FAR
*	1%	*	WE'RE ALREADY SECURE
2%	**1%**	**2%**	**SOCIAL (NET)**
2%	1%	2%	HEALTH CARE
*	—	*	EQUAL OPPORTUNITY
*	—	*	DAY CARE
*	—	*	EDUCATION
1%	**1%**	**1%**	**RELIGIOUS (NET)**
1%	1%	1%	FAITH
*	*	*	JESUS
1%	**1%**	**1%**	**FOREIGN RELATIONS (NET)**
1%	1%	*	TREAT OTHERS FAIRLY
*	1%	*	NOT MAKING ENEMIES
1%	**1%**	**1%**	**PEACE (NET)**
1%	1%	1%	PEACE NO WAR
4%	**4%**	**4%**	**MISCELLANEOUS (NET)**
2%	2%	2%	GOOD HEALTH
1%	*	1%	STABILITY
1%	1%	1%	PERSONAL RESPONSIBILITY
*	1%	—	A MINDSET
*	*	—	AMERICAN
*	—	*	CHARACTER/INTEGRITY
15%	16%	15%	DON'T KNOW

Changing the topic for a moment . . .

7. Which of the following would you most like to have more of in your life?
(ROTATE AND ACCEPT ONE RESPONSE ONLY)

Total	Men	Women	
25%	23%	27%	**PEACE**
16%	18%	13%	TIME
14%	13%	14%	LOVE
12%	14%	11%	MONEY
9%	11%	8%	LAUGHTER
7%	5%	9%	SECURITY
8%	7%	8%	COMBINATION (VOLUNTEERED)
1%	1%	1%	NONE OF THE ABOVE (VOLUNTEERED)
7%	6%	8%	ALL OF THE ABOVE (VOLUNTEERED)
*	1%	*	DON'T KNOW/REFUSED (VOLUNTEERED)

8. Which of the following describes you more accurately: "I am more willing to spend money to save some time," or "I am more willing to spend time to save some money"? (ROTATE)

Total	Men	Women	
56%	54%	59%	**MORE WILLING TO SPEND TIME TO SAVE SOME MONEY**
36%	39%	33%	MORE WILLING TO SPEND MONEY TO SAVE SOME TIME
3%	3%	4%	BOTH (VOLUNTEERED)
2%	2%	1%	NEITHER (VOLUNTEERED)
3%	2%	3%	DO NOT KNOW (VOLUNTEERED)
–	–	–	REFUSED (VOLUNTEERED)

9. And again, you personally, would you rather have more sleep or more sex? (ROTATE "SEX" AND "SLEEP") And would you say definitely or probably more sleep/ sex? I would eliminate the intensity qualifiers on this one and make it a straight "sex or sleep?" question.

Total	Men	Women	
55%	**42%**	**66%**	**TOTAL MORE SLEEP (NET)**
37%	28%	45%	DEFINITELY MORE SLEEP
18%	14%	21%	PROBABLY MORE SLEEP
31%	**44%**	**20%**	**TOTAL MORE SEX (NET)**
10%	14%	7%	PROBABLY MORE SEX
21%	30%	13%	DEFINITELY MORE SEX
7%	7%	8%	DO NOT KNOW (VOLUNTEERED)
7%	6%	7%	REFUSED (VOLUNTEERED)

10. How much control do you feel you have over your life—a great deal of control, a lot of control, some control, a little control, or no control at all?

Total	Men	Women	
96%	**95%**	**97%**	**TOTAL IN CONTROL (NET)**
39%	36%	41%	A GREAT DEAL OF CONTROL
31%	32%	31%	A LOT OF CONTROL
21%	22%	20%	SOME CONTROL
5%	5%	5%	A LITTLE CONTROL
2%	2%	3%	NO CONTROL AT ALL
1%	1%	1%	DEPENDS (VOLUNTEERED)
*	1%	*	DO NOT KNOW (VOLUNTEERED)
–	–	–	REFUSED (VOLUNTEERED)

11. Which area of your life would you say you feel the most in control of—(ROTATE) finance, education, health, career/education, safety, relationship with a spouse or significant other, relationship with children, relationship with friends, or your relationship with family members?

Total	Men	Women	
16%	**15%**	**16%**	**RELATIONSHIP WITH FAMILY MEMBERS**
13%	15%	11%	RELATIONSHIP WITH SPOUSE OR SIGNIFICANT OTHER
13%	15%	11%	FINANCES
10%	6%	14%	RELATIONSHIP WITH CHILDREN
10%	12%	8%	TIME

9%	8%	9%	CAREER/JOB
6%	6%	6%	HEALTH
4%	3%	4%	EDUCATION
4%	4%	3%	RELATIONSHIP WITH FRIENDS
12%	13%	12%	ALL OF THE ABOVE (VOLUNTEERED)
2%	1%	3%	NONE OF THE ABOVE (VOLUNTEERED)
1%	1%	1%	DO NOT KNOW (VOLUNTEERED)
1%	1%	*	REFUSED (VOLUNTEERED)

12. *Which area of your life would you say you feel the* **least** *in control of—
(ROTATE) finance, education, health, career or job, education, relationship with
a significant other, relationship with children, relationship with friends, or your
relationship with family members?*

Total	Men	Women	
25%	**23%**	**26%**	**FINANCES**
18%	19%	17%	HEALTH
16%	17%	16%	TIME
9%	10%	9%	CAREER/JOB
6%	5%	6%	RELATIONSHIP WITH FAMILY MEMBERS
5%	4%	2%	RELATIONSHIP WITH SPOUSE OR SIGNIFICANT OTHER
3%	4%	2%	EDUCATION
3%	2%	4%	RELATIONSHIP WITH CHILDREN
3%	4%	2%	RELATIONSHIP WITH FRIENDS
1%	1%	2%	ALL OF THE ABOVE (VOLUNTEERED)
7%	8%	6%	NONE OF THE ABOVE (VOLUNTEERED)
4%	4%	4%	DO NOT KNOW (VOLUNTEERED)
1%	1%	1%	REFUSED (VOLUNTEERED)

The New Aging/Generational

13. *If given the choice, would you rather* **look** *(ROTATE) younger or thinner?*

Total	Men	Women	
47%	**40%**	**53%**	**THINNER**
36%	41%	31%	YOUNGER
11%	12%	9%	NEITHER (VOLUNTEERED)

4%	4%	5%	BOTH (VOLUNTEERED)
1%	2%	1%	DO NOT KNOW (VOLUNTEERED)
1%	1%	1%	REFUSED (VOLUNTEERED)

14. *If given the choice, would you agree to shave a year off your life if you could be your ideal weight for the rest of your life?*

Total	Men	Women	
32%	30%	33%	YES
63%	**64%**	**63%**	**NO**
5%	6%	4%	DO NOT KNOW)
1%	*	1%	REFUSED (VOLUNTEERED)

15. *Thinking for a moment about women who choose to work after the age of 65, which if a popular age for retirement, what do think is their* **main** *reason for doing so? (READ AND ROTATE)*

Total	Men	Women	
28%	**25%**	**30%**	**CONTINUED FINANCIAL STABILITY**
22%	23%	21%	WANT TO STAY ACTIVE
14%	14%	14%	ENJOY WHAT THEY DO/NOT READY TO STOP
12%	10%	13%	BENEFITS SUCH AS HEALTH INSURANCE
6%	7%	6%	SOCIAL CONTACT
5%	6%	4%	INTELLECTUAL STIMULATION
3%	4%	2%	DON'T WANT TO FACE AGING AND CHANGE
3%	4%	1%	HABIT/CONSISTENCY
1%	1%	1%	ENTERED A NEW FIELD AFTER RETIREMENT
1%	1%	2%	STARTED A NEW BUSINESS AFTER RETIREMENT
1%	*	2%	OTHER (VOLUNTEERED)
3%	3%	2%	DO NOT KNOW (VOLUNTEERED)
1%	2%	1%	REFUSED (VOLUNTEERED)

Unmarried America/Marriage:

16. *Thinking for a moment about single Americans, why do you think people are or remain unmarried? (OPEN-ENDED, PRECODED LIST, ACCEPT MULTIPLE RESPONSES)*

Total	Men	Women	
31%	**28%**	**34%**	**HAVEN'T FOUND THE RIGHT PERSON**
14%	13%	15%	PERSONAL CHOICE/NEVER WANT TO BE MARRIED
8%	7%	9%	WANT INDEPENDENCE FOR A WHILE
8%	8%	8%	WANT TO SPEND TIME ON CAREER
8%	8%	8%	BAD PREVIOUS RELATIONSHIPS
8%	7%	8%	JUST NOT READY FOR SPOUSE AND/ OR CHILDREN
6%	5%	7%	WANT TO GAIN MORE FINANCIAL SECURITY FIRST
5%	5%	6%	DEMANDS OF CAREER AND JOB GET IN THE WAY
5%	5%	4%	DEMANDS OF LIFESTYLE AND OTHER GOALS GET IN THE WAY
2%	2%	2%	SAW OTHERS IN BAD RELATIONSHIPS
2%	2%	1%	GAY OR LESBIAN
1%	1%	2%	OTHER FAMILY RESPONSIBILITIES
4%	6%	3%	OTHER (VOLUNTEERED)
5%	5%	4%	ALL OF THE ABOVE (VOLUNTEERED)
1%	1%	1%	NONE OF THE ABOVE (VOLUNTEERED)
5%	5%	5%	DO NOT KNOW (VOLUNTEERED)
*	*	*	REFUSED (VOLUNTEERED)

17. Regardless of your marital status, which of the following best describes the downside, if any, to remaining single and unmarried? (READ AND ROTATE LIST, ACCEPT MULTIPLE RESPONSES)

Total	Men	Women	
25%	**24%**	**26%**	**LONELINESS OR ISOLATION**
12%	13%	11%	NOTHING/THERE IS NO DOWNSIDE
11%	13%	10%	LACK OF MEANINGFUL RELATIONSHIPS
10%	7%	13%	HANDLING ALL THE RESPONSIBILITIES ALONE
10%	11%	10%	BEING ON YOUR OWN IN DIFFICULT TIMES/WHEN OLDER
7%	7%	7%	NOT HAVING CHILDREN
6%	4%	8%	LESS FINANCIAL SECURITY
5%	5%	5%	DIFFICULTY MEETING PEOPLE LATER IN LIFE
5%	6%	4%	FEELING LIKE YOU'RE "MISSING OUT" BY NOT BEING MARRIED

3%	3%	3%	SOCIETAL PRESSURE
3%	3%	3%	PRESSURE FROM OTHER FAMILY MEMBERS
1%	1%	*	OTHER (VOLUNTEERED)
4%	4%	3%	ALL OF THE ABOVE (VOLUNTEERED)
2%	1%	3%	NONE OF THE ABOVE (VOLUNTEERED)
5%	4%	5%	DO NOT KNOW (VOLUNTEERED)
1%	1%	2%	REFUSED (VOLUNTEERED)

18. For you personally, what is the most important relationship in your life? Your relationship with . . .

Total	Men	Women	
39%	**45%**	**34%**	**SPOUSE OR SIGNIFICANT OTHER**
23%	16%	30%	CHILD
7%	6%	8%	MYSELF
6%	6%	6%	PARENT
6%	7%	5%	EXTENDED FAMILY MEMBER
4%	4%	3%	FRIEND
3%	3%	3%	BROTHER OR SISTER
2%	2%	1%	MEMBER OF THE CLERGY
1%	1%	*	PROFESSIONAL MENTOR
7%	6%	8%	OTHER (VOLUNTEERED)
2%	2%	1%	DO NOT KNOW (VOLUNTEERED)
1%	1%	1%	REFUSED (VOLUNTEERED)

Motherhood

Switching topics for the moment . . .

19. In your opinion, what are the biggest challenges facing mothers who work outside the home full-time? (OPEN-END) ANYTHING ELSE? (PROBE)

Total	Men	Women	
80%	**81%**	**81%**	**FAMILY/CHILDREN (NET)**
23%	23%	24%	TIME WITH CHILDREN
17%	15%	17%	CHILD CARE/DAY CARE/BABYSITTING

6%	9%	5%	TIME TO RAISE/CARE FOR FAMILY
6%	3%	8%	FINDING GOOD CHILD CAREGIVER
3%	4%	3%	FAMILY (NON SPECIFIC)
4%	2%	4%	QUALITY TIME WITH FAMILY
3%	3%	3%	RAISE CHILDREN WELL
2%	3%	2%	CLOSE/RELATIONSHIP WITH CHILDREN
3%	1%	3%	MISS CHILDREN'S MILESTONES
2%	3%	2%	MOTHERLY DUTIES/GOOD MOTHER
2%	2%	2%	CHILDREN (NON SPECIFIC)
1%	1%	1%	RAISE CHILDREN WITH GOOD VALUES
1%	1%	1%	RESPONSIBILITY FOR CHILDREN
1%	1%	1%	RELATIONSHIP WITH SPOUSE
1%	1%	1%	CHILD SAFETY/KNOW LOCATION
1%	1%	1%	AWAY FROM KIDS
1%	1%	1%	KNOW WHAT IS HAPPENING WITH KIDS
1%	1%	1%	LEAVING THE CHILDREN
1%	1%	1%	NOT WATCHING/GUIDING CHILDREN
*	1%	*	CORRECT CHILDREARING
*	1%	*	DISCIPLINING CHILDREN
*	*	*	BE GOOD MOTHER
*	—	*	CHILDREN NEGLECTED
*	*	*	HELP CHILDREN STUDY
*	1%	*	KIDS NOT HOME/LEAVE HOME TOO SOON
*	*	—	KIDS CALL NANNY MOM
*	*	*	MAINTAIN COHESIVE FAMILY
*	1%	—	NOT THERE FOR KIDS
*	—	*	NOT COMMITTED TO FAMILY
1%	1%	*	DISCIPLINE PROBLEMS WITH CHILDREN
25%	**20%**	**27%**	**BALANCE WORK/HOME (NET)**
11%	11%	11%	BALANCE LIFESTYLE/RESPONSIBILITIES
8%	5%	9%	TIME MANAGEMENT
5%	4%	5%	DO EVERYTHING/CONSTANTLY WORKING
1%	*	2%	TIME FOR SELF
*	*	*	CAREER

7%	**9%**	**7%**	**WORK/CAREER (NET)**
7%	8%	7%	JOB/CAREER/WORK
*	1%	*	COMPETE WITH MEN IN WORKFORCE
*	—	*	JOB RETENTION
*	—	*	LACK OF TRAINING/EDUCATION
*	*	—	RESPECT FROM EMPLOYER
*	*	*	WORKING FULL-TIME
*	—	*	GET THINGS DONE
*	1%	*	MAINTAIN SANITY
5%	**8%**	**5%**	**FINANCES/AFFORDABILITY (NET)**
3%	5%	2%	FINANCES/FINANCIAL PROBLEMS
1%	1%	1%	AFFORDABLE/COST OF DAYCARE
1%	1%	1%	MONEY
*	*	1%	HUSBAND DOES NOT PAY CHILD SUPPORT
*	*	*	MAKE ENOUGH TO SUPPORT FAMILY
*	1%	*	SALARY/GOOD PAY
4%	**1%**	**4%**	**NEGATIVE ATTRIBUTES (NET)**
1%	1%	1%	TIRED/EXHAUSTED
1%	*	1%	GUILT/FEELING GUILTY
1%	*	1%	PRESSURED
1%	*	1%	STRESSED
*	—	*	IRRESPONSIBLE
*	—	*	DOUBT
*	*	*	LACK OF ENERGY
*	—	*	IN OWN WORLD/OUT-OF-TOUCH
*	—	*	RUSHED
*	*	—	MISS WORK TO ATTEND KIDS' APPOINTMENTS
*	*	*	TIME DEMANDS
*	*	—	REGRETS
3%	**3%**	**3%**	**HOME(NET)**
2%	1%	2%	KEEP UP WITH HOUSEWORK
1%	2%	1%	HOME (NONSPECIFIC)
*	—	*	HAPPY HOME

4:1%	3%	1%	**POSITIVE ATTRIBUTES (NET)**
1%	2%	1%	RESPONSIBILITY
*	—	*	FREE
*	—	*	INDEPENDENT
*	1%	*	SECURITY
*	*	—	BENEFITS
*	—	*	SENSE OF SELF-IDENTITY
8%	9%	7%	DON'T KNOW/NO ANSWER

20. In your opinion, what are the biggest challenges facing mothers who are at home full-time? (OPEN END) ANYTHING ELSE? (PROBE)

Total	Men	Women	
20%	17%	21%	**SOCIAL/OUTSIDE PRESSURES (NET)**
10%	9%	10%	STIMULATION/ADULT INTELLECT/WORLD
4%	3%	5%	MAINTAIN SANITY
3%	3%	3%	DO EVERYTHING AT ONCE/CONSTANT WORK
2%	1%	2%	BALANCE LIFESTYLE/RESPONSIBILITIES
1%	2%	1%	MISS CHANCE TO LIVE OUT DREAMS/POTENTIAL
1%	*	1%	PEER PRESSURE FROM WORKING MOMS
1%	*	1%	HOME IS HARDER JOB/TWICE THE WORK
*	—	*	DETRACTS FROM OTHER INTERESTS
*	—	*	DEMANDS BECAUSE EXPECTED TO HAVE FREE TIME
*	—	*	SOCIETAL PRESSURE
*	*	*	HOME ROUTINE/RUT
*	*	—	LACK OF DIVERSITY
*	—	*	FAMILY DEPENDS ON HER
*	1%	*	CONTROL/MANAGEMENT
19%	21%	19%	**CHILDREN/FAMILY LIFE (NET)**
5%	4%	5%	TIME WITH CHILDREN
3%	3%	3%	KEEP UP WITH HOUSEWORK
2%	1%	2%	CHILDREN (NONSPECIFIC)
2%	2%	2%	NEED HELP/SUPPORT
1%	1%	1%	RELATIONSHIP WITH SPOUSE
1%	1%	1%	DISCIPLINING CHILDREN

1%	1%	1%	FAMILY (NONSPECIFIC)
1%	1%	1%	MOTHERLY DUTIES/GOOD MOTHER
1%	1%	1%	RAISE CHILDREN WELL
1%	1%	1%	RESPONSIBILITY FOR CHILDREN
1%	*	1%	CHILD CARE/DAY CARE/BABYSITTING
*	1%	*	CORRECT CHILDREARING
*	1%	*	FIND GOOD CHILD CAREGIVER
*	1%	*	LEAVING THE CHILDREN
*	1%	*	MAINTAIN COHESIVE FAMILY
*	1%	*	TIME TO RAISE FAMILY
*	*	*	AWAY FROM KIDS
*	–	*	CHILD SAFETY/KNOW LOCATION
*	*	–	DRUG ABUSE
*	*	*	HOME (NONSPECIFIC)
*	*	–	SACRIFICE HOME APPEARANCE
*	–	*	KIDS NOT HOME/LEAVE HOME TOO SOON
*	*	*	GET ALONG WITH SPOUSE
*	*	*	PROBLEMS WITH HUSBAND
*	–	*	MISS CHILDHOOD MILESTONES
*	*	–	MORE SUPERVISION
*	–	*	NOT ENJOY CHILDREN
*	–	*	NO FATHER/FATHER FIGURE
*	*	–	NOT WATCH/GUIDE CHILDREN
*	*	*	QUALITY TIME
*	*	*	RAISE CHILDREN WITH GOOD VALUES/PRINCIPLES
*	–	*	CLOSE/RELATIONSHIP WITH CHILDREN
*	*	*	SPOIL/SHELTER CHILDREN
*	*	*	TAKE CARE TO RAISE FAMILY
*	*	*	UNDISCIPLINED/REBELLIOUS KIDS
*	–	*	SCHOOL PROBLEMS
18%	**16%**	**20%**	**SELF-IMAGE/SOCIAL LIFE (NET)**
12%	10%	13%	LACK OF SOCIAL LIFE OUTSIDE HOME
4%	4%	4%	DISRESPECT FOR HOMEMAKERS/LACK OF RECOGNITION

2%	2%	2%	SENSE OF SELF/IDENTITY
*	–	1%	CONSTANT FEELING OF INADEQUACY
*	–	*	LOSE YOUR IDENTITY
*	–	*	IN OWN WORLD/OUT-OF-TOUCH
16%	**14%**	**18%**	**FINANCIAL (NET)**
14%	13%	15%	FINANCES/FINANCIAL PROBLEMS
2%	1%	3%	MONEY
11%	**11%**	**11%**	**NEGATIVE CHARACTERISTICS (NET)**
6%	8%	5%	BORED
2%	1%	3%	ISOLATED
1%	1%	1%	STRESSED
1%	*	1%	LONELY
1%	–	1%	PRESSURED
*	1%	*	UNCHALLENGED
*	*	*	FRUSTRATED
*	*	*	DEPRESSED
*	*	*	AGGREVATED
*	–	*	LACK INDEPENDENCE
*	*	–	UNSAFE
*	–	*	OVERWHELMED/FRAZZLED
*	*	*	BURNT OUT
*	–	*	NOT GOOD
*	*	*	INSECURE
*	–	*	INDEPENDENT
*	*	*	LAZY
8%	**5%**	**8%**	**TIME MANAGEMENT (NET)**
5%	3%	5%	TIME FOR SELF/FREE OR PERSONAL TIME
1%	1%	1%	TIME (NONSPECIFIC)
1%	*	1%	TIME MANAGEMENT
1%	1%	1%	TOO MUCH WORK
*	*	*	LOT OF FREE TIME/STAY BUSY
*	*	*	KEEP BUSY
*	–	*	LESS/NO TIME WITH FRIENDS

4%	**5%**	**4%**	**EMPLOYMENT (NET)**
1%	1%	1%	LACK OF WORK EXPERIENCE
1%	1%	1%	MISS CAREER
1%	1%	*	JOB/CAREER/WORK
*	–	*	ANOTHER CAREER
*	*	*	FIND A GOOD JOB
*	*	*	INSURANCE/HEALTH INSURANCE
*	–	*	LACK OF TRAINING
*	*	*	MISS WORKFORCE NETWORK
*	*	*	NO JOB LATER IN LIFE/UPON SPOUSE'S DEATH
4:*	**1%**	*	**POSITIVE CHARACTERISTICS (NET)**
*	1%	–	PEACEFUL
*	–	*	PATIENCE
*	–	*	HAPPY/HAPPINESS
*	*	–	EXCITEMENT
*	*	*	RESPONSIBILITY
*	*	*	**MISCELLANEOUS (NET)**
*	*	–	EAT/GET FAT
*	*	*	SOAP OPERAS/TV
*	*	*	PHYSICAL HEALTH/CAN'T WORK OUT
*	*	–	DEALING WITH REALITY
*	–	*	LACK OF COMMUNICATION
15%	17%	15%	DON'T KNOW

21. *Please tell me if you agree or disagree with the following statement, "It is important for a child to have a mother and father in the home." And would you say you strongly or somewhat agree/disagree?*

Total	Men	Women	
89%	**94%**	**86%**	**TOTAL AGREE (NET)**
75%	80%	71%	STRONGLY AGREE
14%	14%	15%	SOMEWHAT AGREE
7%	**4%**	**11%**	**TOTAL DISAGREE (NET)**
5%	3%	7%	SOMEWHAT DISAGREE

2%	1%	4%	STRONGLY DISAGREE
2%	1%	3%	DEPENDS/DO NOT KNOW (VOLUNTEERED)
*	*	*	REFUSED (VOLUNTEERED)

22. In your view, which word best describes a single woman who decides to have a child, either naturally or by adoption. (READ AND ROTATE LIST)

Total	Men	Women	
27%	24%	30%	**COURAGEOUS**
26%	26%	26%	LOVING
10%	11%	10%	FINANCIALLY SECURE
9%	9%	9%	NAÏVE
8%	8%	8%	MATURE
8%	9%	7%	SELFISH
4%	6%	2%	IMMATURE
3%	3%	2%	OTHER (VOLUNTEERED)
5%	5%	6%	DO NOT KNOW (VOLUNTEERED)
*	1%	*	REFUSED (VOLUNTEERED)

23. In your view, which word best describes a single woman who decides to buy a home on her own? (READ AND ROTATE LIST)

Total	Men	Women	
47%	42%	52%	**A WISE INVESTOR**
25%	24%	25%	FINANCIALLY SECURE
12%	13%	11%	COURAGEOUS
11%	14%	9%	MATURE
1%	2%	1%	NAÏVE
1%	1%	1%	IMMATURE
1%	1%	1%	SELFISH
1%	1%	1%	OTHER (VOLUNTEERED) (SPECIFY) _____
1%	1%	1%	DO NOT KNOW (VOLUNTEERED)
*	1%	*	REFUSED (VOLUNTEERED)

24. Would you say the quality of your family life is better or worse than that of your parents when they were your age?

Total	Men	Women	
81%	**80%**	**82%**	**TOTAL BETTER (NET)**
50%	49%	51%	MUCH BETTER
31%	31%	31%	SOMEWHAT BETTER
11%	**11%**	**10%**	**TOTAL WORSE (NET)**
7%	7%	6%	SOMEWHAT WORSE
4%	4%	4%	MUCH WORSE
8%	8%	8%	DO NOT KNOW (VOLUNTEERED)
1%	1%	1%	REFUSED (VOLUNTEERED)

25. *Would you say the quality of your* work life *is better or worse than that of your parents when they were your age?*

Total	Men	Women	
74%	**72%**	**77%**	**TOTAL BETTER (NET)**
49%	46%	52%	MUCH BETTER
25%	26%	25%	SOMEWHAT BETTER
15%	**17%**	**11%**	**TOTAL WORSE (NET)**
10%	11%	8%	SOMEWHAT WORSE
5%	6%	3%	MUCH WORSE
10%	8%	10%	DO NOT KNOW (VOLUNTEERED)
1%	2%	1%	REFUSED (VOLUNTEERED)

26. *Do you own or are you a partial owner of a small business, or are you self-employed or earn self-employment income?*

Total	Men	Women	
22%	**26%**	**20%**	**TOTAL SMALL BUSINESS OWNER (NET)**
8%	10%	6%	YES, OWNER
4%	3%	4%	YES, PARTIAL OWNER
11%	13%	10%	YES, SELF-EMPLOYED OR SELF-EMPLOYMENT INCOME
76%	72%	80%	NO
1%	1%	1%	DO NOT KNOW (VOLUNTEERED)
1%	1%	1%	REFUSED (VOLUNTEERED)

27a. (Asked of those who answered "YES" to Q26) What prompted you to go into business for yourself? (OPEN-ENDED, RECORD VERBATIM)

Total	Men	Women	
22%	**24%**	**20%**	**FINANCIAL SECURITY (NET)**
8%	10%	5%	BETTER FINANCIALLY
4%	5%	4%	EXTRA INCOME
4%	4%	4%	FINANCIAL SECURITY
2%	2%	3%	NEED MONEY
2%	1%	3%	GOOD BUSINESS OPPORTUNITY
1%	2%	–	TAX ADVANTAGE
1%	–	1%	AN INVESTMENT
18%	**17%**	**20%**	**FLEXIBILITY/MORE TIME (NET)**
5%	5%	6%	FREEDOM
4%	4%	4%	MORE TIME FOR FAMILY/CHILDREN
3%	2%	4%	MORE TIME TO DO OTHER THINGS
2%	2%	2%	OWN SCHEDULE
1%	1%	1%	CAN BE HOME WITH CHILDREN
1%	–	2%	FLEXIBILITY
1%	1%	1%	IN SCHOOL
1%	2%	–	LESS SUPERVISION
18%	**20%**	**15%**	**INDEPENDENCE (NET)**
10%	13%	7%	INDEPENDENCE/WANTED TO BE BOSS
4%	3%	5%	BEING IN MORE CONTROL
2%	2%	2%	DON'T HAVE TO WORRY ABOUT OTHERS
2%	2%	1%	I CAN DO BETTER ON MY OWN
10%	**11%**	**9%**	**CHANGE/NEW CAREER (NET)**
3%	4%	3%	OPPORTUNITY IN FIELD I WAS INTERESTED IN
2%	2%	2%	LACK OF GOOD JOBS
2%	2%	1%	DON'T LIKE CORPORATE LIFE
1%	1%	1%	SECOND CAREER
1%	2%	1%	LOVE MY CAREER
1%	–	1%	TRY SOMETHING NEW
1%	1%	2%	PERSONAL SKILLS

8%	**6%**	**10%**	**RIGHT TIME (NET)**
7%	4%	9%	ENCOURAGED BY FAMILY
1%	2%	*	RETIREMENT
*	–	1%	APPROACHING MIDDLE AGE
6%	**6%**	**7%**	**CHARACTERISTICS (NET)**
3%	5%	3%	DESIRE
2%	1%	3%	CREATIVITY
1%	–	1%	CHALLENGING
6%	**7%**	**6%**	**CIRCUMSTANCE (NET)**
5%	6%	5%	PRE-EXISTING FAMILY BUSINESS/HUSBAND'S FIRM
1%	1%	1%	JUST FELL INTO IT
3%	**3%**	**3%**	**MISCELLANEOUS (NET)**
1%	2%	1%	INSECURITY
1%	–	1%	CHANCE TO MEET PEOPLE
1%	–	1%	CURIOUS
*	1%	–	BETTER TO BE SELF EMPLOYED
11%	9%	12%	DON'T KNOW

27b. *(Asked to those who said "NO" to Q26) Regardless of your current employment status, if given the choice where money was not an object, would you rather stay in the job you are in or start your own business?*

Total	Men	Women	
48%	**51%**	**46%**	**OPEN A SMALL BUSINESS**
38%	35%	41%	STAY IN CURRENT JOB
9%	10%	8%	NEITHER (VOLUNTEERED)
4%	3%	5%	DO NOT KNOW (VOLUNTEERED)
*	–	1%	REFUSED (VOLUNTEERED)

28. *Regardless of whether or not you own your own business or are self-employed, which of the following do you see as the greatest* **challenge** *to starting a business?* *(ACCEPT ONE RESPONSE, READ AND ROTATE RESPONSES)*

Total	Men	Women	
27%	27%	27%	**FINDING FUNDING FOR THE BUSINESS**
16%	16%	15%	FEAR OF FAILURE OR THE UNKNOWN/RISKY DECISION
13%	10%	15%	HAVING NO PAYCHECK OR BENEFITS FOR A WHILE
8%	9%	8%	FINDING CLIENTS
7%	7%	7%	DEVOTING TIME AND ENERGY
7%	8%	6%	FINDING ADEQUATE EMPLOYEES
4%	5%	4%	ENSURING COMPLIANCE WITH AREA LAWS AND CODES
2%	2%	2%	GETTING TECHNICAL ASSISTANCE
1%	1%	1%	ZONING REGULATIONS
1%	*	1%	GENDER OR RACIAL DISCRIMINATION
1%	1%	2%	OTHER (VOLUNTEERED)
3%	4%	2%	COMBINATION (VOLUNTEERED)
4%	3%	4%	ALL OF THE ABOVE (VOLUNTEERED)
1%	1%	1%	NONE OF THE ABOVE (VOLUNTEERED)
3%	3%	3%	DO NOT KNOW (VOLUNTEERED)
1%	1%	1%	REFUSED (VOLUNTEERED)

29. *Regardless of whether or not you own your own business or are self-employed, which of the following do you see as the greatest* benefit *of starting a business?* *(READ AND ROTATE LIST)*

Total	Men	Women	
27%	27%	27%	**BEING YOUR OWN BOSS**
13%	12%	15%	FLEXIBILITY IN WORK SCHEDULE
13%	13%	13%	FREEDOM
10%	10%	10%	CREATIVITY AND EXPRESSING YOURSELF
9%	9%	9%	ENJOYING YOUR WORKDAY MORE
7%	8%	6%	MAKING MORE MONEY
4%	5%	3%	CONTROL OVER WHO YOU WORK WITH
3%	3%	3%	GREATER ABILITY TO ADVANCE
2%	2%	2%	CONTROL OVER HEALTH CARE COVERAGE
1%	1%	1%	OTHER (VOLUNTEERED)
2%	1%	2%	COMBINATION (VOLUNTEERED)

5%	5%	5%	ALL OF THE ABOVE (VOLUNTEERED)
1%	2%	1%	NONE OF THE ABOVE (VOLUNTEERED)
2%	2%	2%	DO NOT KNOW (VOLUNTEERED)
1%	1%	1%	REFUSED (VOLUNTEERED)

30. To the best of your knowledge, which of the following would be the biggest lifestyle benefit of working for a woman-owned business? (READ AND ROTATE LIST)

Total	Men	Women	
12%	13%	11%	**TIME OFF FOR IMPORTANT FAMILY OBLIGATIONS**
11%	6%	16%	WOMEN UNDERSTAND WOMEN BETTER
11%	9%	13%	ROLE MODEL OF WOMEN'S LEADERSHIP
11%	12%	10%	MORE RESPECT FOR FEMALE EMPLOYEES
10%	9%	11%	FLEXIBLE HOURS
8%	7%	9%	CHILD-CARE BENEFITS
7%	7%	7%	MORE FOCUS ON COLLABORATION AND PERSONAL RELATIONSHIPS
*	*	*	OTHER (VOLUNTEERED)
2%	2%	3%	COMBINATION (VOLUNTEERED)
2%	1%	4%	ALL OF THE ABOVE (VOLUNTEERED)
10%	13%	8%	NONE OF THE ABOVE (VOLUNTEERED)
12%	17%	7%	DO NOT KNOW (VOLUNTEERED)
3%	4%	2%	REFUSED (VOLUNTEERED)

31. Regardless of your personal experiences, which of the following best describes why there are few women in top management jobs? (READ AND ROTATE)

Total	Men	Women	
23%	26%	21%	**GENDER DISCRIMINATION IN PROMOTIONS**
21%	17%	24%	MANAGEMENT ROLES PROVIDE LESS FLEXIBILITY FOR WOMEN WITH FAMILIES
17%	17%	17%	EXCLUSION FOR WHAT IS REFERRED TO AS "THE OLD BOYS' NETWORK"
11%	8%	14%	WOMEN ARE THOUGHT TO BE LESS EFFECTIVE IN MANAGEMENT ROLES

11%	13%	9%	MEN ARE MORE AGGRESSIVE IN THEIR CAREER PATHS
4%	4%	4%	WOMEN ARE LESS INTERESTED IN MANAGEMENT ROLES
1%	2%	1%	OTHER (VOLUNTEERED) (SPECIFY) ___
9%	9%	9%	DO NOT KNOW (VOLUNTEERED)
2%	3%	1%	REFUSED (VOLUNTEERED)

32. Generally speaking, what would be your ideal work situation?

Total	Men	Women	
52%	47%	56%	A JOB WITH A LOT OF SECURITY, BUT LITTLE OPPORTUNITY FOR ADVANCEMENT
40%	**46%**	**35%**	**A JOB WITH A LOT OF OPPORTUNITY FOR ADVANCEMENT, BUT LITTLE JOB SECURITY**
6%	**6%**	**7%**	**DO NOT KNOW (VOLUNTEERED)**
1%	**1%**	**2%**	**REFUSED (VOLUNTEERED)**

33. Would you consider your current employment situation to be more of a job or your desired career? (ROTATE)

Total	Men	Women	
44%	**49%**	**39%**	**MY DESIRED CAREER**
34%	32%	36%	MORE OF A JOB
7%	6%	8%	DO NOT WORK OUTSIDE THE HOME (VOLUNTEERED)
2%	1%	2%	BOTH (VOLUNTEERED)
8%	7%	10%	NEITHER (VOLUNTEERED)
3%	2%	4%	DO NOT KNOW (VOLUNTEERED)
1%	2%	1%	REFUSED (VOLUNTEERED)

34. Thinking about your own personal employment experiences, what sacrifices have you made or are willing to make in order to reach the top of your field? (READ AND ROTATE, ACCEPT MULTIPLE RESPONSES)

Total	Men	Women	
27%	21%	32%	**NONE OF THE ABOVE/I WOULD NOT SACRIFICE ANYTHING**

23%	26%	20%	WORK LONG HOURS AND WEEKENDS
14%	13%	15%	HAVE MORE STRESS AND RESPONSIBILITY
12%	11%	12%	SPEND LESS TIME WITH FAMILY AND LOVED ONES
6%	7%	6%	INCREASE WORK TRAVEL
5%	5%	4%	DELAY MARRIAGE
5%	5%	5%	DELAY PARENTHOOD
5%	6%	4%	LOSE TOUCH WITH OLD FRIENDS
3%	4%	6%	OTHER (VOLUNTEERED)
5%	5%	6%	DO NOT KNOW (VOLUNTEERED)
3%	2%	3%	REFUSED (VOLUNTEERED)

35. Thinking about women working or trying to work in fields where women have not been traditionally, which of the following do you think represents the greatest barrier to a woman's success in a nontraditional field?

Total	Men	Women	
24%	26%	22%	**STEREOTYPICAL ATTITUDES**
15%	14%	16%	LACK OF SUPPORT FROM SUPERIORS
11%	9%	13%	LACK OF SUPPORT FROM COWORKERS
10%	11%	10%	HER OWN FEARS OR SHORTCOMINGS
8%	7%	8%	HABIT/TRADITION
6%	6%	7%	FEELINGS OF ISOLATION OR NOT BELONGING
6%	6%	6%	LACK OF ROLE MODELS
4%	5%	4%	LACK OF SUPPORT FROM CUSTOMERS AND CLIENTS
3%	3%	4%	TOOLS OR EQUIPMENT NOT ADAPTED FOR USE BY A WOMAN
1%	2%	1%	OTHER (VOLUNTEERED)
8%	9%	7%	DO NOT KNOW (VOLUNTEERED)
3%	3%	2%	REFUSED (VOLUNTEERED)

36. Which of these statements do you agree with more? (READ AND ROTATE)

Statement A. I'd prefer a job with regular hours where I have time for my family and/or my leisure time interests, even if this means I'll make less money.

Statement B. I'd prefer a job with a good income even if this means I have to work longer hours and therefore have less time for my family and/or my leisure time interests.

And would you say that you strongly or somewhat agree with statement A/B?

Total	Men	Women	
77%	**71%**	**83%**	**TOTAL AGREE STATEMENT A (NET)**
64%	56%	71%	STRONGLY AGREE STATEMENT A
13%	15%	12%	SOMEWHAT AGREE STATEMENT A
20%	**26%**	**14%**	**TOTAL AGREE STATEMENT B (NET)**
13%	18%	8%	SOMEWHAT AGREE STATEMENT B
7%	8%	6%	STRONGLY AGREE STATEMENT B
2%	3%	2%	DO NOT KNOW (VOLUNTEEZRED)
1%	1%	2%	REFUSED (VOLUNTEERED)

37. What do you think is the biggest problem facing women at work today? (OPEN END, PRECODED LIST)

Total	Men	Women	
36%	**34%**	**37%**	**COMBINING WORK AND FAMILY**
15%	12%	17%	RECEIVING EQUAL PAY FOR EQUAL WORK
11%	12%	9%	DISCRIMINATION IN HIRING AND PROMOTIONS
9%	9%	9%	LACK OF AFFORDABLE, QUALITY CHILD CARE
5%	5%	5%	STRESS GENERALLY
4%	6%	3%	SEXUAL HARASSMENT
4%	4%	4%	LOW PAY AND WAGES
2%	1%	2%	NOT ENOUGH OPPORTUNITIES FOR EDUCATION AND TRAINING
2%	2%	1%	LACK OF JOB SECURITY
1%	1%	1%	POOR HEALTH CARE BENEFITS
1%	*	1%	POOR RETIREMENT BENEFITS
4%	4%	4%	OTHER (VOLUNTEERED)
6%	7%	6%	DO NOT KNOW (VOLUNTEERED)
1%	2%	1%	REFUSED (VOLUNTEERED)

38. Thinking about your ideal job, would you prefer to have greater security or have greater flexibility? (ROTATE)

Total	Men	Women	
51%	**51%**	**51%**	**GREATER FLEXIBILITY**
45%	45%	45%	GREATER SECURITY
3%	3%	3%	DO NOT KNOW (VOLUNTEERED)
1%	1%	1%	REFUSED (DOT READ)

39. If you had the choice, would you prefer to work full-time, part-time, or would you prefer to not work at all?

Total	Men	Women	
41%	**50%**	**32%**	**WORK FULL-TIME**
30%	23%	37%	WORK PART-TIME
26%	24%	28%	NOT WORK AT ALL
1%	1%	1%	DO NOT KNOW (VOLUNTEERED)
1%	1%	1%	REFUSED (VOLUNTEERED)

Demographics

40. What is your age, please? (CODE RESPONSE)

Total	Men	Women	
10%	9%	11%	18–24
9%	7%	10%	25–29
9%	10%	7%	30–34
9%	10%	9%	35–39
10%	10%	10%	40–44
9%	10	9%	45–49
10%	11%	10%	50–54
14%	14%	14%	55–64
9%	9%	9%	65–74
8%	7%	8%	75+
3%	3%	3%	REFUSED (VOLUNTEERED)

41. *In politics today, do you consider yourself to be a Republican, Independent, or Democrat? (ROTATE)*

Total	Men	Women	
36%	27%	35%	**TOTAL REPUBLICAN (NET)**
20%	19%	21%	STRONG REPUBLICAN
11%	12%	10%	NOT-SO-STRONG REPUBLICAN
5%	6%	4%	INDEPENDENT-LEANING REPUBLICAN
16%	18%	15%	INDEPENDENT
38%	35%	40%	**TOTAL DEMOCRAT (NET)**
7%	7%	7%	INDEPENDENT-LEANING DEMOCRAT
10%	10%	10%	NOT-SO-STRONG DEMOCRAT
21%	18%	23%	STRONG DEMOCRAT
1%	1%	1%	OTHER _____ (VOLUNTEERED)
10%	10%	10%	DON'T KNOW/REFUSED (VOLUNTEERED)

42. *Thinking for a moment about your social, economic, and political views, do you generally consider yourself to be conservative or liberal?*

Total	Men	Women	
42%	43%	42%	**TOTAL CONSERVATIVE (NET)**
21%	23%	20%	VERY CONSERVATIVE
21%	20%	22%	SOMEWHAT CONSERVATIVE
20%	21%	19%	MODERATE
29%	27%	30%	**TOTAL LIBERAL (NET)**
17%	15%	19%	SOMEWHAT LIBERAL
12%	12%	11%	VERY LIBERAL
*	1%	*	OTHER (VOLUNTEERED)
3%	3%	4%	DON'T KNOW (VOLUNTEERED)
4%	5%	4%	REFUSED (VOLUNTEERED)

43. *Are you currently . . . (CODE "ENGAGED" AS "SINGLE") (CODE "LIVING WITH SIGNIFICANT OTHER" AS "SINGLE")*

Total	Men	Women	
65%	58%	52%	MARRIED
24%	23%	24%	SINGLE
9%	9%	9%	DIVORCED
1%	1%	2%	SEPARATED
8%	5%	9%	WIDOWED
3%	3%	3%	REFUSED (VOLUNTEERED)

44. What is the last grade of formal education you completed?

Total	Men	Women	
6%	6%	7%	LESS THAN HIGH SCHOOL
25%	24%	26%	HIGH SCHOOL GRADUATE
28%	29%	28%	SOME COLLEGE/VOCATIONAL SCHOOL
24%	24%	24%	COLLEGE GRADUATE
13%	14%	12%	POSTGRADUATE
3%	4%	3%	DON'T KNOW/REFUSED (VOLUNTEERED)

45. Which of the following media sources do you consider your primary source of news and information? Would it be . . . ?

Total	Men	Women	
22%	21%	23%	A LOCAL NEWSPAPER
4%	5%	3%	A NATIONAL NEWSPAPER SUCH AS *USA TODAY*
21%	16%	25%	YOUR LOCAL EVENING TV NEWS
16%	17%	15%	CABLE TELEVISION NEWS CHANNELS
8%	8%	7%	NATIONAL NETWORK EVENING NEWS
9%	11%	8%	RADIO
9%	10%	8%	INTERNET
7%	7%	6%	ALL (VOLUNTEERED)
*	*	*	NONE (VOLUNTEERED)
1%	1%	*	DON'T KNOW (VOLUNTEERED)
3%	4%	3%	REFUSED (VOLUNTEERED)

46. Do you have any children? (IF YES: HOW MANY?)

Total	Men	Women	
71%	**68%**	**74%**	**TOTAL WITH CHILDREN (NET)**
16%	18%	14%	YES, 1
27%	24%	30%	YES, 2
28%	26%	30%	YES, 3 OR MORE
25%	29%	22%	NO CHILDREN
3%	3%	3%	REFUSED (VOLUNTEERED)

47. How likely are you to have children in the next five years?

Total	Men	Women	
20%	**23%**	**18%**	**TOTAL LIKELY (NET)**
10%	12%	9%	VERY LIKELY
5%	6%	5%	SOMEWHAT LIKELY
5%	5%	4%	JUST A LITTLE BIT LIKELY
72%	69%	75%	NOT AT ALL LIKELY
4%	6%	3%	DON'T KNOW (VOLUNTEERED)
3%	3%	3%	REFUSED (VOLUNTEERED)

48. Do you have any grandchildren? (IF YES: HOW MANY?)

Total	Men	Women	
35%	**33%**	**35%**	**TOTAL GRANDCHILDREN (NET)**
7%	7%	7%	YES, 1
7%	7%	6%	YES, 2
21%	19%	22%	YES, 3 OR MORE
62%	63%	62%	NO
3%	4%	3%	REFUSED (VOLUNTEERED)

49. Would you describe your racial or ethnic background as:

Total	Men	Women	
76%	76%	76%	WHITE/CAUCASIAN
11%	10%	12%	BLACK/AFRICAN AMERICAN
6%	6%	6%	HISPANIC/LATINO

1%	2%	1%	ASIAN
*	*	*	MIDDLE EASTERN
2%	2%	2%	NATIVE AMERICAN
1%	1%	1%	OTHER (VOLUNTEERED)
3%	4%	3%	DON'T KNOW/REFUSED (VOLUNTEERED)

50. Are you . . . ? (READ CATEGORIES)

Total	Men	Women	
23%	22%	24%	CATHOLIC
23%	21%	25%	CHRISTIAN
30%	30%	30%	PROTESTANT
2%	3%	2%	JEWISH
3%	4%	2%	AGNOSTIC/ATHEIST
*	–	1%	MUSLIM
2%	1%	2%	MORMON
4%	4%	4%	OTHER (SPECIFY) (VOLUNTEERED)
8%	9%	6%	NONE/UNAFFILIATED (VOLUNTEERED)
5%	5%	5%	REFUSED (VOLUNTEERED)

51. (ASKED ONLY TO "PROTESTANTS" OR "CHRISTIANS") And do you consider yourself to be BORN AGAIN or EVANGELICAL?

Total	Men	Women	
N=643	N=205	N=438	
41%	35%	45%	BORN AGAIN
14%	17%	11%	EVANGELICAL
34%	37%	32%	NEITHER (VOLUNTEERED)
6%	5%	8%	DO NOT KNOW (VOLUNTEERED)
1%	1%	1%	REFUSED (VOLUNTEERED)

52. How often do you attend religious services?

Total	Men	Women	
4%	3%	4%	EVERY DAY
27%	23%	31%	A FEW TIMES PER WEEK

19%	17%	21%	A FEW TIMES PER MONTH
17%	20%	14%	A FEW TIMES PER YEAR
28%	31%	26%	SELDOM/NEVER
5%	6%	4%	DON'T KNOW/REFUSED (VOLUNTEERED)

53. How would you describe the community in which you live?

Total	Men	Women	
24%	26%	22%	URBAN
39%	41%	38%	SUBURBAN
30%	28%	32%	RURAL
3%	1%	5%	DON'T KNOW (VOLUNTEERED)
3%	3%	3%	REFUSED (VOLUNTEERED)

54. Which of the following best describes your current work status or occupation?

Total	Men	Women	
30%	29%	31%	PROFESSIONAL/EXECUTIVE/OWNER
14%	13%	15%	WHITE-COLLAR/ADMINISTRATIVE/CLERICAL
14%	19%	10%	BLUE-COLLAR/SERVICE/MANUFACTURING
7%	5%	9%	PART-TIME WORK OUTSIDE OF THE HOME
4%	1%	7%	STAY-AT-HOME/DO NOT WORK
4%	3%	4%	UNEMPLOYED
3%	4%	3%	STUDENT
18%	21%	17%	RETIRED
2%	2%	1%	OTHER___(RECORD VERBATIM-VOLUNTEERED)
1%	*	1%	NOT SURE (VOLUNTEERED)
3%	4%	3%	REFUSED (VOLUNTEERED)

55. Do you, or does anyone in your household, belong to a labor union or teachers' association? [IF YES] And do they work in the PUBLIC SECTOR or the PRIVATE SECTOR?

Total	Men	Women	
20%	**22%**	**19%**	**YES, UNION (NET)**
16%	15%	16%	YES, PUBLIC-SECTOR UNION

4%	7%	3%	YES, PRIVATE-SECTOR UNION
68%	68%	68%	NOT A MEMBER OF A LABOR UNION
8%	6%	9%	DON'T KNOW (VOLUNTEERED)
4%	4%	4%	REFUSED (VOLUNTEERED)

(SPLIT SAMPLE)

56a. Which of the following statements most closely reflects your position on the issue of abortion? (ROTATE TOP TO BOTTOM AND BOTTOM TO TOP)

Total	Men	Women	
N=396	N=198	N=396	
55%	**54%**	**56%**	**TOTAL PRO-LIFE (NET)**
16%	14%	17%	ABORTIONS SHOULD BE PROHIBITED IN ALL CIRCUMSTANCES
15%	16%	14%	ABORTION SHOULD BE LEGAL ONLY TO SAVE THE LIFE OF THE MOTHER
24%	24%	25%	ABORTIONS SHOULD ONLY BE LEGAL IN CASES OF RAPE, INCEST, OR TO SAVE THE LIFE OF THE MOTHER
37%	**34%**	**38%**	**TOTAL PRO-CHOICE (NET)**
21%	18%	23%	ABORTIONS SHOULD BE LEGAL FOR ANY REASON, BUT NOT AFTER THE FIRST THREE MONTHS OF PREGNANCY
7%	8%	6%	ABORTIONS SHOULD BE LEGAL FOR ANY REASON, BUT NOT AFTER THE FIRST SIX MONTHS OF PREGNANCY
9%	8%	9%	ABORTIONS SHOULD BE ALLOWED AT ANY TIME DURING A WOMAN'S PREGNANCY AND FOR ANY REASON
9%	11%	6%	DON'T KNOW/REFUSED (VOLUNTEERED)

56b. I am going to read you four statements: Listen carefully. When I've finished, please tell me which of them is CLOSEST to your own view: 1, 2, 3, or 4.

Total	Men	Women	
N=405	N=203	N=405	
46%	**46%**	**55%**	**TOTAL PRO-CHOICE (NET)**
27%	29%	26%	ABORTIONS SHOULD BE LEGAL AND GENERALLY AVAILABLE AND SUBJECT TO ONLY LIMITED REGULATION
19%	17%	21%	REGULATION OF ABORTION IS NECESSARY, ALTHOUGH IT SHOULD REMAIN LEGAL IN MANY CIRCUMSTANCES
47%	**48%**	**45%**	**TOTAL PRO-LIFE (NET)**
36%	41%	32%	ABORTION SHOULD BE LEGAL ONLY IN THE MOST EXTREME CASES, SUCH AS TO SAVE THE LIFE OF THE WOMAN OR IN CASES OF RAPE AND INCEST
11%	9%	13%	ALL ABORTIONS SHOULD BE MADE ILLEGAL
6%	5%	7%	DO NOT KNOW/REFUSED (VOLUNTEERED)

57. And regarding your family's annual income, please tell me which of the following categories best describes your family's total annual household income before taxes.

Total	Men	Women	
13%	10%	17%	LESS THAN $25,000
9%	8%	9%	$25,000 TO $29,999
12%	12%	12%	$30,000 TO $39,999
10%	11%	10%	$40,000 TO $49,999
11%	15%	8%	$50,000 TO $59,999
7%	8%	7%	$60,000 TO $69,999
4%	4%	4%	$70,000 TO $79,999
4%	5%	4%	$80,000 TO $89,999
14%	17%	11%	$90,000 OR HIGHER
3%	2%	4%	DO NOT KNOW (VOLUNTEERED)
12%	10%	14%	REFUSED (VOLUNTEERED)

58. Do you currently hold any investments in stocks or stock mutual funds either directly or through a 401(k) or pension plan?

Total	Men	Women	
50%	52%	49%	YES
43%	43%	44%	NO
6%	5%	7%	DON'T KNOW/REFUSED (VOLUNTEERED)

59. Region

Total	Men	Women	
5%	6%	5%	NEW ENGLAND
13%	15%	12%	MIDATLANTIC
20%	23%	18%	EAST NORTH CENTRAL
7%	6%	7%	WEST NORTH CENTRAL
15%	12%	17%	SOUTH ATLANTIC
7%	6%	7%	EAST SOUTH CENTRAL
9%	8%	10%	WEST SOUTH CENTRAL
7%	7%	8%	MOUNTAIN
16%	18%	15%	PACIFIC

60. Gender

Total	
48%	MALE
52%	FEMALE

TWO SIDES SPEAK: THE 2004 ELECTION

The first presidential election after the 9/11 terrorist attacks was a benchmark for the future. With voters closely divided, no ringing consensus emerged about national priorities in the years to come. However, Republican pollster Kellyanne Conway, and Democratic pollster Celinda Lake, reached some intriguing conclusions in their Election Day polling, especially related to women. Their results, taken from two very different perspectives, present a fascinating picture of the American voter.

KELLYANNE CONWAY
THE POLLING COMPANY, INC.

The postelection survey was fielded on Election Day, November 2, 2004, at a computer-assisted telephone interviewing (CATI) phone facility using live callers. The survey is not an exit poll of voters as they exit the voting booth, but rather a telephone survey of actual voters. Participants were drawn from a random digit dialing sample of registered voters nationally and then screened to ensure that they did vote in the November 2, 2004, general election. Sampling controls were used to ensure that a proportional and representative number of people were interviewed from such demographic groups as age, gender, race, and ethnicity and geographic region. Rotational patterns for questions where respondents were offered choices were employed to reduce natural biases sometimes associated with first or final responses. Of the 800 actual voters randomly selected from a national sample of telephone exchanges, 51% voted to reelect President George W. Bush, 48% supported Democrat John Kerry, and 1% backed Ralph Nader, who was running as an independent. In congressional races, 48% of actual voters supported the Republican candidate, while 45% pulled the lever for the Democrat; 2% reportedly voted for "other" congressional candidates, while 3% did not vote in these elections.

A reverse gender gap was at work. "Values voters," small business owners, and security moms helped push President Bush past 50%, as a reverse gender gap emerged; "Iraq" voters heavily favor Kerry, "terrorism" voters supported Bush. According to an Election Night survey of 800 actual voters nationwide, President Bush's win on Election Day Tuesday was due in large part to his support among values voters, mothers, and those most concerned about terrorism. Senator Kerry performed well among those who cited the "situation in Iraq" as their most important issue and traditional Democratic constituencies, including Blacks and single women.

More than three-quarters of voters had made a decision for president by Labor Day. A full 78% said they knew whom they would support before September. Only 22% needed extra insurance in October and November, a sharp contrast from the 36% of the 2000 electorate who were still undecided between George W. Bush and Al Gore after the conventions that year.

Iraq and terrorism dominated voter concerns, followed by "morality and family values." A full 40% of the electorate focused most on the situation in Iraq (17%) or the war on terror (23%). Difference in candidate support emerged between these voters, as those who believe the "war on terror" is most important voted for President Bush over Senator Kerry (78% to 22%) and voters who cited "the situation in Iraq" supported Kerry over Bush (75% to 25%). Another 17% said "jobs/economy" was most important, while "morality and family values" influenced 16% of the electorate, including 29% of 25 to 34-year-olds. Health care, including Medicare and prescription drugs, was mentioned by 7% of the electorate, including 9% of seniors.

Most important issue

Voters most likely to say "the war on terror" include (total 23%) Republicans, self-identified conservatives, security moms, Bush supporters, 35- to 44-year-olds, gun owners.

Voters most likely to say "the situation in Iraq" include (total 17%) self-identified liberals, Democrats, 45- to 54-year-olds.

Voters most likely to say "jobs/ the economy" include (total 17%) Black voters, Democrats, Self-identified liberals, union households, unmarried adults.

Voters most likely to say "morality/family values" are most important, include (net 16%) Republicans, Self-identified conservatives, 25- to 34-year-olds, Southerners, gun owners, married adults.

Voters most likely to say "Health care/ Medicare/Prescription Drugs" include (net 7%) Seniors aged 65 and older, Democrats, and unmarried women between the ages of 18 and 34.

Congressional Vote. In the race for the U.S. Congress, American voters supported the Republican candidate over the Democrat 48% to 45%. Men were more likely than women to endorse Republican congressional candidates (51% to 45%), while women favored Democrats by a similar margin as compared to men (47% to 42%). Gun owners were more likely to support the Republican congressional candidates over the Democrat by more than 2 to 1 (63% to 29%). Labor union members were more likely to back Democrats over Republicans for Congress, but only by an 11 point margin (52% to 41%).

**Religious faith played a sole. The religious faith of the two presi-
dential candidates had a measurable impact on the election results,
particularly among those who supported President Bush. Let
Freedom Ring,** a 527Group, commissioned the polling company, inc.
to ask voters nationwide to rate, on a 1-to-5 scale, the relative importance of the religious faith of the man they chose for president in making
their decision to do so. When considering both George W. Bush and
John Kerry, there are some clear similarities among those who feel that
the religious faith of the candidate is a very important part of the deci-
sion-making process. Among those who cast a ballot for George W.
Bush, over one-half (52%) reported that his religious faith was "very important" in their presidential selection, a figure that was 3.5 times
greater than the number (15%) of John Kerry voters that said the same
about the senator's faith. Two-fifths (40%) of John Kerry supporters acknowledged that religious faith was a nonissue in their consideration for
president, stating that it was "not at all important" in their decision to
vote for him. In contrast, a scant 8% of those who voted for Bush said
that the president's faith mattered not to them. Bush supporters that
were more likely to cite religious faith as being "very important" in their
decision to vote for the president include: Those with household income
of $30,000 a year or lower, pro-life voters, people living in the south-
central regime, those who attend religious services weekly.

Interestingly, among Kerry voters, Blacks and Hispanics were much
more likely than whites to state the senator's religious faith as being
"very important" in their decision to vote for him. Other Kerry voters
who were more likely to cite his religious faith as being "very important"
in their decision to vote for him included: Those who attend weekly services, pro-life voters, those with household income of $30,000 a year or
lower. Only 17% of Catholics who voted for the senator stated that his
religiosity was a "very important" factor in giving him their support.

Morality Matters. A series of questions were added to the postelection
survey by American Values, a nonprofit organization, to discern the extent to which, if at all, matters of morality and moral character influenced the national electorate. With so much riding on the 2004

presidential election, voters sent a clear message: the moral direction of this country is slipping. Nearly 6 in 10 respondents (59%) indicated they felt the country's moral standards and values had "gone off on the wrong track," compared to 31% who felt the country was "headed in the right direction" with respect to its moral compass, marking an almost 2-to-1 differential. Bush voters were nearly twice as likely as Kerry voters to express confidence in the country's moral direction (41% vs. 21%).

While concern for the country's overall moral direction was shared by a majority of the general voting population, the value placed on the moral character and values of the individual presidential candidates was not spread evenly across the electorate. Large majorities of supporters of each candidate rated his "values" of high importance (90% for Bush, 74% for Kerry). However, among Bush voters the intensity was 25 points more palpable, with 72% of Bush backers rating his character as a "very important" factor, compared to just 47% of Kerry voters who said the same.

The Political Currency of Traditional Marriage. We asked a series of questions regarding same-sex marriage. Despite the claim that Mr. Bush and Mr. Kerry are of a single mind on the matter of same-sex marriage, voters deciphered clear differences between the two men on this critical issue in 2004. When voters were asked to indicate which statement regarding same-sex marriage was closest to the position of the candidate they endorsed, two-thirds of those surveyed indicated a clear understanding of the Kerry position. The president had made clear that he opposed same-sex marriage and supported a constitutional amendment protected traditional marriage as being between one man and one woman. However, the president's position on civil unions was a bit less obvious, perhaps fueled in part by his claim in the waning days of the campaign that he would be open to its possibility. The Kerry team, on the other hand, made their acceptance of civil unions clear from the start, but took a weaker stance on the issue of same-sex marriage overall, saying it was an issue that should be left to the states. A majority of actual voters (52%) said they would vote for the candidate who was against allowing same-sex couples to marry, which is more than double the number (23%) who reported that they would pick the candidate who supported same-sex unions. A notable 23% were unsure and indicated they would need more information before making such a choice.

Amending the Constitution. Though voters overwhelmingly indicated their desire to protect traditional marriage and restrict the sacred institution to couples composed of one man and one woman, they were evenly split in their support to amend the U.S. Constitution. All survey respondents were asked about their opinions on a constitutional amendment; however, half were asked about an amendment "banning same-sex marriage," while the other half were queried on an amendment "defining marriage as between one man and one woman." Support and opposition for an amendment of any kind differed virtually imperceptibly between the two phraseologies: 48% of voters would support an amendment "banning same-sex marriage," while 46% would oppose. Similarly, 49% would be in favor of an amendment "defining marriage as between one man and one woman," compared to 46% who would be against.

The "Station-in-Life" Factor. Married voters supported President Bush over John Kerry by a 13-point margin (56% to 43%) and those with children were 19 points more likely to support the president over John Kerry (59% to 40%). Unmarried voters were more likely to side with Kerry (57% to 42%) and single women favored the senator by considerable margins.

The Gender Gap Gets the Pink Slip. Senator Kerry posted just a 3% advantage (51% to 48%) over President Bush among women, a significant difference from the 11-point margin for Al Gore over Mr. Bush in 2000. Security moms (married women with children who cite the war in Iraq or terrorism as the most important issue in deciding their vote) supported the president over Kerry by 18 points (59% to 41%). Single women between the ages of 18 and 34 sided with Kerry over Bush by a 3-to-1 margin.

American Small Businesses Favored President Bush. The Small Business & Entrepreneurship Council (SBEC) took part in the polling company, inc. postelection survey. More than one-quarter (27%) of actual voters surveyed on Election Night 2004 characterized themselves as "small business owners" (SBOs). This broke down as follows: 12% own a small business, 4% partially own a small business, and 11% report they are self-employed or earn self-employment income. Small business owners (SBO) favored George W. Bush by 16 points over John Kerry (57% to 41%).

CELINDA LAKE
LAKE SNELL PERRY & ASSOCIATES

Lake Snell Perry & Associates designed and administered this survey, which was conducted by phone using professional interviewers. The survey reached 1,000 definite voters nationwide in the November 2004 general election for president. The survey was conducted on November 1–2, 2004. Telephone numbers for the survey were drawn using random digit dial (RDD). The interviews consisted of a base sample of 1,000 men and women who are likely voters nationwide. The data were weighted slightly by age, race, gender, party identification, marital status, and religion in order to ensure that it accurately reflects the demographic configuration of these populations. The margin of error for the survey is +/- 3.1%.

The Gender Gap

Votes for Women 2004, a nonpartisan network of women's organizations created to monitor the gender gap in the 2004 presidential elections, commissioned an election omnibus survey to evaluate the gender gap in voting preferences and in priorities for the future among voters in the 2004 presidential election. This research found that there continues to be a strong gender divide not only when it comes to voting behavior, but also on opinions of which policies should take precedence in the next four years.

The gender gap is alive and well. The electorate favored President Bush over John Kerry by a 3-point margin (51% to 48%). But among

men and women there exists a 7-point divide—55% of men voted for
Bush, while 48% of women supported him. Forty-four percent of men
favored Kerry, while a majority of women (51%) voted for Kerry. The
2004 gender gap is somewhat smaller than the 10-point gap in the 2000
election, when 43% of women versus 53% of men voted for Bush. In
2000, 54% of women voted for Gore, as did 42% of men. Support for
the Democratic candidate has eroded among white women, working
women, married women, and older women. This year, 44% of white
women voted for Kerry, compared with 48% who voted for Gore in
2000. There was a similar decline among working women—58% of
working women voted for Gore, while 51% voted for Kerry.

This division is also evident along marital lines. Married voters
tended to support Bush and a large proportion of unmarried voters supported Kerry. Married men voted for Bush by a 21-point margin (60%
Bush to 39% Kerry), while married women voted for Bush by a smaller
11-point margin (55% Bush to 44% Kerry). A similar gap exists among
unmarried men and women. Unmarried men voted for Kerry by 8
points (53% to 45%), while Kerry prevailed among unmarried women
by 25 points (62% to 37%).

There is also a gender gap along racial lines. Although both white
men and women broke for Bush, white men were considerably more in
Bush's camp than white women. White men favored Bush by 25 points
(62% for Bush to 37% for Kerry), while white women favored Bush by
11 points (55% for Bush to 44% for Kerry). The same trend exists
among minority men and women in their support for Kerry. Nonwhite
men supported Kerry by a 37-point margin (67% for Kerry to 30% for
Bush), while nonwhite women voted for Kerry by a wider margin of 51
points (75% for Kerry to 24% for Bush).

Additionally, there is a gender gap within every age group. Although both younger men and women favored Kerry, young women
were significantly more for Kerry. Men age 18 to 29 voted for Kerry by
4 points (51% to 47%), while women showed a 13-point margin for

Kerry (56% to 43%). Men age 30 to 44 were 14 points for Bush (56% Bush to 42% Kerry) and women in that age range split (50% Bush, 49% Kerry). We see the same trend among men and women age 45–59 (men 45 to 59 years: 54% Bush, 45% Kerry; women age 45–59 years; 49% Bush, 50% Kerry). There is also a significant gap between adults over 60 years old (men 60 years and older: 60% Bush, 39% Kerry; women: 49% Bush, 51% Kerry).

Top Issues: Putting "Moral Values" in Perspective

Much has been made of the role moral values played in this election based on exits that tended to use a limited list of concerns. The CNN exit poll identified moral values as the most important issue to voters (22% say most important issue), although it was followed closely by the economy and jobs (20%), terrorism (19%), Iraq (15%), health care (8%), taxes (5%), and education (4%). It should be noted that roughly 70% of voters identify something other than moral values as the most important issue. However, when using a more complete list of concerns—like Social Security and prescription drugs—our research indicates that economic and security considerations took precedence in voters' minds in deciding for whom to vote. Voters identify jobs and the economy as the top issue for determining their vote for president (23%), followed by homeland security and terrorism (19%), Iraq (13%), and moral values (10%). There is little difference between men and women in ranking these top-tier issues.

Rounding out the list of top concerns are health care and prescription drugs (8%), Social Security and Medicare (6%), taxes (5%), education (4%), national defense and veterans' issues (3%), federal budget deficit (3%), and gay and lesbian rights issues (2%).

There are some interesting differences among women of different political orientations. Democratic women, who widely favored Kerry, placed the most importance on the economy and jobs (38%), health care and prescription drugs (14%), and Iraq (11%), while Republican women, most of whom broke for Bush, showed more concern for homeland security and terrorism (24%), followed by moral values (15%), and jobs and the economy (13%). Independent women—who split between Bush and Kerry—placed greatest importance on homeland security and terrorism (27%), jobs and the economy (20%), and Iraq (17%).

Women's Issues Shortchanged in the Campaign

Voters believe a range of women's issues were shortchanged in this presidential campaign. This belief is particularly prevalent among women. In particular, voters say equal pay for women, prevention of domestic violence against women, women's equality under the law, and appointing women to leadership positions in the administration are issues that were not adequately addressed. This perception is driven by the intense belief among women that not enough attention was placed on these issues.

There is a significant gender gap on perceptions of how much attention the campaign spent on women's issues. By a wide margin, women were more likely than men to say the candidates did not focus enough on equal pay for women (60% not enough to 41% not enough), prevention of violence against women (58% to 38%), women's equality under the law (61% to 36%), appointing women to leadership positions in the administration (54% to 36%), and education (46% to 35%).

Younger women were more likely than older women to believe there was not enough attention given to women's issues, but majorities of older women feel similarly—equal pay (67% not enough younger women to 55% not enough for older women), prevention of violence against women (69% to 46%), appointing women to leadership positions (57% to 52%), and women's equality under the law (65% to 56%).

Similarly, married women and unmarried women are in agreement that the issues of equal pay for women (63% and 58%, respectively), prevention of violence against women (61% and 54%), appointing women to leadership positions (53% and 56%), and women's equality under the law (61% for each) were not discussed enough during the campaign.

Majorities of Democratic women, Republican women, and Independent women say that equal pay for women, prevention of violence against women, and women's equality under the law were not discussed enough during the campaign.

Voter's Agenda for the Future

Voters' agenda for the future involves not only top issues such as the economy, security, and health care, but also a desire for women's equity and the prevention of violence against women. These issues resonate widely and cut across generational and ideological lines. Not surprisingly, women express the most intense reactions to the importance of women's equity.

Voters identify health care, education, and the economy and jobs as the top issues they want the President to focus on over the next four years. Women and men share the same top priorities for the president, though women place more importance on health care (65% to 57% very high, top priority), and men would like to see the greatest focus placed on the economy and jobs (62% to 50%).

The survey findings also indicate a significant priority for women's equity. Roughly 4 in 10 voters say prevention of violence against women, women's equality under the law, and equal pay for women should be top priorities for the administration. Again, the intensity for the women's equity agenda comes from women.

There is a dramatic gender gap in the perceived importance of women's equity, with women rating each of the women's rights issues presented significantly higher than men. The gender gap is greatest when it comes to the perceived importance of women's equality under the law (13-point gap: 45% of women to 32% of men rate as a top priority), appointing women to leadership positions in the administration (14-point gap: 38% to 24%), and equal pay for women (10-point gap: 43% to 33%).

Women also place somewhat more importance on the issue of abortion (9-point gap: 42% to 33%) and on prevention of violence against women (9-point gap: 47% to 38%).

Younger women and older women share similar priorities around women's equity, with pluralities of both groups rating the items as a top priority. Married women and unmarried women also respond similarly, with pluralities of unmarried women saying equal pay, prevention of violence and women's equality should be top priority, while pluralities of married women say equal pay and women's equality should be top priority, and a majority say prevention of violence against women should be a priority.

Equal Rights for Women and Economic Security

Voters tend to recognize the relationship between equal rights for women and their economic security. By a wide margin, voters agree with a statement that if American women had equal rights under the law it would strengthen their economic well-being over a statement that while equal rights are important, this does not really make a difference for women's economic well-being. A majority (55%) agree with the former position, compared to 29% who take the opposing view.

Opinion on the connection between women's rights and economic well-being splits clearly along gender lines. Two-thirds of women (64%) favor the argument that equal rights for women would strengthen their economic well-being, while only 43% of men hold this view. Women split along partisan lines as well. Large proportions of Democratic and Independent women see the connection between women's equal rights and economic well-being (76% and 72%, respectively). While Republican women also tend to hold this view over the argument that equal rights do not make a difference for women's economic well-being, they express significantly less intensity than their Democratic and Independent counterparts (among Republican women: 48% say there is a connection between rights and economic well-being to 33% who say rights do not really make a difference for women's economic well-being).

APPENDIX C

SELECTED NOTES

For further information about the research and polling organizations and activities of the authors, visit our Web sites: for Celinda Lake, www.lakesnellperry.com; for Kellyanne Conway, www.pollingcompany .com. At THE POLLING COMPANY site, you can also find information about WOMANTREND, a highly respected research and consulting company, under the auspices of TPC, and subscribe to the quarterly newsletter, *WomanTrends*.

The major findings in this book are based on surveys detailed in Appendix A. The following are selected additional references.

TREND 1

Sources include: Lake Snell Perry Mermin & Associates study for the Unmarried Women's Project, 2004; *The Japan Times:* "Better Left on the Shelf Than a Downtrodden Wife?" by Kaori Shoji, June 2, 2005; Janice Witzel, Ph.D, The Family Institute at Northwestern University, Evanston, Illinois; *Business Week* Special Report: "Unmarried America," October 20, 2003; *American Demographics:* "A Place For One," by James Morrow, November 2003; quirkyalone.net; *Quirkyalone: A Manifesto for Uncompromising Romantics*, by Sasha Cagen (HarperSanFrancisco, 2004); American Association for Single People; the U.S. Census Bureau.

TREND 2

Sources include: *Newsweek* report: "State of Our Unions," March 1, 2004; The National Center of Health Statistics; The National Marriage Project at Rutgers University, David Popenoe and Barbara Dafoe Whitehead, co-directors; *New York Times:* "When Richer Weds Poorer, Money Isn't the Only Difference," by Tamar Lewin, May 19, 2005; Brandeis University Women's Studies Research Center; Centers for Disease Control; American Jewish Committee's Surrvey of American Jewish Opinion; *Public Perspective:* "Leaving Tradition Behind," by Claudia Deane et al., May/June 2005; *AARP:* "Split Decisions," January/February 2005; *AARP Bulletin:* "Unmarried Together," by Linda Greider, October 2004; *New York Times:* "O.K. It's Over. So Now Let's Party," by Rachel Dodes, February 13, 2005; Society for Human Resource Management: 2002 Benefits Survey; Human Rights Campaign Foundation, 2004 (domestic partner benefits); *Journal of Marriage and the Family*; U.S. General Accounting Office; the U.S. Census Bureau.

TREND 3

Sources include: the Institute for American Values, "The Motherhood Project"; *American Demographics:* "Soccer Mom is Dead. Gen-X Parents are Redefining Parental Roles," by David Myron, September 2004; University of Connecticut and University of Minnesota joint research project (Martha Farrell, principle investigator); *New York Magazine:* "The Bitch on the Playground," by Amy Sohn; Purina and Healthy Pets Consortium: "State of the American Pet," August 2003; Single Mothers by Choice (org.); *New York Times:* "Perfect Madness—The Mommy Trap," by Judith Shulevitz, February 20, 2005; *U.S. News & World Report:* "Making Babies," by Anna Mulrine, September 27, 2004; *New York Magazine:* "The Perfect Little Bump," by Laurie Abraham, September 27, 2004; National Adoption Center; *New York Times:* "As Bills Mount, Debt on Homes Rise for the Elderly," by Jennifer Bayot, July 4, 2004; *Perfect Madness: Motherhood in the Age of Anxiety*, by Judith Warner (Riverhead 2005); *Conceive* magazine; American Society of Reproductive

Medicine; Society for Assisted Reproductive Technology; Breastfeeding Works; Institute for Women's Policy Research; the U.S. Census Bureau.

TREND 4

Sources include: THE POLLING COMPANY, INC.: Department of Labor Intercept Study of 260 Women Entrepreneurs, March 2002; THE POLLING COMPANY, INC.: AWED survey of 201 AWED members and alumni, November 2001; Lake Snell Perry Mermin & Associates survey for AAUW (salary); THE POLLING COMPANY, INC./WOMANTREND with Event Strategies, Inc., for NE Regional Conference on Women Entrepreneurship in the 21st Century, August 2002; salary.com; National Council for Research on Women; Center for Women's Business Research; *New York Times Magazine:* The Opt-Out Revolution," by Lisa Belkin, October 24, 2003; *Business Week* cover story: "Old. Smart. Productive. Surprise! The Graying of the Workforce is Better News Than You Think," by Peter Coy with Diane Brady in New York, June 27, 2005; *The Public Interest:* "What Do Women Really Want," by Neil Gilbert, Winter 2005; *AARP Bulletin:* "Hollywood Writers, You're Fired," by Barbara Basler, January 2005; *American Demographics:* "Retirement Goes Boom," by Christopher Reynolds, April 2004; *AARP:* "Hire Calling," by Mary Quigley and Loretta E. Kaufman, November/ December 2004; *USA Today:* "The New Entrepreneurs—Americans Over 50," by Jim Hopkins, January 27, 2005; Center for Women's Business Research: Top 10 Facts About Women Business Owners, 2003; *American Demographics:* "Brains and Gender," by Peter Francese, September 2004; Institute for Women's Policy Research; CBS Market Watch: "Values at Work Differ by Gender," by Andrea Coombes, June 21, 2004; *AARP:* "Ready, Net Go," by Karen Hube, March/April 2005; Telework.gov; *Managed Health Care Executive:* "As More Women Enter Medicine, Culture Will Change," by Tina Wardrop, February 1, 2004; Catalyst Foundation; CareerWomen.com; Women Unlimited; Wiserwoman.com; CareerWoman.com; WomentorSM Group; National Federation of Independent Businesses; Small Business and Entrepreneurship Council; American Small Business Association; National Association of Small Businesses; Center for Women's Business Research; Travel Industry Association of America; the U.S. Census Bureau.

TREND 5

Sources include: THE POLLING COMPANY, INC.: Lifestyle and Projection Report, prepared for *Martha Stewart Living*, Omnimedia Inc., presented by Kellyanne Conway, December 10, 2003; Harvard's Joint Center for Housing Studies: The State of the Nation's Housing 2003; *People:* "The Substance of Style. How the Rise of Aesthetic Value is Remaking Commerce, Culture, and Consciousness," by Virginia Postrel, November 3, 2003; U.S. Department of Education, National Center for Education Statistics (home schooling); *American Demographics:* "Gen X Wants No-Debt Home Ec," by Matthew Grimm, April 2004; *American Demographics:* "X-It Plans," by James Morrow, May 2004; *American Demographics:* "House Arrest," by David G. Kennedy, May 2004; *American Demographics:* Single Family, Condo Style," by Peter Francese, October 2004; *American Demographics:* Manifest Destiny 3.0," by Dr. Jim Taylor, September 2004; *American Demographics:* "The Math of Moving," by Christopher Reynolds, July/August 2004; www.cohousing.org; International Housewares Association; the U.S. Census Bureau.

TREND 6

Sources include: Family and Work Institute: "Overwork in America," 2004; *AARP Bulletin:* "Too Many Choices," by Barry Schwartz, April 2005; THE POLLING COMPANY, INC.: surveys for The Better Sleep Council—September 2004, November 2004, February 2005; *Ad Age:* "What American Consumers Do on the Weekend," by Bradley Johnson, May 16, 2005; *Las Vegas Review-Journal:* "Technology's Role Seen to Grow in Women's Work-Family Balancing Act," by Emily Kumler, November 1, 2004; Lifetime television; the U.S. Census Bureau.

TREND 7

Sources include: Lake Snell Perry Mermin & Associates report: "Why 30s are Unique," March 29, 2005; THE POLLING COMPANY, INC.: Lifestyle and Projection Report, prepared for *Martha Stewart Living*, Omnimedia Inc., presented by Kellyanne Conway, December 10, 2003; *Time:* "Midlife Crisis? Bring It On," May 16, 2005; *American Demographics:* "Overlooked and Under X-ploited," May 2004; *American Demographics:* "A Different Dream. For Young Americans It's Not Financial Security But Living in Freedom That Most Defines the American Dream," by Noah Rubin Brier, May 2004; *New York Times:* "Need Turns Aging Strangers Into Roommates," by David W. Chen, April 17, 2005; *Reaching Women* newsletter: "Reach Aging Women with Ageless Relevance," by Andrea Learned, February 28, 2003; *Buffalo News:* "Millenials Go To College," by Holly Auer, December 18, 2003; *Time:* "Grow Up? Not So Fast," by Lev Grossman, January 24, 2005; The Gallup Organization: "Angst Aplenty. Top Worries of Young Americans," by Linda Lyons, July 15, 2003; *AARP:* "Across the Divide," by Melissa Gotthardt, March/April 2005; *American Demographics:* "A Second Coming of Age," by Dr. Jim Taylor, June 2004; *American Demographics:* "Gen X—The Unbeholden," by Christopher Reynolds, May 2004; *American Demographics:* "Odd Gen Out," by Joan Engebretson, May 2004; *American Demographics:* "In the Shadow of the Boom," by Peter Francese, May 2004; *Primer:* Gender Differences Among 30s, by Joel Benenson and Amy Levin, February 7, 2005; the U.S. Census Bureau.

TREND 8

Sources include: THE POLLING COMPANY, INC.: Lifestyle and Projection Report, prepared for *Martha Stewart Living*, Omnimedia Inc., presented by Kellyanne Conway, December 10, 2003; Harrris Interactive, the Harris Poll, October 16, 2003: "Most Americans Believe in God, But There is No Consensus on His/Her Gender, Form or Degree of Control Over Events"; U.S. Surgeon General's Report: Exercise in

America (1996–8); Kalorama Information Market Report: "The Market for Physical Fitness Equipment," November 1999; *LA Times/Washington Post* Service: "Girlfriends," by Melissa Healy, June 7, 2005; *Newsweek:* "House Calls," by Peg Tyre, February 7, 2005; *U.S. News & World Report* Special Report: "Who Will Take Care of You?" February 7, 2005; the U.S. Census Bureau.

TREND 9

Sources include: THE POLLING COMPANY, INC.: The Dole Poll for the Dole Nutrition Institute, 2004; THE POLLING COMPANY, INC. and PBS "To the Contrary": "What Women Want in 2004," released May 14, 2004; THE POLLING COMPANY, INC.: Lifestyle and Projection Report, prepared for *Martha Stewart Living,* Omnimedia Inc., presented by Kellyanne Conway, December 10, 2003; Millward Brown Intelliquest/MSN: "How Women Use the Internet," 2002; *Wall Street Journal:* "The New Family Portfolio Manager—Mom," by Hilary Stout, February 10, 2005; *Reaching Women* newsletter: "Tell Me More," by Lisa Johnson, April 2005; *Time:* "The Real Face of Homelessness," by Joel Stein, January 20, 2003; Yahoo and Starcom Mediavest Group: Internet Use Statistics; *Good Housekeeping:* "What Women Want in Cars Today," October 2004; IHT: "The Feminist Future of the Automobile," by Mary Blume, October 7, 2004; *The Journal:* "Women Steer Towards Cars with Family Appeal," by Steve Hughes, October 23, 2004; "Equality in Cyberspace. Women and the Internet," by Patricia K. Bowers, April 23, 1995; WebSiteJournal.com: "What Women Want," by Heidi Pollock, June 9, 1999; TNS Media Research and Just Ask a Woman studies on women's use of the Internet; Department of Commerce Minority Business Agency Report, *American Demographics* 2002; *New York Times:* "What Women Want—More Horses," by Alex Williams, June 12, 2005; *New York Times:* "When the Joneses Wear Jeans," by Jennifer Steinhauer, May 29, 2005; Fraser Forum: "Welfare and Poverty—Family Matters, March 2004; *Business Week* online: "How Tech Helps Liberate Women," by Christopher Farrell, October 18, 2004; *U.S. News & World Report:* "Oldies But Goodies," by Kristin Davis, March 14, 2005; *AARP*

Bulletin: "50-Plus and Going Broke," by Russell Wild, January 2005; *American Demographics:* "The Only Way Into the Fast Lane," by David J. Kiley, April 2004; *American Demographics:* "Spending Trending," April 2004; American Demographics: "Coming of Age," by Noah Rubin Brier, November 2004; *USA Today:* "Ad Campaigns Tell Women to Celebrate Who They Are," by Theresa Howard, July 11, 2005; National Endowment for Financial Education and AARP, A Women & Money Program Incubator: "Frozen in the Headlights—The Dynamics of Women and Money," February 2000; Jump$tart Coalition for Personal Financial Literacy; *People en Espanol* Hispanic Opinion Tracker; the U.S. Census Bureau.

TREND 10

Sources include: Lake Snell Perry Mermin & Associates: "The Middle Class Squeeze," July 26, 2004; THE POLLING COMPANY, INC/WOMAN TREND: Voter Models: Updating the Prism. New Modes of Analysis for Retaining and Attracting Voters, Winter 2004; Lake Snell Perry Mermin & Associates: "The Role of Moral Values in the 2004 Election," November 24, 2004; THE POLLING COMPANY, INC. study for the Home School Legal Defense Association: "Same-Sex Marriage, Civil Unions and the Federal Marriage Amendment," released April 7, 2004; THE POLLING COMPANY, INC.: Survey for *More* Magazine, September 1999; Lake Snell Perry Mermin & Associates: "Public Attitudes Toward Stem Cell Research," May 2005; *Trinity:* "Gender Politics: Hazardous to the Political Health of Female Candidates," by Kellyanne Conway; *The Nation:* "Money Talks," by Celinda Lake and Robert Borosage, August 21, 2000; Lake Snell Perry Mermin & Associates: "Value and the Democratic Party," January 28, 2005; *National Review:* "Outlook 2004-How Things Change," by Kellyanne Conway, December 30, 2003 Lake Snell Perry Mermin & Associates: "The Gender Gap and Women's Agenda for Moving Forward," November 9, 2004; *New York Times:* "Sex and the Single Voter," by Bella M. DePaulo, June 18, 2004; Women's Voices, Women's Vote, 2004; *Women's Quarterly:* "Are Office Park Dads for Real?" by Karlyn Bowman, Autumn 2002; The Pluralism Project at

Harvard University: "Religious Women and Election 2004," September 2004; *American Demographics:* "How Do You Define Morality?" June 2004; *American Demographics:* "The Art of Cultural Correctness," by William F. Gloede, November 2004; Lifetime Television and Policy Alternatives: Women's Voices Survey 2000; Pew Research Center survey, July 14-August 5, 2003; *Time*/CNN Poll: May 21–22, 2003; CBS News Poll: February 24–25, May 27–28, 2003; THE POLLING COMPANY, INC.: Studies for *Ladies Home Journal:* January 2000, September 2001, January 2002; *Christian Science Monitor:* "Playing Against Type. Women Link Family Security with Being Tough on Iraq," December 2, 2002; *Washington Post:* "Security Mom Bloc Proves Hard to Find," by Richard Morin and Dan Balz; *American Demographics:* "Voter 2004-The Morning After," by Alicia Mundy, April 2004; *American Demographics:* "The Net Difference," by Noah Rubin Brier, October 2004; *U.S. News & World Report:* "Female Persuasion," by Kenneth T. Walsh, October 4, 2004; *Christian Science Monitor:* "Why Women Are Edging Toward Bush," by Linda Feldmann, September 23, 2004; *Boston Globe:* "A New Condescension Greets Women Voters," by Cathy Young, September 27, 2004; *AARP Bulletin:* "How Older Voters Could Make a Difference," by Bill Hogan, October 2004; *Ms.:* "Portraits of Women Voters," Winter 2004; *American Demographics:* "The Voting Youth," by Noah Rubin Brier, October 2004; *Time:* "What Do Women Want?" by Nancy Gibbs, October 11, 2004; *National Review:* "The Gender Gap," by Myrna Blythe, September 16, 2004; the U.S. Census Bureau.

INDEX

AARP (American Association of Retired Persons), 41, 97, 98, 147
Abortion, 59, 60, 200–201
Acupuncture, 178
Adecco, 98
Adoption, 26, 51, 54
Age, 7
  cosmetic surgery and, 173
  feeling younger than current, 154–157
  generational compression, 7, 141–165
  levels of control and, 124–126
  motherhood and, 46–49
  retirement and, 97–99
  self-employment and, 66
  of single women, 13, 18, 26
  voting behavior and, 209, 296–297
  weekends and, 136
Age discrimination, 147
Ah ring, 23
Alienated Single archetype, 5–6, 26, 201, 219
  control level and, 122
  financial status of, 185
  job versus career, 7
  single women, 12
Alpha moms, 56–58
Alpha-Striver archetype, 4
  control level and, 121
  financial status of, 184
  job versus career, 78
  single women, 12
  voting behavior, 201

Alternative health care, 169, 178
Altinkemer, Cheryl, 187
American Association for Single People, 32
American Association of University Women, 93
American College of Obstetricians and Gynecologists, 50
American Jewish Committee, 33
American Psychoanalytic Association, 178
American Small Business Association, 67
American Society of Reproductive Medicine, 51
American Values, 292
Anderson, Teresa, 51–52
Anthony, Susan B., 194
Appearance. *See* Health and beauty
Appliances
  high-tech, 106
  testing, 111–112
Arthur Andersen/Ameritech, 69
Asian women
  consumer spending and, 183
  feeling age, 154
At-home testing, 107
Automobile clubs, 32
Automobile purchases, 187–190

Babies "R" Us, 56
"Baby M" case, 52
Barbie, 179
Beanpole families, 144–145

Beauty. *See* Health and beauty
Be Jane, Inc., 115
Berry, Halle, 173
Bipolar disorders, 178
Birthing tubs, 55
Birth rates, 59
Black women
 aging and wisdom, 151
 consumer spending and, 184
 cosmetic surgery and, 172–173
 feeling age, 154
 intermarriages, 33
 need for peace and, 134
 reasons for not marrying, 16
Botox, 170, 172
Breast augmentation and reduction,
 171
Breast feeding, 56, 88, 100
Breastfeeding Works, 88
Budget Living magazine, 113
Bush, George W., 43, 290–298
Business ownership, 64–70,
 100

Cagen, Sasha, 23–24
Candidates, sex of, 204–208, 217
CareerWomen.com, 71
Caretaker mentality, 39
Car purchases, 187–190
Catalyst Foundation, 81, 94
CBS Evening News, 12
Census 2000 data, 31
Center for Women's Business Research,
 96
Center of Philanthropy, Indiana
 University, 187
Centers for Disease Control (CDC), 48,
 50
Cesarian delivery, 55
Charitable giving, 187
Charles Schwab, 183
Checkbook, balancing, 186
Chemical peel, 172
Childbirth, 55
Child care, 82, 86
Childlessness, incidence of, 49
Child protection, 61
Child support, 54
Choices, increase in, 137–138
Church attendance, 170, 212
Citigroup Women & Co., 183
Cocooning, 105

Cohabitation
 as alternate to marriage, 34
 demographic of, 34–35
 elderly and, 35–36
 incidence of, 32
 premarital, 34, 35, 38
Cohousing Association of the United
 States, 117
Cohousing communities, 116–117
Coleman, Thomas, 32–33
Collaborative divorce, 43
Collagen injection, 172
Commitment ceremonies, 26, 215
Computer technology, 126, 190–191
Conceive magazine, 50
Concierge physicians, 171
Condominium ownership, 116
Construction firms, 96
Consumer discounts, 33
Consumer spending, 181–195
 car purchases, 187–190
 computers, 190–191
 financial literacy, 185–186
 financial status of different groups,
  184–185
 future and, 195
 multi-cultural boom, 183–184
 online shopping, 192–193
Control, feelings of, 120–126
Cosmetics, 173
Cosmetic surgery, 170–173, 180
Country clubs, 32
Credit card debt, 126, 186
Cross-training, 69
Cruz, Penelope, 173
Curves, 170

Deadbeat dads, 61
Death penalty, 213
Dental schools, 95
Depression, 178
Dickinson, Emily, 24
Distance learning, 106
Divorce, 13, 36
 collaborative, 43
 finances and, 183
 home ownership and, 108
 initiation of, 42
 parental, 34, 43
 rates, 15, 41–42, 44
 risk factors for, 38
Do-it-yourselfers, 113–115

Domestic partner benefits, 43–44, 44,
    215, 216
Doulas, 55
Dream Dinners, 112

Eating disorders, 57, 179
eBay, 85
Echo boomers, 161–162
Ecological lifestyles, 169
Ectopic pregnancy, 51
Education, 2, 47, 61, 90, 218
    business ownership and, 68
    cohabitation and, 34
    control over, 121, 123, 124
    feeling age, 156
    law schools, 91–92
    multigenerational households and,
        148
    single women and, 16, 18
    of stay-at-home moms, 80, 81
    successful marriages and, 38
    voting behavior and, 199–200, 209
Education, U.S. Department of, 106
Elderly. See also Age
    as caregivers, 7, 146
    cohabitation and, 35–36
    parents, 31, 146
Emotional infidelity, 39–40
Employment benefits, 33
Encore workplace, 97–98
Entrepreneurship, 66–70, 100
Epidurals, 55
Ernst & Young, 81
Ethnicity. See Race and ethnicity
Executive-management positions,
    90–94, 100, 216
Exercise, 107, 170
Extramarital affairs, 41, 42
Extreme Homes (television show), 114
Eyelid surgery, 171

Falleroni, Lisa, 115
Families and Work Institute, 119
Family life, 3, 27, 43–44, 215–216. See
    also Homes
    beanpole families, 144–145
    cohabitation. See Cohabitation
    gay and lesbian households, 29, 31, 32
    stepfamilies, 29, 32, 58
    traditional nuclear family, 28, 29, 31,
        34
Familymoon, 57, 58

Farm owners, 95
Fatherlessness, 35
Fein, Ellen, 25
Female norms, eight archetypes of, 3–6
Feminism, 11
Feminist Champion archetype, 3–4
    control level and, 121
    financial status of, 184
    job versus career, 78
    single women, 11–12
    voting behavior, 201
Fertility technology, 26, 46, 48–52, 215
Financial Literacy for Youth Month, 186
Fitness center, home as, 107
Flexible working hours, 68, 216
Florida State University, 114
Fortune magazine, 85
401(k)s, 101, 183
Fox, Ruva, 23

Gary, Indiana, 34
Gay and lesbian households, 29, 31, 32,
    215
Gay marriage, 33, 43–44, 60, 293–294
Gender bias, 71
General Accounting Office (GAO), 32
Generational compression, 7, 141–165
Gilbert, Neil, 48–49
Glass, Shirley, 40–41
Glass ceiling, 66, 89–94
Gonzalez, Luisa, 51–52
Gore, Al, 294, 296
Grandparents, 12, 144, 146, 148, 154,
    157
Grass ceiling, 94

Hair straightening, 172
Hallelujah Diet (Malkums), 174
Harris Interactive study, 20, 145
Health, control over, 121–126
Health and beauty, 167–180
    cosmetic surgery, 170–173, 180
    exercise, 170
    future and, 178, 179
    LOHAS (lifestyles of health and
        sustainability), 168, 169
    thinner versus younger, 175–177
    weight loss, 167, 173–174
Health care, 35, 47, 67, 69, 97, 100–101
    alternative, 169, 178
    at home, 107
    as number one challenge, 150–151

Health care (*cont.*)
   proxies, 26, 31
   voting behavior and, 199, 217
Health clubs, 32
Health insurance, 171, 178
Healthy Marriage Initiative, 43
Helicopter parent, 57
HERS (health, education, retirement,
      and security) agenda, 199–200
Hispanics
   consumer spending and, 183–184
   feeling age, 154
   home ownership and, 108
Holistic disease prevention, 169
Home Again (television show), 114
Home Depot, 98, 113, 114
HomeGenie, 111
Home maintenance firms, 116
Homeopathy, 169
Homepreneuring trend, 117
Homes, 31, 103–118
   cohousing communities, 116–117
   condominium ownership, 116
   do-it-yourselfers, 113–115
   future and, 118
   hiving, 104–107
   improvement, 113–115
   kitchens, 106
   prepared meal services, 112
   robots in, 110–111
   as school, 80, 106–107
   second homes, 108, 109
   single women and, 103, 107–110, 118
   as spa and fitness center, 107
   testing appliances, 111–112
   as workplace, 106
Home schooling, 80, 106–107
Household relationships. *See* Family life
Huppie, 203

Income
   aging and wisdom, 152
   cohabitation and, 34
   control over, 119, 122–126
   feeling age, 156
   important relationships and, 37
   need for more, 132–133
   poverty, 54–55
   single women and, 18, 21
   spending time to save money, 129–131
   voting behavior and, 209
   wage gap, 92–94

Incredibles, The (film), 64
Individuality, importance of, 24
Infidelity
   emotional, 39–40
   incidence of, 40–42
Institute for Women's Policy Research
      (IWPR), 54
Insurance, 32, 171, 178
Intelligent Oven, 106, 111
Interest rates, 109
Intermarriage, openness to, 33
International Quirkyalone Day
      (February 14), 23
Internet
   affairs, 40, 41
   car buying, 189
   dating, 12, 24, 42, 43
   education, 106, 218
   female use of, 191, 193–194
   medical information, 171, 180
   pedophiles, 61
   as resource and shopping center,
      105
   shopping, 139, 192–193
In vitro fertilization, 46, 48, 50–51
IRAs (individual retirement accounts),
      183
iRobot, 110
Isolation and loneliness, 19–21

Japan
   single women in, 18–19
   Yumel doll in, 59
Job share, 71
Job spoil, 94
Joint tenants with right of survivorship,
      31
Journal of Marriage and the Family, 35
Jump$tart Coalition for Personal
      Financial Literacy, 186
Jupiter Media Matrix, 43
Just-in-time work cycles, 69

Kerry, John, 290–298
Kitchens, 106
K-Mart, 93
Kunin, Madeleine, 205

Labor and delivery, 55
Labor Statistics, Bureau of, 137
Laser hair removal, 172
"The Last Exodus" program, 174

Latchkey kids, 81, 158
Law firms, 92
Law schools, 91–92, 95
Let's Dish, 112
Lewin, Tamar, 33
Lewinsky, Monica, 211
Life magazine, 136
Lifetime Television, 137
Liposuction, 171, 180
Living wills, 26
LOHAS (lifestyles of health and
    sustainability), 168, 169
Loneliness and isolation, 19–21
Longevity, 97, 148, 150
Lopez, Jennifer, 173
Lowe's, 113, 114
Luppie, 203

Maker's Diet, The (Rubin),
    174
Malkums, George, 174
Marriage, 27–44. *See also* Divorce;
    Family life
  average duration of first, 42
  delayed, 14, 27, 29–30, 46, 143, 144,
      164, 215
  emotional infidelity, 39–40
  evolution of institution of, 28–29
  federal laws and, 32
  future and, 44
  key factors in success or failure of,
      38
  median age of, 30, 44
  mixed, 33
  rates in geographic areas, 34
  remarriage, 13, 35, 42, 44, 58
  size of wedding, 27–28
  social class and, 33
Marriage penalty tax, 32
Mary Tyler Moore Show (television
    series), 22
Massage, 178
Mass Connections, 112
Match.com, 12, 24
Maternity leave, 71
Mattel, 179
Maytag, 111, 112
Medicaid, 31
Medicare, 31, 126, 201
Meditation, 178
Mental health coverage, 180
Mentors, 70–72

Merrill Lynch, 93
  Women's Business Development
      division, 183
Microdermabrasion, 172
Midlife crisis, 157
Military, 2, 95
Mind-body connection, 169, 178
Miscarriage, 51
Mommy Entrepreneur, 7
Mommy Telecommuter, 7
Moreno, Enrique, 52
Mortgage options, 108, 109
Motherhood, 45–61
  age and, 46–49
  breast feeding, 56, 88
  child aversion and, 45–46
  childbirth, 55
  fertility technology and, 26, 46, 48–
      52
  future and, 61
  remarriage and, 58
  single. *See* Single mothers
  stay-at-home moms, 79–81
  surrogate, 46, 51–52
Mouse race, 119–139, 217
  future and, 139
  increase in choices, 137–138
  money versus time, 129–132
  multitasking, 120, 137
  need for peace, 133–135
  search for control, 120–126
  sleep versus sex, 127–129
  voluntary simplicity movement and,
      135–136
  weekends, 136
Multiculturalism, 159
Multicultural Maverick archetype, 4
  control level and, 121
  financial status of, 185
  job versus career, 78
  single women, 12
  voting behavior, 201
Multigenerational households, 7, 146,
    148
Multiskilling, 94
Multitasking, 120, 137, 189

Nanny-cam, 57
Naperville, Illinois, 34
Nascar dads, 26, 203, 217
National Association of Realtors, 107,
    108

National Federation of Independent
    Businesses, 67
National Federation of Small Businesses,
    67
National Marriage Project, 34
National security, 197, 200, 201, 203,
    290–291
National Service, 165
Naturopathy, 169
Netflix, 195
New Passages (Sheehy), 146
New York Times, 33, 47
9/11 terrorist attacks, 138–139, 163–165,
    200, 289
Non-bridal registries, 26
Nontraditional jobs, 95–97
NOPE (not on planet earth), 203
Northeast Regional Conference on
    Women Entrepreneurship in the
    21st Century, 69
Not Just Friends (Glass), 40
Nuclear family, 28, 29, 31, 34

Office of Equal Employment
    Opportunity (EEO), 91
Old Bachelor card game, 9
Old boys' network, 90, 91
Old Maid card game, 9
Online. *See* Internet
Opportunity cost, 30–31
Organic foods and products, 169
Overwork. *See* Mouse race

Parallel parenting, 57
Parental divorce, 34, 43
Parental leave, 81
Parenting, delayed, 46–49, 162–164, 215
Partnership for Public Service, 163, 164
Part-time work, 86–87, 101
Patriotism, 163, 164
Peace, need for, 132–136
Pedophiles, 61, 216
Pensions, 35, 44, 101, 185, 200
People en Espanol, 183
*Perfect Madness: Motherhood in the Age of
    Anxiety* (Warner), 57
Perfect mom syndrome, 57
Perot, Ross, 72
Persian Gulf War, 200
Personal organizers, 131
Pets, 58–60
Pew Charitable Trusts, 210

Physical appearance. *See* Health and
    beauty
Plum, 50
Political affiliation, aging and wisdom
    and, 153
Politics, 2, 197–213, 217
    abortion issue, 59, 60, 200–201
    blogs, 211
    of different groups, 201
    future and, 212–213
    grass-tops citizenry, 202, 204–206
    HERS (health, education, retirement,
        and security) agenda, 199–200
    religion and, 211–212
    sex of candidates, 204–208, 217
    single women and, 25–26, 209
    voting behavior, 197, 199–202,
        204–205, 208–212
Polling methodology and results,
    221–288
The Polling Company,
    Inc./WomanTrend (tpc/WT), 69,
    112
Popcorn, Faith, 105
Popenoe, David, 38
Population Research Center, 170
Portfolio managers, 183
Powers of attorney, 31
Pregnancy Discrimination Act, 88
Premarital cohabitation, 34, 35, 38
Prepared meal services, 112
Prescription drugs, 46, 47
Presidential elections
    1992, 26, 217
    2000, 294, 296
    2004, 26, 67, 199, 201, 202, 212, 217,
        289–300
    2006, 25, 212
Priest, Ivy Baker, 194
Property taxes, 110
Prudential Financial, 183
Psychology Today, 20
Purple state, 203

*Quirkyalone: A Manifesto for
    Uncompromising Romantics* (Cagen),
    23–24

Race and ethnicity. *See also* Black
    women; Hispanics
    business ownership and, 68
    important relationships and, 37

voting behavior and, 296
workplace and, 77, 90, 91
Rape, 287
Relationships. *See also* Family life;
    Marriage
    control over, 121–124
    most significant, 37, 39
Religion, 170
    church attendance, 170, 212
    cohabitation and, 34–35
    in public schools, 60
    voting behavior and, 211–212, 292
Religious Crusader archetype, 4–5
    control level and, 121
    financial status of, 185
    job versus career, 78
    voting behavior, 201
Remarriage, 13, 35, 42, 44, 58
Reproductive technologies, 26, 46,
    48–52, 215
Retirement, 116, 126, 154, 215, 217
    age at, 97–99
    funding, 47
    voting behavior and, 200
Rhinoplasty, 171
Right to die issue, 213
Robots, 110–111
Rooma robots, 110–111
Rosenbluth, Frances, 18–19
Rubin, Jordan S., 174
*Rules, The: Time-Tested Secrets for
    Capturing the Heart of Mr. Right*
    (Fein and Schneider), 25
Rutgers University, 34, 210

St. James, Elaine, 135
Salary.com, 93
Salton IceBox, 106
Sandwich generation, 7, 146
Saturn automobile, 188–189
Savings, 187
Schlesinger, Arthur, 7
Schneider, Sherrie, 25
Seabiscuit candidate, 203
Sears Roebuck, 115
Second-home ownership, 108, 109
Second Time Around Parents, 164
Security moms, 203, 294
Self-employment, 64–70, 86, 106, 108
Senior Survivor archetype, 5
    control level and, 122
    financial status of, 185

single women, 12
    voting behavior, 201
Sex and the City (television series), 16
Sex discrimination lawsuits, 93
Sexual activity, 127–128
Shakespeare, William, 148
Sheehy, Gail, 146
Silver ceiling, 94
*Simplify Your Life: 100 Ways to Slow
    Down and Enjoy the Things
    That Really Matter* (St. James),
    135
Single mothers, 15, 20, 21, 29
    adoption and, 54
    attitudes toward, 52–54
    incidence of, 48, 61
    in poverty, 54–55
Single women, 9–26
    age of, 13, 18, 26
    aging and wisdom and, 152, 153
    "aha" moments of, 22–23
    charitable giving and, 187
    demographics of, 10–12
    education and, 16, 18
    as fastest-growing segment, 14
    feeling age and, 154
    feelings of control and, 122–123
    friendships and, 24
    future and, 25–26
    growing population of, 6
    home ownership and, 103, 107–110,
        118
    incidence of, 10, 13
    income and, 18, 21, 183
    involvement with children, 55
    Japanese, 18–19
    loneliness and isolation of, 19–21
    as mothers. *See* Single mothers
    quirkyalones, 23–24
    reasons for not marrying, 15–19
    voting behavior and, 25–26, 209
    workplace and, 72–73, 89
Sleep, 119, 127–129
Small Business Entrepreneurship
    Council, 67
Small Business & Entrepreneurship
    Council (SBEC), 294
Snowflake Necklace, 23
Soccer moms, 26, 217
Social class, marriage and, 33
Social Security benefits, 32, 35, 44, 98,
    126, 163, 185, 197, 201

Society for Assisted Reproductive
    Technology, 51
Spa, home as, 107
Stay-at-home moms. *See also*
    Motherhood
  challenges facing, 83–84
  versus working mothers, 79–80
Stealth parenting, 57
Stem-cell research, 51, 60, 213
Stepfamilies, 29, 32, 58
Stier, Max, 164
Stillbirth, 51
Stress. *See* Mouse race
Suburban Caretaker archetype, 4
  control level and, 121
  financial status of, 184
  job versus career, 78
  voting behavior, 201
Super Suppers, 112
Surrogate mothers, 46, 51–52
Survey of American Jewish Opinion, 33
Sustainable economy, 169
SUVs, 188

Taxation breaks, 33
Teach for America, 163
Techno-etiquette, 217
Teen People magazine, 179
Telecommuting, 69, 106
Television viewing, 137
Television writers, 147
Testing appliances, at-home, 107
Theocon, 203
Therapy, 278
This Old House (television show), 114
Thresholders, 161–162
Time
  control over, 121–125
  need for more, 132–134, 136
  spending to save money, 129–131
Time magazine, 162
"To-do" list, 131
Trading Spaces (television show), 114
Traditional nuclear family, 28, 29, 31,
    34
Tranquility Cross, 23
Travel Industry Association of America,
    88
Tripartisanship, 203
Trophy child, 57
Trump, Donald, 72
Twixters, 161–162

University of Connecticut, 46
University of Minnesota, 46
University of Texas, 170
Unmarried partners, committed, 29, 31.
    See also Cohabitation
  incidence of, 32
Unmarried women. *See* Single women
Unmarried Women's Project, 97

Valentine's Day, 23
Veterinary schools, 95
Vila, Bob, 115
Voluntary simplicity movement,
    135–136
Volunteerism, 187, 210, 213
Volvo Democrat, 203
Volvo YCC, 190
Votes for Women 2004, 295
Voting behavior, 3, 25–26, 197, 199–202,
    204–205, 208–212

Wage gap, 92–94
Waitress Mom archetype, 5, 203, 219
  control level and, 121
  financial status of, 185
  job versus career, 78
  single women, 12
  voting behavior, 201
Walgreens, 98
Wall Street Journal, 211
Walters, Barbara, 56
Warner, Judith, 57
Washington Post, 64, 79
Weddings. *See* Marriage
Weekends, 136
Weigh Down Workshop, Inc., 174
Weight loss, 167, 173–174, 179
Welty, Eudora, 8
Whitehead, Barbara Dafoe, 38
White House Project, 205
Whitman, Meg, 85
Widowed women, 13, 26, 35, 36, 44
  finances and, 181, 183
  home ownership and, 108
Wife abuse, 28
Wilkins, Jennifer, 27
Winfrey, Oprah, 23, 59
Wisdom, aging and, 151–154
Wisewoman.org, 97
Women's movement, 2
Women's Philanthropy Institute, 187
WomentorSM Group, 72

WOMEN Unlimited, 72
Working mothers, 64, 77–79. *See also*
    Motherhood; Workplace
  challenges facing, 81–83
  versus stay-at-home moms, 79–80
Working poor, 63
Workplace, 3, 6–7, 63–101, 139, 216
  breastfeeding and, 88, 100
  business trips with children, 88
  eBay business, 85
  executive-management positions,
    90–94, 100, 216
  flexible hours, 68, 216
  future and, 100–101
  glass ceiling, 66, 89–94
  graying of workforce, 97–98
  home as, 106
  ideal job and family situation, 75–76

  job versus career, 76–78
  mentors, 70–72
  nontraditional jobs, 95–97
  parental leave, 81
  part-time work, 86–87, 101
  quality of work life, 73–76
  self-employment, 64–70, 86, 106,
    108
  single women in, 72–73
  taking kids to, 69, 88
  time off for family obligations, 68
  wage gap, 92–94
  work-family balance, 85–88, 99, 100
Wrinkles, 173, 175

Yumel doll, 59

Zero-down loans, 109

ABOUT THE AUTHORS

Celinda Lake is president of Lake Snell Perry Mermin/Decision Research, a research-based strategy firm in Washington, D.C., working with a wide range of clients that require high-quality research. She is one of the Democratic Party's leading political strategists, and has worked with a number of progressive organizations, including EMILY's List, The White House Project, Planned Parenthood, The Unmarried Women's Project, Sierra Club, The AFL-CIO, Human Rights Campaign, and SEIU. Lake is one of the nation's foremost experts on electing women candidates and on framing issues to women voters. Lake has also been partner and vice president at Greenberg-Lake and has served as political director of the Women's Campaign Fund.

Kellyanne Conway is president and CEO of THE POLLING COMPANY, INC./WOMANTREND. She has provided primary research and advice for clients in 46 or the 50 states and has directed hundreds of demographic and attitudinal survey projects for political races, trade associations, and Fortune 100 companies. Kellyanne is an attorney, a nationally regarded expert on women consumers, and a regular commentator on network and cable television. Kellyanne has worked for a diverse portfolio of corporate, political and non-profit entities, including Major League Baseball, ABC News, Lifetime Television, Martha Stewart Living Omnimedia, Cendant, Grocery Manufacturers of America, Mass Connections, Heritage Foundation, Republican National Committee, National Rifle Association, and Family Research Council.

Catherine Whitney is a New York nonfiction author who has written, cowritten, and ghost-written more than 40 books in a variety of fields, including biography, women's issues, health and medicine, business, parenting, law and the courts, and social history. In 2000, she collaborated with the women of the U.S. Senate on *Nine and Counting*, an unprecedented collaborative effort of women from both sides of the aisle. Whitney's own books include *The Calling: A Year in the Life of an Order of Nuns and Whose Life? A Balanced, Comprehensive View of Abortion from Its Historical Context to the Current Debate.*